MW00835044

J. M. Synge

J. M. Synge

Nature, Politics, Modernism

SEÁN HEWITT

OXFORD
UNIVERSITY PRESS

UNIVERSITY PRESS

Great Clarendon Street, Oxford, OX2 6DP,
United Kingdom

Oxford University Press is a department of the University of Oxford.
It furthers the University's objective of excellence in research, scholarship,
and education by publishing worldwide. Oxford is a registered trade mark of
Oxford University Press in the UK and in certain other countries

First Edition published in 2021

Impression: 1

Published in the United States of America by Oxford University Press
198 Madison Avenue, New York, NY 10016, United States of America

British Library Cataloguing in Publication Data
Data available

Library of Congress Control Number: 2020935563

ISBN 978-0-19-886209-3

DOI: 10.1093/oso/9780198862093.001.0001

Printed and bound by
CPI Group (UK) Ltd, Croydon, CR0 4YY

In memory of my father
Paul Hewitt (1957–2019)

Isn't there the light of seven heavens in your heart alone, the way you'll be an angel's lamp to me from this out, and I abroad in the darkness...

J. M. Synge, *The Playboy of the Western World*, 1907

Acknowledgements

This research was made possible by the help and support of many individuals and institutions. The Arts and Humanities Research Council, UK, funded the PhD on which this book is based, and the Leverhulme Trust supported postdoctoral research which fed into the work here.

I would like to thank the archivists and librarians at the following institutions, whose insight and support made this book possible: the Archives of Trinity College Dublin; the Berg Collection at the New York Public Library; the Harry Ransom Center, University of Texas; the John Rylands Library, University of Manchester; the University of Liverpool special collections and the Sydney Jones Library; Liverpool Central Library; the British Library; the library of Newnham College, Cambridge.

Thanks to the British Association of Irish Studies for a bursary to fund archival study, and to the North West Consortium Doctoral Training Programme (AHRC), which provided a grant to fund overseas research. The School of Histories, Languages and Cultures, and the Institute of Irish Studies, at University of Liverpool also provided funding to enable research trips.

The Willson Center for Humanities & Arts, University of Georgia, supported my research through a visiting fellowship, and I would like to thank their staff, and especially Nicholas Allen, for supporting my work there. I would also like to acknowledge the help of the Cambridge Group for Irish Studies, at which part of this book was presented and received generous feedback.

Many colleagues have discussed and offered advice and insights into the work here. In particular, I would like to thank Lauren Arrington, Frank Shovlin, Ben Levitas, Diane Urquhart, Sinéad Garrigan Mattar, Tom Walker, Alison Garden, Katie Mishler, Anna Pilz, Liss Farrell, and Elliot Ramsey. The anonymous peer reviewers at various journals and at Oxford University Press did much to improve my arguments. I am grateful, too, for the expert editorship of Jacqueline Norton and the editorial and production teams at Oxford University Press.

A personal thank you, too, to my parents, for their love and support.

Contents

List of Figures

List of Abbreviations

CL I	J. M. Synge, *The Collected Letters of John Millington Synge: Vol. I, 1871–1907*, ed. Ann Saddlemyer (Oxford: Clarendon Press, 1983)
CL II	J. M. Synge, *The Collected Letters of John Millington Synge: Volume II, 1907–1909*, ed. Ann Saddlemyer (Oxford: Clarendon Press, 1984)
CW I	J. M. Synge, *Collected Works, Volume I: Poems*, ed. Robin Skelton (Gerrards Cross: Colin Smythe, 1982)
CW II	J. M. Synge, *Collected Works, Volume II: Prose*, ed. Alan Price (London: Oxford University Press, 1966)
CW III	J. M. Synge, *Collected Works, Volume III: Plays, Book I*, ed. Ann Saddlemyer (Gerrards Cross: Colin Smythe, 1982)
CW IV	J. M. Synge, *Collected Works, Volume IV: Plays, Book II*, ed. Ann Saddlemyer (London: Oxford University Press, 1968)
NYPL MS	Berg Collection, New York Public Library
TCD MS	Papers of John Millington Synge, Trinity College Dublin
TCD SSMS	Synge-Stephens Papers, Trinity College Dublin
VP	W. B. Yeats, *The Variorum Edition of the Poems of W. B. Yeats*, ed. Peter Allt and Russell K. Alspach (New York: Macmillan, 1977)
VPl	W. B. Yeats, *The Variorum Edition of the Plays of W. B. Yeats*, ed. Russell K. Alspach (London: Macmillan, 1966)

Introduction

While staying at Coole Park with his Abbey co-directors W. B. Yeats and
Lady Gregory, J. M. Synge spent much of his time 'wandering in woods
where many shy creatures still find their homes—marten cats and squirrels
and otters and badgers,—and by the lake where wild swans come and go'.
The demesne, spanning a thousand acres, with its famous, incantatory
inventory of seven woods, certainly provided ample opportunities for walking. In this recollection, from Lady Gregory's *Our Irish Theatre*, Synge
(a quiet man, by most accounts) is aligned with those gentle, reluctant
animals, and with the Romantic transience and freedom of the swans. As
in Yeats's later poem, in which the swans at Coole are 'mysterious, beautiful'
and independent of will, here Synge is a recluse, with apparently little
interest in the daily life of the other writers (though in fact they often revised
their playscripts together).[1] While staying at her house, Gregory continues,
the younger writer 'hardly looked at a newspaper'. In fact, he seemed 'to look
on politics and reforms with a sort of tolerant indifference'. Signalling his
aloofness, he had even gone so far as to shun wearing black clothes, then
highly fashionable amongst the literati, 'thinking they were not in harmony
with nature'.[2]

The image we are presented with here, already being promulgated by
Synge's contemporaries within a few short years of his death, is that of a man
detached from the sways of the modern world: apolitical, solitary, even
insouciant. But there is something more to Gregory's final, almost throw-
away, remark about Synge's clothing than might first be credited. In fact, the
act of refusing to wear black, of being wary about being out of (spiritual,
aesthetic) 'harmony' with nature, is evidence of a constellation of ideals
central to Synge and his work and fundamental to his political, aesthetic, and

---

[1] 'The Wild Swans at Coole', in *The Variorum Edition of the Poems of W. B. Yeats*, ed. Peter
Allt and Russell K. Alspach (New York: Macmillan, 1977), pp. 322–33. All future references to
Yeats's poems are taken from this edition, and referenced in the body of the text using *VP* and
page number.
[2] Lady Gregory, *Our Irish Theatre: A Chapter of Autobiography* (New York and London:
G.P. Putnam's Sons, 1913), p. 123.

J. M. Synge: Nature, Politics, Modernism. Seán Hewitt, Oxford University Press (2021). © Seán Hewitt.
DOI: 10.1093/oso/9780198862093.003.0001

philosophical values. Hardly comparable to W. B. Yeats, whose posturing, curated public persona and appearance was kept intact by a carefully planned wardrobe, Synge is not remembered as a man conscious of his dress in any artistic or philosophical sense. On the contrary, he believed (according to his nephew) that 'it was the duty of everyone to make himself as picturesque as possible'.[3] He appeared in a tableau of a gypsy camp while staying with friends in Oberwerth, Germany, and later dressed in a bohemian style on his return from the Continent.[4] In Lady Gregory's recollection, however, we get an insight into the values behind Synge's sartorial aesthetic. By shunning the colour black, he was in fact expressing a form of aesthetic pantheism that was at the heart of what this book calls his artistic philosophy—a set of closely held and guarded principles that guided the development of his writing from the bucolic poetic Romanticism of his youth to the combative theatrical modernism of his mature work. Taking primary political influences from William Morris, and primary spiritual influences from Spinoza, Synge insists on a pantheistic set of correspondences between nature and mankind. For him, the 'Universe is a divine unconsciousness', and 'All art that is not conceived by a soul in harmony with some mood of the earth is without value' (*CW* II, 35).[5] In that small sartorial decision, then, Synge gives us an insight into how seriously he took the values he formulated for himself, and how pervasive they were in both his life and his work.

Compounding Yeats's claim that Synge was a man 'by nature unfitted to think a political thought', enshrining him as a pure, inspired artist, a national genius for the new theatre, Gregory's recollected vision of Synge also forms part of a stubborn tendency over the course of the twentieth century to emphasize him as an apolitical writer.[6] T. R. Henn, for example, suggested that Synge was 'not concerned with the politics of his Ireland'.[7] Although some friends argued that Synge was 'most intensely Nationalist', or 'a keen observer of political conditions', others suggested that he 'cared

---

[3] Edward Stephens, *My Uncle John: Edward Stephens's Life of J. M. Synge*, ed. Andrew Carpenter (London: Oxford University Press, 1974), p. 176.

[4] Stephens, *My Uncle John*, pp. 91, 176.

[5] TCD MS 4392, quoted in Ann Saddlemyer, 'Synge and the Doors of Perception', in Andrew Carpenter, ed., *Place, Personality and the Irish Writer* (Gerrards Cross: Colin Smythe, 1977), 97–120, p. 103.

[6] W. B. Yeats, 'J. M. Synge and the Ireland of his Time', *Essays and Introductions* (New York: Macmillan, 1961), 311–42, p. 319.

[7] T. R. Henn, *Last Essays* (Gerrards Cross: Colin Smythe, 1976), p. 205.

nothing for either the political or the religious issue'.[8] These conflicting views arose from Synge's often slippery political statements and concerns, which must be understood alongside his aesthetic philosophy to be fully appreciated. Since the 1980s, however, a more historicist criticism has resulted in a wealth of nuanced discussions of Synge as political, unweaving the previously held Yeatsian image. By situating his work in the contexts of international modernism, critics have focused attention on the increasing tenor of Synge's works as a form of 'modernist provocation'.[9] Synge's politics, as Christopher Collins has recently argued, were 'channelled into aesthetics', though the sense of a one-way relationship suggested by the verb 'channelled' is misleading.[10] As this study shows, the influences of aesthetic and political thought, for Synge, existed in a much more fluid and mutually affecting relationship.

Synge belongs to a generation of writers who embraced socialism in the 1880s and 1890s, and for whom aesthetics, ethics, and politics were intimately related.[11] In rejecting Victorian materialism and positivism, fin de siècle socialists often hoped for a spiritual as well as a democratic revolution. Thomas Linehan suggests that, setting itself against the supposedly decadent values of the Victorian era, 'British socialism was a species of modernism in its own right'.[12] The complex relationship between ethics and aesthetics, a prominent feature of fin de siècle socialism, was professed captivatingly in the aesthetic democracy of William Morris, and Morrisian thought recurs throughout Synge's texts.[13] The desire for a reintegration between humankind and nature, especially, was fundamental to the socialism of both men. In fact, of the few photographs left in Synge's archives at Trinity College

---

[8] Quotations from Stephen MacKenna, John Quinn, and Arthur Lynch, respectively. See E. H. Mikhail, ed., *J. M. Synge: Interviews and Recollections*, with a foreword by Robin Skelton (London and Basingstoke: Macmillan, 1977), pp. 14, 80; and letter from John Quinn to F.J. Gregg, 1 April 1909, NYPL MS 2513.

[9] Mary Burke, 'The Riot of Spring: Synge's "Failed Realism" and the Peasant Drama', in Nicholas Grene and Chris Morash, eds., *The Oxford Handbook of Modern Irish Theatre* (Oxford: Oxford University Press, 2016), 87–102, p. 89.

[10] Christopher Collins, *Theatre and Residual Culture: J. M. Synge and Pre-Christian Ireland* (London: Palgrave Macmillan, 2016), p. 16.

[11] Ruth Livesey offers a solid introduction to this generation of writers in 'Socialism in Bloomsbury: Virginia Woolf and the Political Aesthetics of the 1880s', *The Yearbook of English Studies*, Vol. 37, No. 1 (2007), pp. 126–44.

[12] Thomas Linehan, *Modernism and British Socialism* (Basingstoke and New York: Palgrave Macmillan, 2012), p. 6.

[13] For more on Morris's aesthetic democracy, see Linda C. Dowling, *The Vulgarization of Art: The Victorians and Aesthetic Democracy* (London and Charlottesville, VA: University Press of Virginia, 1996), p. 51.

Dublin that were not taken by the writer himself, one is a portrait of William Morris, who died in 1896.[14] Though there is no evidence to suggest that Synge, unlike Yeats, ever met Morris, the importance of aesthetic socialism to his work should not be understated.[15] Like Synge's work, fin de siècle socialism was often rife with Romanticism (moments of heightened spirituality, a valorization of the child and the primitive), bringing into question Linehan's claim for it as a specifically modernist phenomenon. Rather, I argue that it is specifically in the difficulty of this ideal—in the places where it comes under political and social pressure—that it results in the development of a modernist aesthetic.

In a notebook entry written circa 1900, during which time he was composing his first play, *When the Moon Has Set* (1900–3), Synge summarized the three systems of thought with which he was working at the time:

> Hegelian and all other mystic dogmatisms give way before a pantheistic emotion which is spread so widely before the path we follow that it seems the inevitable and ultimate mood of all ~~literature~~ art. William Morris. Breton Mysteries. Spinoza.[16]

The rejection of dogmatic or organized religion, and the revealing triad of socialism, peasant culture, and pantheism, form an apt summary of the core features of Synge's philosophy. Although G. J. Watson has hinted cryptically at Synge's 'value system', no critic has fully undertaken the task of defining, and exploring the implications of, this system.[17] In an early poem, Synge writes that 'For my own soul I would a world create, / A Christless creed, incredulous, divine'; however, unlike his contemporary W. B. Yeats, who prepared various complex and detailed expositions of his artistic philosophy, from *Per Anima Silentia Lunae* (1918) to his vast work *A Vision* (1925 and 1937), Synge left no protracted and explicit statement of his aesthetic, spiritual, or political 'creed'. Rather, despite the prefaces to his plays being read recently as a form of manifesto, Synge's philosophy was never worked

---

[14] TCD MS 4367, item 40.

[15] Roy Foster suggests that Morris became a sort of 'heroic leader' for the young Yeats, who briefly adopted Morrisite communism before rejecting it for its attitude to religion. For more on W. B. Yeats's interactions with Morris and his political and aesthetic thought, see Roy Foster, *W. B. Yeats: A Life, I: The Apprentice Mage, 1865–1914* (Oxford and New York: Oxford University Press, 1997), pp. 59–64, 87.

[16] TCD MS 4389, f. 53v.

[17] G. J. Watson, *Irish Identity and the Literary Revival: Synge, Yeats, Joyce and O'Casey*, 2nd edn. (Washington, DC: The Catholic University Press of America, 1979, 1994), p. 47.

into a static 'system'.[18] The development of his work over the space of his short career, however, cannot be fully appreciated without first understanding the foundational positions which underscore it. Synge spent many years of philosophical, political, and aesthetic theorization before his first successful works were produced, and formulated various axioms for 'healthy' art, meaning that as the tenets of his philosophy were tested by the realities of a fraught political and social landscape, his literary work became increasingly defensive. As he perceived that the dominant political, social, and aesthetic trends might threaten the integrity of his philosophy, Synge redoubled his protests against them.

This study thus charts the development of Synge's modernist art as a fraught reactive battle between aesthetic socialism and the increasing pressures of capitalist modernization and restrictive political nationalism. Many studies have posited right-wing views as a political corollary to modernism, and have highlighted a tendency towards authoritarianism, and even fascism, particularly amongst canonical figures such as Yeats, Eliot, and Pound.[19] Where Elizabeth Cullingford suggests that Yeats's early enthusiasm for William Morris, and his desire for revolution, laid the groundwork for his anti-capitalist interest in fascism, this book argues that Synge's socialism led him to a rebellious modernism that remained rooted in left-wing politics through an awareness of the importance of economic and industrial reforms.[20] In contrast to a proposed 'religion of socialism', or a Yeatsian 'church of poetic tradition', Synge constructed a set of values that fetishized nature and saw harmony with nature as the prerequisite factor for a healthy society.[21] That he saw societal and physical degeneration as symptoms of a disconnection from nature eventually brought him into flirtation with contemporary debates around eugenics, though he avoided succumbing to positing genetic solutions through his belief in socialist principles of economic reform. In an article published in *The Speaker*, Synge contrasted the works of the novelists Joris-Karl Huysmans and

---

[18] Levitas, 'The Abbey and the Idea of a Theatre', p. 49.

[19] See, in particular, Charles Ferrall, *Modernist Writing and Reactionary Politics* (Cambridge: Cambridge University Press, 2001); Michael North, *The Political Aesthetic of Yeats, Eliot, and Pound* (Cambridge: Cambridge University Press, 1991); Annalisa Zox-Weaver, *Women Modernists and Facism* (Cambridge: Cambridge University Press, 2011).

[20] Elizabeth Cullingford, *Yeats, Ireland, and Fascism* (London and Basingstoke: Macmillan, 1981), p. 16.

[21] The phrase 'religion of socialism' is taken from Stephen Yeo, 'A New Life: The Religion of Socialism in Britain, 1883-1896', *History Workshop Journal*, 4 (1977), 5–55. Yeats's discusses his building of a 'church of poetic tradition' as a response to loss of orthodox religious faith in *Autobiographies: Memories and Reflections* (London: Macmillan, 1955), pp. 115–16.

Pierre Loti with the works of Anatole France. Huysmans and Loti, he suggests, produce a 'feeling of unreality'; by contrast, the ironical novels of Anatole France manifest a 'half-cynical optimism' alongside 'socialistic ideals', which combine to form 'a practical philosophy...that is fearless and perfectly healthy'.[22] However true this may be of France, it is certainly indicative of Synge's own artistic values.

No doubt inculcated by his time in Paris, a city experiencing the emergence of a theatrical modernism that raised aesthetic and political challenges to the French government as well as to the structures of literary drama, Synge's views were ardently socialist, even leaning towards anarchism at times. He was, in his own words, a 'radical', someone who 'want[ed] change root and branch'.[23] His socialism preceded his nationalism in terms of immediate importance: as he told Maud Gonne in Paris, he opposed militant nationalism, and he assured his mother that, for him, home rule would be a natural development from the spread of socialism. As she related in a letter to his brother, Robert, 'he thinks Ireland will come to its own in years to come when socialistic ideas spread in England, but he does not at all approve of fighting for freedom.'[24] The sense that socialistic ideas would coalesce with anti-imperialist thought was, as Fintan Lane notes, common to William Morris's writings on the Irish question.[25]

Synge was well read in contemporary socialism and showed a marked concern for workers' rights and a nuanced attention to class politics from an early age.[26] He convinced his mother to change the family subscription from the *Daily Express* to *The Irish Times*, which, though still Unionist, was more liberal in its politics. He must have been fervent enough in his argument, since his mother changed the subscription despite the fact that she thought

[22] 'Three French Writers', in *CW* II, 395–6, p. 395. The original article was entitled 'Loti and Huysmans', *The Speaker*, 18 April 1903.

[23] *CL* I, p. xiii.

[24] Letter from Kathleen Synge to Robert Synge, quoted in David H. Greene and Edward M. Stephens, *J. M. Synge, 1871–1909* (New York: Macmillan, 1959), p. 63. No date given.

[25] Fintan Lane, *The Origins of Modern Irish Socialism, 1881–1896* (Cork: Cork University Press, 1997), pp. 105–43.

[26] Between 1893 and 1897 Synge read John A. Hobson's *Problems of Poverty: An Inquiry into the Industrial Condition of the Poor* (1891), various works by William Morris and Karl Marx, and works on socialism and 'individualism' more broadly, such as Edward Caird's *Individualism and Socialism* (1897), Benjamin Kidd's *Social Evolution* (1894), and Isaac Taylor's *Ultimate Civilization and other essays* (1860). See TCD MSS 4414, 4416, 4418, 4379. He also read Victor Considerant's *Principes du socialisme* (1843), Henri Brissac and Alfred Naquet's *Pour et contre le collectivisme* (1895), Gabriel Deville's 'L'État et le socialisme' (1895), and other works on socialism and anarchy. For more on Synge's reading in socialism, see Declan Kiberd, *Inventing Ireland: The Literature of the Modern Nation* (London: Vintage, 1996), p. 175.

The Irish Times was 'a rebel paper'.[27] Indeed, Synge was 'not only nationalist but socialist in principle'.[28] While it has been posited that 'Synge's dramatization of peasant life simply does not reflect the socialism he had evidently read about', this book argues stridently that his reading in socialism, alongside his engagement with sociology, anthropology, and contemporary politics, is integral to the particular drama that he produced, and also to the development of that drama.[29]

In Paris, the riots over the first performance of Alfred Jarry's *Ubu Roi* (1896), an avant-garde play considered to be 'an assault on the audience, upsetting expectations, meant to create antagonism and discredit authority', would certainly have come to Synge's attention, even if he was not in attendance.[30] In fact, Jarry's collapsing of the distinction between noble and ignoble, between 'primitive' and civilized, finds a striking afterlife in Synge's own riot-inducing masterpiece, *The Playboy of the Western World*, first performed just over a decade later. In Dublin, the establishment of an Irish Literary Theatre sought, like the Théâtre Libre and the Théâtre de l'Œuvre, to offer an experimental and more overtly literary alternative to the popular fare of melodrama and, as Lauren Arrington has shown, its contentious relations with the state characterized its development.[31] Synge's exposure to modernist, symbolist theatre in Paris (where he lived in the countercultural Rive Gauche, in the Latin quarter) certainly contributed to his understanding of modern theatre, even if the techniques he used would be different to those employed by the modernist directors in France, who tended to focus the theatre away from language, and to use staging to suggest interior states. His combination of Rabelaisian humour with the dreaminess of fin de siècle mysticism is what sets him apart from contemporaries such as Maeterlinck, Yeats, and Arthur Symons, but it is only through the crucible of the Revival and the pressure of Irish politics that this Rabelaisian streak, which was also the defining essence of Synge's modernism, would be activated. Understanding theatre as a political art was fundamental to

---

[27] Greene and Stephens, *J. M. Synge, 1871–1909*, p. 26.
[28] Nicholas Grene, 'On the Margins: Synge and Wicklow', in Nicholas Grene, ed., *Interpreting Synge: Essays from the Synge Summer School, 1991–2000* (Dublin: Lilliput Press, 2000), 20–40, p. 22.
[29] Paul Murphy, *Hegemony and Fantasy in Irish Drama, 1899–1949* (Basingstoke: Palgrave Macmillan, 2008), p. 39.
[30] Sally Debra Charnow, *Theatre, Politics, and Markets in Fin-de-Siècle Paris* (Basingstoke: Palgrave Macmillan, 2005), p. 140.
[31] See, in particular, the first chapter of Lauren Arrington, *W. B. Yeats, the Abbey Theatre, Censorship, and the Irish State: Adding the Half-Pence to the Pence* (Oxford and New York: Oxford University Press, 2010).

Synge and, as Ben Levitas has argued, his writing was at times specifically engaged in a form of protest, of 'interventionism', the famous riotous responses being orchestrated with intent.[32] Though Nicholas Grene sees little evidence to suggest that *The Playboy* was written with the audience reaction in mind, Synge's conception of his own literary project did become increasingly political.[33] This is not to say for certain that he intended riots; rather, it demonstrates that the rioters reacted to a consciously combative strain in Synge's work.

The Decadent emphasis on rejuvenation, both physical and literary, became a constant touchstone for Synge's theorizing. As Patrick McGuinness notes, Anatole Baju (editor of *Le Décadent*) and his collaborators 'repeatedly sought to distinguish between the "*decadence*" of the ruling class and ideology, of the republican body politic, and the modernity and progressiveness of the *decadent* writer'.[34] Synge's claim to progressiveness takes similar tenets, lambasting the malaise of the Irish political classes and the monotonizing effect of capitalist modernization, though his flirtation with composing 'decadent' writing was relatively short-lived. The Revivalist concern with racial characteristics, with how the 'Celtic race' might prove its difference from the Anglo-Saxon and thus be placed in innate opposition to both anglicization and modernity, was coupled with a simultaneous fear of degeneration, which for many Revivalists (most notably Douglas Hyde) was characterized by the insidious workings of anglicization on the colonized mind.[35] The rejuvenation of the national body was thus central to Revivalism, and the language of regeneration is prevalent throughout its texts.[36] As across Europe, the source of rejuvenation was generally seen as

---

[32] Ben Levitas, 'The Abbey and the Idea of a Theatre', in Grene and Morash, eds., *Oxford Handbook*, 41–57, p. 49. See also Ben Levitas, *The Theatre of Nation: Irish Drama and Cultural Nationalism, 1890–1916* (Oxford: Clarendon Press, 2002), pp. 115–36.

[33] Nicholas Grene, 'J. M. Synge: Late Romantic or Protomodernist?', in Gregory Castle and Patrick Bixby, eds., *A History of Irish Modernism* (Cambridge: Cambridge University Press, 2019), 78–90, p. 87.

[34] Patrick McGuinness, 'Introduction', in Patrick McGuinness, ed., *Symbolism, Decadence and the Fin de Siècle: French and European Perspectives* (Exeter: University of Exeter Press, 2000), p. 6.

[35] See especially Douglas Hyde, 'The Necessity for De-Anglicising Ireland', in Charles Gavan Duffy, George Sigerson, and Douglas Hyde, *The Revival of Irish Literature* (London: T. F. Unwin, 1894), pp. 115–61.

[36] Joep Leerssen writes, 'The horizon of expectation of the Abbey audiences was habituated, through a thousand turns of phrase and metaphor, to see Irish cultural nationalism as aiming at a *revival*, a *rejuvenation*, turning Kathleen Ní Houlihan from an old hag into a young queen.' *Remembrance and Imagination: Patterns in the Historical and Literary Representation of Ireland in the Nineteenth Century* (Cork: Cork University Press, 1996), p. 222.

the natural environment and the peasantry (who, by extension, were deemed more 'natural' by their close association with nature), both of which were held as being untainted by modernity.[37] Yeats, when he first visited Coole, for example, described in his journal 'servants and labourers who seemed themselves natural, as bird and tree are natural'.[38] The discursive processes of the Revival, in seeking in the natural and in the 'pre-modern' a source of revitalization, a sort of primitive corrective to modernity, are attempts to establish (and attain primacy for) a distinctive vision of racial and cultural 'authenticity'. As is well known, the question of national identity formation in this period was fought out in the alembic of the theatre, where rivalling visions of 'authentic' Irishness could be sanctioned, legitimized, and (sometimes violently) critiqued.

Synge's protest was thus twofold. His artistic experiment was conceived, in many ways, as a protest against existing literary conditions: against the prosaic language of realism; the morbidity of fin de siècle Decadence; the idealized spiritual detachment of the Celtic Twilight; the dull moralism of Victorianism and Romantic visions of the peasantry. But along with this literary protest, which led him into modernist experimentation, came a more overtly political form of protest: an attack on nationalist orthodoxies regarding Irish moral superiority; an attack on the modernization schemes of constructive unionism; an attack on what he called the 'ungodly ruck of fat-faced, sweaty-headed swine' that constituted the middle class of Irish Catholics (CL I, 328-9). Synge's invective against a homogeneous audience, and his hatred for the Catholic bourgeoisie, are mirrored not only in the form of his drama but in his political aggression towards the introduction of increasingly capitalist forms of modernization into rural areas. This book thus shows that Synge's drama is as much a form of political as of literary protest. Over his career, the very plays that came to fracture the tenuously held image of a homogeneous audience would also blow apart the image of a pious, compliant peasantry; and the very bourgeois Catholic nationalists Synge hoped to offend are also those he held partially responsible for the increasing degeneration of rural communities. Synge's socialist politics, in this way, are fundamental to his turn towards a combative theatrical modernism.

---

[37] See Marius Turda, *Modernism and Eugenics* (New York: Palgrave Macmillan, 2012), p. 4. For a wide-ranging exploration of discourses of degeneration in European culture, see Daniel Pick, *Faces of Degeneration: A European Disorder, c.1848—c.1918* (Cambridge: Cambridge University Press, 1989).

[38] W. B. Yeats, *Memoirs*, ed. Denis Donoghue (London: Macmillan, 1972), pp. 101-2.

Ever since Yeats made that false claim regarding Synge's apolitical mind-set, a current of critical thought was established which read Synge's plays, too, as being disconnected from contemporary politics, presenting a dehistoricized peasantry existing outside of economic or social change.[39] Over the past few decades, however, such a view has been gradually subjected to critical pressure. This has in part been effected through pioneering work in the theatre itself. Through the directorial work of Irish director Garry Hynes, whose productions of Synge in the 1980s, and later with *DruidSynge*, seemed 'to discover Synge's modernity', Synge began to be freed from the image of the Romantic wanderer, and his dark brutality revealed.[40] The later work of Martin McDonagh (many of whose plays were also directed by Hynes), and to a lesser degree Marina Carr, has helped to realign Synge with a modern Irish tradition of politically engaged theatrical violence and satire.

Emilie Morin has recently challenged the notion that Samuel Beckett's plays were evidence of a writer 'peculiarly unqualified for political activity'. The critical inheritance Morin charts, which has tended to see Beckett's works as 'expressions of a tortured psyche' detached from political concerns, is similar to Synge's fate in literary criticism over the majority of the twentieth century, which becomes more striking when we consider the many similarities between the two writers (not least their use of silence, empty space, and their preoccupation with characters thrust into a sort of existential dread).[41] Maurice Bourgeois, Synge's first biographer, was one of the first to argue for Synge's drama as apolitical, writing that 'Synge has no wish to change or reform anything: his contention is that the theatre, even in a land of controversy like Ireland, must remain in its purely artistic sphere.'[42] The function of art, the primacy of an artistic life and the artistic imagination, however, are political in Synge's thought. Nicholas Grene has best summed up the prevailing view of Synge's drama, even now, as being 'associated with a late romantic cult of the peasant, a pastoral kitsch particularly distasteful in a country bent on establishing its credentials as a fully

[39] Seamus Deane, for example, sees Synge's drama as exhibiting an 'almost total absence of historical references'. *Celtic Revivals: Essays in Modern Irish Literature, 1880–1980* (London: Faber & Faber, 1985), p. 55.

[40] Normand Berlin, 'Traffic of Our Stage: DruidSynge', *Massachusetts Review*, Vol. 48, No. 1 (Spring, 2007), 90–102, p. 90.

[41] Emilie Morin, *Beckett's Political Imagination* (Cambridge: Cambridge University Press, 2017), pp. 1–2.

[42] Maurice Bourgeois, *John Millington Synge and the Irish Theatre* (London: Constable & Company, 1913), p. 139.

modernized urban society'.[43] Alarmingly, this idea of a dehistoricized peasantry in Revivalist literature has, on occasion, even been reapplied to the actual historical circumstances of the peasantry themselves. Thus, Weldon Thornton, discussing Synge's *The Aran Islands*, suggests that 'we can safely say that the Aran Islands, especially the smaller two, were in Synge's day as uninfluenced by modern communication, transportation, and technology as any part of Europe, and that they differed little from what they had been a thousand years before.'[44] One might argue that this historical inaccuracy is merely the result of a too-close application of the vision of the islands presented in Synge's text to actual historical conditions. However, as later critics have demonstrated, such views are inaccurate not only historically but also in terms of the rural world as presented in Synge's works, which are constantly alive to the pressures of modernity and social change.

The damage carried out to our understanding of Synge and his place within Revivalism and modernism by this view of him as an apolitical writer is currently being redressed in criticism, and this book works to continue that reassessment. Although the project of recovering a political Synge was begun by one of his most attentive critics and editors, Robin Skelton, recent critical work has allowed for a much more thorough reconsideration of Synge's achievement by engaging more closely with historical contexts.[45] Brian Cliff and Nicholas Grene's *Synge and Edwardian Ireland* collects essays that foreground the rapid processes of modernization during the Revival period, and offer a number of readings of Synge's work which reveal him to be an artist in constant dialogue with modernity, politics, and technological advancement.[46] Such a reassessment has necessarily been accompanied by a heightened awareness of Synge as a man much concerned with politics, and as a man with a carefully reasoned set of political values. Nelson O'Ceallaigh Ritschel suggests a 'socialistic bridge' between George Bernard Shaw, Synge, and James Connolly, and draws on the new image of a 'leftist, socially liberal Synge' in order to read *The Playboy of the Western World* as a 'nationalist socialist' play written in opposition to the 'bourgeois

[43] Nicholas Grene, 'Introduction', in Grene, ed., *Interpreting Synge*, 11–16, p. 12.

[44] Weldon Thornton, *J. M. Synge and the Western Mind* (Gerrards Cross: Colin Smythe, 1979), p. 60.

[45] See Robin Skelton, 'The Politics of J. M. Synge', *The Massachusetts Review*, Vol. 18, No. 1 (Spring, 1977), 7–22.

[46] Brian Cliff and Nicholas Grene, eds., *Synge and Edwardian Ireland* (Oxford: Oxford University Press, 2012). The essays collected here, for example, assess Synge's photography, his use of a typewriter, and his engagement with modernization on the Aran Islands.

nationalist' world of its detractors.[47] Even more recently, Susan Cannon Harris has shown how Synge's drama, particularly *Riders to the Sea* (1904), influenced leftist theatre groups across Europe and was adapted by Bertolt Brecht into a revolutionary narrative in his play *Señora Carrar's Rifles* (1937).[48]

There has been a similar disagreement regarding Synge's attitude to modernization, so much so that, within a single volume, David Fitzpatrick can argue that 'as a celebrant of tradition, [Synge] instinctively deplored factors tending to reduce deprivation and promote modernization, such as state-sponsored investment, emigration, and linguistic change' and, to the contrary, Nicholas Allen can assert that Synge was 'open to the idea of transition in language, culture, and economy'.[49] This book suggests that Synge was, in fact, open to social modernization, though he did oppose schemes of modernization that he saw as homogenizing, capitalist, and 'inorganic', by which he understood that they were imposed on communities by the state rather than being natural progressions of community traditions towards modernity. He opposes what Joe Cleary describes as the particular 'diffusionist model' of modernization which Ireland experienced, in which the modern is transferred and disseminated via the expansion of the British state and its colonial representatives, as opposed to through any concerted effort or exertion of the existing culture to modernize on its own terms.[50]

It could be argued that Synge was ready to adopt the benefits of modernity for himself, but not willing to allow it to the peasantry he wrote about. He bought his first camera in the 1890s, used a typewriter, and travelled regularly by train. All of these technologies aided Synge's writing, and marked him as a modern writer amongst the rural communities in which he travelled. He also, however, advocated the construction of a free railway between Leixlip and Dublin, as well as a new housing estate, in order to ease overcrowding in the city, and came to develop a nuanced stance on

---

[47]   Nelson O'Ceallaigh Ritschel, *Shaw, Synge, Connolly, and Socialist Provocation* (Gainesville, FL: University of Florida Press, 2011), pp. 5, 76.

[48]   See Susan Cannon Harris, *Irish Drama and the Other Revolutions: Playwrights, Sexual Politics, and the International Left, 1892–1964* (Edinburgh: Edinburgh University Press, 2017), pp. 135–68.

[49]   Cliff and Grene, eds., *Synge and Edwardian Ireland*, pp. 137, 170.

[50]   Joe Cleary, 'Introduction: Ireland and Modernity', in Joe Cleary and Claire Connolly, eds., *The Cambridge Companion to Modern Irish Culture* (Cambridge: Cambridge University Press, 2005), 1–24, see especially pp. 3–7.

modernization and state intervention.[51] Far from focusing on areas untouched by the 'filthy modern tide' (*VP*, 610), Synge punctuated his career with travels through the 'congested districts' of Ireland, which were undergoing a process of modernization overseen by a recently established government board for the purpose, the Congested Districts Board for Ireland (1891–1923). It is no coincidence that the progressions in Synge's dramatic works roughly coincide with periods of travel in these modernizing districts, during which he wrote prose works which explored the problems faced by the communities on the western seaboard and elsewhere. The two most recent book-length studies of Synge, by Christopher Collins and Giulia Bruna, focus on the dramatic works and the travel writing respectively. In taking a holistic approach to Synge's oeuvre, I hope to demonstrate not only that such a distinction is arbitrary, but that it maintains a false divide between sociopolitical engagement and artistic experiment that hinders a full appreciation of Synge's writings.[52] His reactions to, and observations of, modernization are key to understanding the development of his work, which displays a sharp awareness of changing social conditions and processes of modernization in the cultural, geographical, and literary fields. Synge sought out the places where the old and new interacted, and it is from these moments that he found his greatest inspiration. In fact, for him, the 'old and new' constituted the 'two streams of humanity', and it was on the interaction of these currents that art, and the 'purer movements of mankind', depended (*CW* II, 394).

It is clear from his notebooks that Synge was preoccupied not solely with social modernity but also with artistic modernity. In noting down the titles of the works he was reading, for example, he miswrote some of them to include the word 'modern'. Ferdinand Brunetière's *Le Symbolisme contemporain* (1891), for example, is miswritten as 'Le Symbolisme modern'; Victor Charbonnel's *Les mystiques dans la littérature présente* (1897) becomes 'Les mystiques dans la littérature moderne'.[53] This small evidence at least contributes to our understanding of Synge's awareness of, and preoccupation with, the idea of the modern in literature and with the challenges being undertaken in some movements of contemporary writing. Attempting to define the tangible sense of a 'modern' art in a notebook used in 1900, Synge

---

[51] In his diary for 1892. TCD MS 4413, f. 17v.

[52] Christopher Collins, *Theatre and Residual Culture: J. M. Synge and Pre-Christian Ireland* (London: Palgrave Macmillan, 2016); Giulia Bruna, *J. M. Synge and Travel Writing of the Irish Revival* (New York: Syracuse University Press, 2017).

[53] TCD MS 4419, ff. 27r., 29v.

asked himself, 'How does modern literature exist in the chaos of root ideas?'[54] Synge was thus theorizing a relationship between modern literature and chaos, between what we now term modernism and the complex of ideas which it is its mission to express. The feeling that the 'root ideas' of society were in a state of chaos—that religious, social, and political norms were being destabilized by modernity—is recurrent in Synge's early notebooks and essays. His questioning of how 'modern literature' has adapted to this chaos, or at least how it exists within it, is paramount to understanding that Synge did have a critical sense of the modern, and that in this sense he displays many of the key preoccupations of an early modernist writer.[55] In fact, Synge's early theorization of the Revival and its cultural precursors reveals that he saw the movement in terms commensurate with our critical understanding of the impulses of early modernism, pinpointing evolutionism and 'freed thought', alongside a 'new creative force', as the potential causes of the movement.[56]

It has often been suggested that Synge's reading was largely orthodox, consisting mostly of the classics of the Western canon; that his appetite for contemporary works was small. Grene notes that 'the books in the family library had all passed the strictest entrance requirements...and there were no magazines, current novels or other frivolous reading matter'.[57] Commenting on Synge's later reading habits, McCormack insists that Synge 'had a small appetite for contemporary literature'.[58] Indeed, Synge was primarily a reader of canonical literature. However, alongside Yeats's comments that Synge did not 'admit the existence of other writers' and that 'in the arts he knew no language but his own', these claims (however true) have contributed to an underlying assumption of Synge's artistic insularity. By referring to Synge's journals, in which he details his day-to-day reading, and to his notebooks, in which he summarizes and comments on the arguments of various thinkers, this book shows that Synge cannot be fully understood without regarding the influence of a large number of other writers, both the canonical and the relatively obscure. Making sustained use of archival materials to uncover the intimate connections between Synge's reading, his drafts and his published works, this book reveals

---

[54] TCD MS 4392, f. 2r.

[55] The idea of modernism as a cultural response to the perception of modernity as a crisis is central to many critical examinations of the movement. See, for example, Tonning, *Modernism and Christianity*, pp. 1–2.

[56] TCD MS 4393, f. 1r.   [57] Greene and Stephens, *J. M. Synge, 1871–1909*, p. 15.

[58] McCormack, *Fool of the Family*, p. 24.

Synge as engaged in many currents of contemporary political, aesthetic, and spiritual thought, and shows just how closely his artistic production is influenced by, and responsive to, such discourses. Rather than being the product of a man with 'no life outside his imagination', Synge's drama is the culmination of an intimate engagement with political and social change.[59] In each chapter, Synge's early drafts, his aesthetic notes, his letters, his notes on reading, and the lists of books which he read are used to unravel the complex political and aesthetic philosophy he developed. In turn, this work allows us to better understand the shifts in his drama, which are responses to various threats, both literary and political, to his fundamental values. One of the main innovations of this book is its attempt to explore, with a broad scope, the underpinning values of Synge's art. Rather than focusing on his engagement with any discrete subject, I examine the confluence of various themes in Synge's work to suggest a broader underlying set of artistic and political concerns, through which we can better understand his work and its relationship to both Revivalism and early modernism.

For Synge, Revivalism was specifically linked to the peculiar temporal categories of a modernizing Ireland. Cóilín Parsons has recently noted the prevalence of overlapping timescales in Synge's prose, seeing Synge's modernism as being occasioned by the fact that the community he encountered on the Aran Islands was one 'that doesn't resist, but rather *defines* modernity'.[60] 'The tension between the archaic and the modern', as Gregory Castle demonstrates, 'characterizes Irish modernism generally.'[61] This is partly because, as David Lloyd has claimed, post-Famine Irish culture remained resistant to certain 'obliterative' forms of modernization 'both in the invention of social formations and imaginaries that project temporal horizons and ethical frames that are out of kilter with modernity and in the displaced structures of memory that refuse to succumb to forgetting and moving on'.[62] Synge was acutely aware of this. Indeed, in one of his first published articles, written after his first visit to the Aran Islands in 1898, Synge makes a comparison between the position of the Breton folklorist and translator Anatole Le Braz (1859–1926) and his own, contrasting the temporal

[59] Yeats, *Essays and Introductions*, p. 329.

[60] Cóilín Parsons, *The Ordnance Survey and Modern Irish Literature* (Oxford: Oxford University Press, 2016), p. 122.

[61] Gregory Castle, for example, argues that 'the tension between the archaic and the modern...characterizes Irish modernism generally'. See *Modernism and the Celtic Revival* (Cambridge: Cambridge University Press, 2001), p. 207.

[62] Lloyd, *Irish Times*, p. 6.

experiences of a writer in Ireland and in Brittany. Whereas Le Braz grew up amongst the peasantry, speaking mainly their language, by the turn of the nineteenth century the majority of the Irish population could not enjoy such a privilege, and so became more conscious of the stratification of time and its cultural effects:

> In Ireland it is different. The same survivals of the old have not for us the charms of lingering regret, but rather the incitement of a thing that is rare and beautiful, and still apart from our habitual domain. If an Irishman of modern culture dwells for a while on Inishmaan, or Inisheer, or, perhaps, anywhere among the mountains of Connaught, he will not find there any trace of an external at-homeness, but will rather yield himself up to the entrancing newness of the old.   (CW II, 394)

The culture shock is facilitated by the time shock, and the presence of the old, seen as a 'survival' of modernization, is recognized as pertaining to an entirely different culture from that of the anglicized writer. Continuity is compromised. The world of the old in Ireland is not Synge's past—he is separated from it by language, culture, and heritage to such a degree that it becomes 'new'. The fact that it is a remnant of the old means that it has resisted anglicization and is strange to the 'modern' visitor because it represents a tradition and culture largely unrepresented in contemporary urban Ireland.[63] What Synge called the 'shock of new material', therefore, need not necessarily be interpreted in the sense typical to understanding modernism as a reaction to the newness of technological and scientific advancement; rather, the fact that Ireland consisted of geographies where uneven temporalities coexisted meant that the 'modern' mind of the city dweller met the remnants of the 'old' in the Gaelic culture of the western counties. The effects of the modernization process in Ireland, therefore, allowed the 'old' to be redesignated as 'new', but also emphasized its contrariness to certain forms of modernity.[64]

Synge's continuous study of the Irish language, both through immersion during his visits to the Aran Islands and West Kerry, and through scholarly

[63] For more on this idea, see David Lloyd, *Irish Times: Temporalities of Modernity* (Dublin: Keough-Naughton Institute for Irish Studies, University of Notre Dame/Field Day, 2008), pp. 10–21.

[64] Recalled by W. B. Yeats in 'The Bounty of Sweden', in *Autobiographies: Memories and Reflections* (London: Macmillan, 1955), 529–72, p. 531.

study in Dublin and Paris, informed his sense of the 'old' and its uses, in many ways setting him apart from his contemporaries and working as a catalyst for his 'brutal' drama. In his preface to *Beside the Fire*, his collection of Irish folk tales, Douglas Hyde referred to this Irish-language tradition as 'part of the flotsam and jetsam of the ages, still beating feebly against the shore of the nineteenth century, swallowed up at last in England by the waves of materialism and civilization combined; but still surviving unengulfed on the western coasts of Ireland'.[65] Yeats, reviewing the book, figured the lyrical world of the Irish-speaking peasantry and their culture as prelapsarian, even tinged with the animism of a 'pre-civilised' people: 'We stand outside the wall of Eden and hear the trees talking together within, and their talk is sweet in our ears.'[66] In similar fashion, Synge weaponized Irish-language culture as a 'survival of the old' which could be set in opposition to anglicization, materialism, and the homogenizing effects of civilizing imperatives. For Synge, however, who studied 'Celtic' literature and was much less perturbed by the tradition's sex, violence, and depiction of women than many of his contemporaries, Irish-language culture was both lyrical and brutal, poetic and wild. Its revitalizing possibilities were based not only in its Romantic and idealized forms, but (as Sinéad Garrigan Mattar has shown) in its oppositional nature, in 'what is most brutal, sexual, and contrary'.[67]

Following on from Parsons, this book examines the effect of overlapping temporalities on Synge's drama, demonstrating the correlation between modernization and the new formal characteristics of literary modernism, examining the interactions between this vital world of the 'old' and the civilizing world of the 'new'. However, the aesthetic influences on Synge's modernism are also brought to the fore. Tom Walker has noted the prevalent Marxist narrative in studies of Irish modernism that suggests that artistic change is rooted in uneven development, in social and political fracture, hence 'Irish artists' innovative search, whether as revivalists, modernists or (now more complexly) both, to find an adequate means of expressing such social contradictions'.[68] Walker counters by suggesting

---

[65] Douglas Hyde, *Beside the Fire: A Collection of Irish Gaelic Folk Stories*, with notes by Alfred Nutt (London: David Nutt, 1890), p. x.

[66] *Uncollected Prose, Volume I: First Reviews and Articles, 1886–1896*, collected and edited by John P. Frayne (London: Macmillan, 1970), p. 295.

[67] Sinéad Garrigan Mattar, *Primitivism, Science, and the Irish Revival* (Oxford: Clarendon Press, 2004), p. 4.

[68] Tom Walker, 'The culture of art in 1880s Ireland and the genealogy of Irish modernism', *Irish Studies Review*, Vol. 26, No. 3 (2018), 304–17, p. 306. Key proponents of the 'uneven

the importance of new aesthetic ideology and conditions on the development of modernist art, drawing particular attention to William Morris's influence and the intersections of Revivalism, modernism, cultural nationalism, and art in the 1880s. Synge's experimentation with, and deployment of, new aesthetic principles, and the dialectic between aesthetics and politics, are fundamental to understanding the complex interplays between Romanticism, modernism, modernity, and political radicalism that this study foregrounds.

The argument that Synge was an acute and careful commentator on the effects of modernization is coupled, in this book, with an attempt to establish Synge as a mystical thinker, and with the insistence that these two facets of his writings are inextricable. Though Synge's mystical tendencies might appear obvious to readers familiar with the rapturous visions of the natural world in plays like *The Shadow of the Glen* and *The Well of the Saints*, it is important to emphasize that this spirituality is inscribed as a reaction to modernity and the pressures of communal dissolution. As Synge's most recent biographer, W. J. McCormack, suggests:

> Synge's spiritualist interests do not derive from his friend Yeats's commitment to the world of faery; they precipitate from the dissolution of communities (including his own family) throughout the nineteenth century, from dissolution and phantasmal resolution. In reciprocal fashion, his declared sympathy with socialism is partly a revulsion *against* society (as he knew it, mainly in Ireland) and partly a contribution to the reconstruction of some framing outlook... in which spiritual, aesthetic, and ethical values might constellate.[69]

The first two chapters of this book explore this idea in detail, demonstrating that Synge's deployment of various spiritualist discourses constitutes a way of bridging, even if only momentarily, the temporal and cultural ruptures resultant from the processes of modernization. In both his use of spirituality as an attempt to bridge the divisions of modernity and his harnessing of modern scientific knowledge and rejection of occult ritual, Synge's

---

development' narrative of Irish modernism include David Lloyd's *Irish Times* and Terry Eagleton's essay 'The Archaic Avant-Garde', in *Heathcliff and the Great Hunger: Studies in Irish Culture* (London and New York: Verso, 1995), 273–319.

[69] W. J. McCormack, *Fool of the Family: A Life of J. M. Synge* (London: Weidenfeld & Nicolson, 2000), p. 27.

mysticism aims at the Romantic but constantly registers its own inability to access a transcendent world. Unlike the peasant figures he observes, Synge's own modernity prohibits an unconscious spirituality.

It is this coexistence of Romanticism and modernity in Synge's works which has perhaps obscured the ways in which his drama exhibits an increasing modernism over the course of his career. Katherine Worth, in her important exploration of the European influences on modern Irish drama (and particularly on Irish modernism), suggests that Synge might at first seem out of place in a discussion of modernist playwrights, noting his lack of radical experiment in dance, masks and music.[70] For Thomas Kilroy, Synge is 'technically conservative', and this distinguishes him from his 'modernist contemporaries', who embarked on a 'progressive search for new forms to match the radical programme of the new drama'.[71] Where one critic argues that Synge was 'a Romantic through and through', another makes the claim that Synge's project 'is ultimately modernist and not Romantic'.[72] This book argues that Synge was a dramatist who was formally experimental, and who persistently sought to produce a literature that he saw as adapted to present conditions and concerns. Though he may, at heart, have been a 'Romantic through and through', his experience of modernization, of political, social, and cultural tensions, and his belief in the truth of modern scientific knowledge, meant that he was constantly questioning his own Romanticism and his own attraction to the picturesque. Synge's project historicizes the peasantry, deconstructs and protests against what he perceives as the discursive violence of Romantic cultural nationalism, and is ultimately modernist because it insistently registers the growing impossibility of the Romantic.

This book, then, argues that it is perhaps most helpful to consider Synge as a Romantic in temperament but a modernist in practice. The Irish Revival is now being understood 'less as the diametric antithesis of modernism than as its discursive sibling', as 'contiguous with modernism rather than merely

[70] Katherine Worth, *The Irish Drama of Europe from Yeats to Beckett* (London: The Athlone Press, 1986), p. 120.

[71] Thomas Kilroy, 'Synge and Modernism', in Maurice Harmon, ed., *J. M. Synge Centenary Papers, 1971* (Dublin: Dolmen Press, 1972), 167–79, p. 171.

[72] Elizabeth Coxhead, 'Synge and Lady Gregory', in Suheil Badi Bushrui, ed., *Sunshine and the Moon's Delight: A Centenary Tribute to John Millington Synge, 1871–1909* (Gerrards Cross and Beirut: Colin Smythe and American University of Beirut, 1972), 153–8, p. 154; Barry McCrea, 'Style and Idiom', in Cleary, ed., *The Cambridge Companion to Irish Modernism*, 63–74, p. 67.

concurrent'.[73] Traditionally, the historical narrative of modernism has relied on a set of binaries or tensions as explanatory constructs: nationalism and internationalism; popular culture and elite culture; civilized and primitive; archaic and modern; radical and conservative.[74] Following suit, earlier critical works saw Revivalism and modernism as inherently opposed, with Revivalism seeking to revive the past and modernism choosing 'to rewrite or repudiate it altogether'.[75] However, as Paige Reynolds has shown, there are numerous 'conceptual and practical overlaps' between the two movements.[76] Synge is a Revivalist, but is constantly fighting against the dominant tenets of that movement. This does not, of course, mean that his work does not exhibit characteristic features of both Romanticism and Revivalism: it returns constantly to spiritual harmony in nature, to the rural, to the cult of the peasant, and to an emphasis on the Irish as equipped, in some instances, to counter anglicized modernity. On the other hand, it also exhibits many of the key traits of modernism: it subjects dramatic form to the pressures of modernity; it emphasizes the evolutionary imperative in both literary and social terms; it satirizes Romantic primitivism almost as often as it deploys it; it is eventually combative, unconcerned with popularity and preoccupied with the freedoms of the artistic imagination. In other words, his work plays ironically with its own Romanticism, and sits within our typical understanding of Revivalism as a wolf in sheep's clothing. The intense pressures of the Revival, both in aesthetic and political terms, compelled Synge into modernism, and into a dramatic experimentation which was as much a form of political and literary protest.

---

[73] Joe Cleary, 'Introduction', in Cleary, ed., *The Cambridge Companion to Irish Modernism*, 1–18, p. 12; Terence Brown, 'Ireland, Modernism and the 1930s', in Patricia Coughlan and Alex Davis, eds., *Modernism and Ireland: The Poetry of the 1930s* (Cork: Cork University Press, 1995), 24–42, p. 36.

[74] Tim Armstrong draws out these 'seeming contradictions' in his *Modernism: A Cultural History* (Cambridge: Polity, 2005), especially pp. 4–5.

[75] Richard Kearney, *Transitions: Narratives in Modern Irish Culture* (Manchester: Manchester University Press, 1988), p. 10.

[76] Paige Reynolds, *Modernism, Drama, and the Audience for Irish Spectacle* (Cambridge: Cambridge University Press, 2007), p. 7.

1

'An Initiated Mystic'

Occultism and Modernization in *The Aran Islands*

In December 1897, having returned from Paris to Dublin, Synge underwent an operation for the removal of a swollen gland in his neck, the first sign of the Hodgkin's disease which would eventually kill him just over a decade later. During this time he was still pursuing Cherrie Matheson, who had already turned down two of his marriage proposals, partly if not wholly due to Synge's abandonment of Protestantism. In a recollection written in 1924 and published in *The Irish Statesman*, Cherrie (who was by this time married and using the name C. H. Houghton) remembered a peculiar incident from the day of the operation:

> Somewhere about this time he had an operation on his throat and looked very delicate. I saw him not long after, and he said to me: 'I tried to send you a telepathic message just before I went under ether. Did you get it?' I had not. He looked disappointed and sad.[1]

In anecdotal accounts, we find many instances of Synge affecting telepathy and phantasms in those he knew and loved. Lady Gregory, for instance, felt a foreboding sense of evil on the morning of Synge's death, and Yeats's sister Lolly had a prophetic dream of a ship running aground. Molly Allgood, the actress to whom Synge became engaged shortly before his death, recalled to Yeats three 'pre-visions' of Synge's death: in one, Synge's face fell off during afternoon tea, revealing his bare skull; later, she dreamt of a coffin being lowered into the ground with 'a sort a strange cross' over it; and in another, she dreamt she saw Synge on a boat and waved, but the boat went away.[2] Edie Harmar, a friend of the Synge family, saw him three times in a mirror,

---

[1] C. H. Houghton, 'John Synge as I Knew Him', in Mikhail, ed., *J. M. Synge: Interviews and Recollections*, 3–7, p. 5.

[2] All of these reports are recounted in W. B. Yeats, 'The Death of Synge: Extracts from a Diary kept in 1909', in *Autobiographies*, 497–528, pp. 508, 517–18.

J. M. Synge: Nature, Politics, Modernism. Seán Hewitt, Oxford University Press (2021). © Seán Hewitt. DOI: 10.1093/oso/9780198862093.003.0002

at three different stages of his life.[3] In fact, even as long after Synge's death as 1923, when Yeats gave his Nobel speech to the Swedish Academy, the elder poet imagined that 'a young man's ghost should have stood upon one side of me'.[4]

The prevalence of spiritualist practices amongst the Anglo-Irish did not bypass Synge's strictly evangelical family. As Edward Stephens notes, 'the reality of psychic phenomena was tacitly assumed by the members of the [Synge] family'.[5] His father, in fact, claimed second sight.[6] However, Cherrie Matheson's is the only account of Synge which suggests that he actively attempted to communicate telepathically, and thus asks us to take more seriously the question of Synge's own engagement with occult phenomena. Synge's interest in occultism and theosophy has most usually been seen as a passing phase in his development as a writer. Maurice Bourgeois grants that Synge 'dabbled' in occultism, Buddhism, theosophy, and magic, and Greene and Stephens suggest that the young writer attended at least one meeting of the Theosophical Society with AE.[7] Arguing that 'the stimulus of the Aran experience would have elicited little response had not Synge spent most of his earlier life preparing for it', Vivian Mercier finds an exception in the influence of Helena Blavatsky's theosophy on Synge's works. Mercier notes that Synge 'looked into the work of that shameless charlatan Mme Blavatsky, who temporarily fascinated Yeats and A.E. but not Joyce nor, I imagine, Synge'.[8] In recent years, criticism has provided us with readings of Synge as a primitivist, an anthropologist, an ethnographer; however, Synge the occultist has never really been granted credence.[9] Rather than being a transient interest, Synge's engagement with the occult had a profound impact on his

---

[3] Edward Stephens, *My Uncle John: Edward Stephens's Life of J. M. Synge*, ed. Andrew Carpenter (London: Oxford University Press, 1974), p. 130.

[4] Yeats, 'The Bounty of Sweden', in *Autobiographies*, 529–72, p. 571.

[5] Edward Stephens, *My Uncle John*, p. 68. For one example of the spiritualist interests of the Anglo-Irish, in this instance the Gore-Booths, see Lauren Arrington, *Revolutionary Lives: Constance and Casimir Markievicz* (Princeton: Princeton University Press, 2015), pp. 6–7.

[6] Edward Stephens, *My Uncle John*, p. 68.

[7] Bourgeois, *John Millington Synge and the Irish Theatre*, p. 44; Greene and Stephens, *J. M. Synge, 1871–1909*, p. 69.

[8] Vivian Mercier, *Modern Irish Literature: Sources and Founders*, ed. Eilís Dillon (Oxford: Clarendon Press, 1994), pp. 212–15. Synge notes reading Blavatsky in his diary, TCD MS 4379.

[9] See Sinéad Garrigan Mattar, *Primitivism, Science, and the Irish Revival* (Oxford: Clarendon Press, 2004); Deirdre Toomey, '"Killing the da": J. M. Synge and *The Golden Bough*', in Robert Fraser, ed., *Sir James Frazer and the Literary Imagination: Essays in Affinity and Influence* (London and Basingstoke: Macmillan, 1990), 154–71; Castle, *Modernism and the Celtic Revival*. Mary Bryson, for example, does not mention Synge in her synoptic article 'Metaphors for Freedom: Theosophy and the Irish Revival', *The Canadian Journal of Irish Studies*, Vol. 3, No. 1 (June 1977), 32–40.

writing and was internalized into his approach as a way of reconciling his own contradictory reactions of the ongoing modernization of the west of Ireland. As Parsons argues, 'Synge oversteps the spatial and temporal boundaries of his narrative—life in the present moment of these islands— because he is confronted when he arrives on the islands with a community that doesn't resist, but rather *defines* modernity.'[10] This is part of a wider and much more far-reaching tendency in Synge's works, which return to spiritualism and notions of transcendence into an atemporal zone in order to model and attain a new relationship with the natural world.

A short early prose work, 'Under Ether' (1897–8), combines his interest in occultism and theosophy with an implicit social concern. 'Under Ether' is an account of an operation, in which the narrator is placed under anaesthetic and undergoes a sort of visionary experience. That Synge's account of his operation and Cherrie's account of his attempt at telepathy coincide must hardly be surprising when we consider the piece in question. 'Under Ether' is the most artistically successful of Synge's early prose works, though it gives a very different feeling for him as a writer than his plays and *The Aran Islands* (1907). Yeats, after reading Synge's early poetry and prose in Paris, wrote: 'I have but a vague impression, as of a man trying to look out of a window and blurring all that he sees by breathing upon the window.'[11] In fact, many critics have seen these early works as self-conscious, overly aesthetic, and generally unsuccessful.[12] 'Under Ether' is an exception to this characterization, and is Synge's first work to break from the stilted archaisms and melodrama of, for example, 'Vita Vecchia' (1895–7) and 'Étude Morbide' (1899); it is self-reflexive, even playful, in a way that these other early works are not, and does not attempt to reach beyond the scope of a single scene, a single experience, and so avoids falling flat. Unlike his 'Étude Morbide', which is also heavily influenced by the Symbolist and Decadent movements, 'Under Ether' avoids self-aggrandizement, and where 'Étude Morbide' feels like a contrived imitation of the Symbolist style, 'Under Ether' is more convincingly authentic, perhaps because the frame of the waking narrator's voice adds a layer of irony to the image of the serious mystic. The tendency in Synge studies has generally been to segment his literary career into

---

[10] Parsons, *The Ordnance Survey and Modern Irish Literature*, p. 122.

[11] 'The Trembling of the Veil', in *Autobiographies*, 107–352, p. 344.

[12] Nicholas Grene, *Synge: A Critical Study of the Plays* (London: Macmillan, 1975), p. 22; Robin Skelton, *The Writings of J. M. Synge* (London: Thames & Hudson, 1971), p. 16; Ann Saddlemyer, 'The Poeticizing of Synge', in Patrick Lonergan, ed., *Synge and His Influences: Centenary Essays from the Synge Summer School* (Dublin: Carysfort Press, 2011), 7–32, p. 15.

definable stages, and *The Aran Islands* has often been seen as a moment of departure, a clear-cut break into genius.[13] However, as Ben Levitas has noted, the stages of Synge's progress are not so easy to compartmentalize.[14] By beginning with Synge's work in the Symbolist mode, associated with his stay in Paris, and tracing a trajectory through to *The Aran Islands*, I want to highlight many intrinsic concerns which complicate our understanding of Synge's progress through literary styles and movements.

Beginning with the narrator being directed by hospital nurses to wait for the operating theatre to be readied, 'Under Ether' details the grotesque and threatening world of the hospital before moving into a sort of dream vision wherein the narrator takes flight through a symbolic world. Borrowing from the dream-vision tradition, Synge describes the revelatory nature of the other world, and his narrator is finally brought back to the hospital as the anaesthetic wears off, changed and inspired. However important it might be not to overplay the autobiographical nature of any text, it is illuminating for our study of Synge to recognize it here. Synge's narrator sits down in the waiting room to read the ethics of 'the great pantheist' Spinoza; Synge himself had read Spinoza earlier that year.[15] Synge's narrator undergoes an operation under ether; Synge had undergone the same operation just days before beginning to compose the piece.[16] Synge's narrator cries out, 'I'm an initiated mystic... I could rend the groundwork of your souls' (*CW* II, 42); likewise, Synge himself had by this time undergone his own tentative conversion to occult mysticism.

During 1897, Synge and his friend Stephen MacKenna corresponded about their mutual interest in psychical phenomena, and MacKenna sent Synge a reading list, advocating Paris as the best place for such studies due to its 'immense *richesse* of the literature of the subject from the elementary matter of Magnetism, Hypnotism *etc.* to deepest Magic'. Furthermore, he offered to introduce Synge to Richard Best ('who lives the things of the spirit'), an offer Synge took up when he returned to Paris in January 1898, announcing himself at Best's door in the rue d'Assas with the famous and telling line, 'Je suis Synge—pas singe.'[17] Synge's reading in 1897 hints at this

---

[13] See, for example, Thornton, *J. M. Synge and the Western Mind*, pp. 43–4; Greene and Stephens, *J. M. Synge, 1871–1909*, p. 74.

[14] Ben Levitas, 'J. M. Synge: European Encounters', in P. J. Mathews, ed., *The Cambridge Companion to J. M. Synge* (Cambridge: Cambridge University Press, 2009), 77–91, p. 78.

[15] TCD MS 4418.

[16] TCD MS 4418. 'Operation on neck by C.B. Ball', entry for 11 Dec 1897, f. 76v.

[17] Greene and Stephens, *J. M. Synge, 1871–1909*, p. 69.

new interest, though his study of theosophical and psychical texts was to grow in 1898 and culminate in an intense course of reading in 1899. In 1897, though still heavily concerned with the canonical texts of Western literature, Synge notes for the first time reading Maeterlinck (who appears another eight times throughout the year), Villiers de l'Isle-Adam, Nietzsche, Yeats, and Blake. His interest in the Symbolist writers overlaps quite naturally with his interests in mysticism and the occult, and also with an early interest in theosophy.[18] The claim of the narrator of 'Under Ether' to being an 'initiated mystic' could quite easily have come from Synge's own mouth, though his 'initiation' seems to have been only through study rather than via any occult ritual. Even as late as October 1904, Synge was corresponding with MacKenna about his 'researches' into 'so-called occult phenomena'. Even though MacKenna admitted that Synge was a 'lean sceptic', it seems that Synge 'admit[ted] their reality'.[19]

In theosophical writings, the effect of anaesthetics is often theorized as having some connection with the ability to provoke 'out-of-body' experiences, and even 'astral travel', where the patient visits remote places, either known or unknown in the physical world. The effects of anaesthetics are discussed by Helena Blavatsky in *Isis, Unveiled* (1877), and also in works such as Annie Besant's *The Ancient Wisdom* (1897), which Synge read in January 1899.[20] That such discussions are found in many theosophical works, some of which Synge himself encountered, and others which would have undoubtedly been encountered by friends such as MacKenna and AE, make it very probable that Synge's reading in theosophy gave him a hint at the possible effects of ether, and provided him with a conceptual platform from which he could explore the idea of non-physical, symbolic worlds. That a dislocation from the physical body might result in the connection with another world is common to both Symbolist and theosophical thought, and anaesthetics were considered to be a method via which this dislocation might occur. Ether in particular was a drug 'widely associated with the visionary experience', and Maeterlinck was demonstrating how physical

---

[18] Synge attended at least one meeting of the Theosophical Society with AE in October 1897. See Greene and Stephens, *J. M. Synge, 1871–1909*, p. 69. Synge had also read and made brief notes on the work of Helena Blavatsky in 1895. See TCD MS 4379.

[19] Letter from Stephen MacKenna to J. M. Synge, October 1904. TCD MS 4424–4426, item 154, ff. 154r-v.

[20] H. P. Blavatsky, *Isis Unveiled: A Master-Key to the Mysteries of Ancient and Modern Science and Technology, Vol. I: Science* (London: Bernard Quaritch, 1877), pp. 539–40; Annie Besant, *The Ancient Wisdom: an Outline of Theosophical Teachings* (London: Theosophical Publishing House, 1897), p. 55.

illness and decadence (both pressing preoccupations for Synge during this time) could be harnessed to produce the terrifying mystical revelations of his 'Visions Typhoïdes' (1888), in which the narrator traverses subaquatic forests and eventually experiences graphic and gruesome torture.[21] Annie Besant summarized the contemporary theory behind this for readers unable to access or commit to a reading of Blavatsky's larger and more difficult volume, *The Secret Doctrine* (1888):

> Anaesthetics drive out the greater part of the etheric double, so that consciousness cannot affect or be affected by the dense body, its bridge of communication being broken. In the abnormally organized persons called mediums, dislocation of the etheric and dense bodies easily occurs, and the etheric double, when extruded, largely supplies the physical basis for 'materializations.'[22]

Under anaesthetic, the veil between the two worlds is lifted, and the patient, just like the medium, is able to connect with the spiritual, astral plane.

The aesthetics of Symbolism provided a literary mode which allowed Synge to easily weave theosophy into his text. In 'Under Ether', the first effects of the anaesthetic are described in vivid detail as the narrator feels the gradual dislocation of his self from his body. Most importantly in the context of Synge's later exploration with mysticism in *The Aran Islands*, the whole sequence is conceived in terms of a terrifying loss of self-control, of volition, and of a move between solipsism towards a greater, more expansive, and unifying world view. The loss of physical control is delineated by Synge in terms of both surgical and philosophical anxiety: the patient is subject to the will of the operating surgeons, but also to the inevitable draw of the non-physical world. He has lost his volition on both counts, and the narrative tension of 'Under Ether' sees him attempting to reclaim himself in the face of both threats to his self-control and self-determination. The freedom of the symbolic world is configured by the context of the operating theatre as being simultaneously liberating and terrifying. After the first dose of ether, the effect is not complete, and the narrator details the horror of existing halfway between two worlds:

---

[21] Alex Owen, *The Place of Enchantment: British Occultism and the Culture of the Modern* (Chicago and London: University of Chicago Press, 2004), p. 161. For Maeterlinck's 'Visions', see Maurice Maeterlinck, *Introduction à une psychologie des songes, 1886–1896*, compiled with notes by Stefan Gross (Brussels: Labor, 1985).

[22] Annie Besant, *The Ancient Wisdom*, p. 55.

Speech was gone. Volition was gone. I was a dead weight; a subject on a board; toy of other wills. It was agony. My eyes rolled swiftly from one side to the other, seeing now with phantasmal and horrible distortion.... The ceiling, which now shone with terrible distinctness, seemed bending over the nurses; and the nurses, some without heads, some with two, were floating in the air. Voices were behind me. Fifty suggestions flashed through my brain; had the ether apparatus broken? Did they think me insensible? Would I have to lie feeling all with treble intensity, unable to speak or move?   (*CW* II, 40–1)

In a state similar to dream paralysis, the narrator is able to experience both the physical and non-physical worlds, one in which pain is a terrifying reality and one in which the features of the physical world are distorted to nightmarish effect. Phantasms and two-headed nurses float around the operating room, symbolizing the fractured nature of the modern world. The narrator lies caught between two modes of experience, neither of which allows him self-control. After another dose of ether, however, his dislocation from the physical is complete: 'clouds of luminous mist were swirling round me, through which heads broke only at intervals'. The mist that descends here signals the movement from one world to the next in a similar way to how the sea mist comes to function as a veil between worlds, and between temporal zones, in *The Aran Islands*.[23] It is when the nurses and doctors begin to laugh at the narrator, mocking him, that he cries out, 'I'm an initiated mystic.' Asserting himself as being endowed with some heightened knowledge, the narrator again cries out: '"Ha, ha, ha!" I roared in ironical triumph, "now you're serious. Now you know what you have to deal with"' (*CW* II, 42). After this, the clouds of mist come back more completely, 'now heavy, now opaque', and Synge enters the symbolic, revelatory world in which the laws of time, force, and matter are contravened, transforming the narrator into a godlike and prophetic traveller:

---

[23] Emily Lawless uses the returning of sea mist to similar effect in her Aran novel *Grania* (1892), in which the heroine rows through 'odd-looking vortexes and currents' of fog which seem to move in a psychedelic manner: 'fragments ... breaking capriciously off, joining together again, gathering into interlaced patterns, sweeping up and down, expanding, converging.' In the world of the fog in *Grania*, as in Synge's Wicklow essays (discussed in the following chapter of this book), 'reality and unreality had become one'. Emily Lawless, *Grania: The Story of an Island*, edited with notes and an introduction by Michael O'Flynn (Brighton: Victorian Secrets, 2014), pp. 232–3.

The next period I remember but vaguely. I seemed to traverse whole epochs of desolation and bliss. All secrets were open before me, and simple as the universe is to its God. Now and then something recalled my physical life, and I smiled at what seemed a moment of sickly infancy. At other times I felt I might return to earth, and laughed aloud to think what a god I should be among men. For there could be no terror in my life. I was a light, a joy.

These earthly recollections were few and faint, for the rest I was in raptures I have no power to translate. At last clouds came over me again. My joy seemed slipping from my grasp, and at times I touched the memory of the operation as one gropes for a forgotten dream.   (CW II, 41)

The world that the narrator enters via the symbolic shroud of mist is timeless, unbound, and opposite in all senses to the clinical world of the operating theatre, with its 'faint jingle of tram bells' outside, but its existence is also facilitated by this world. The two exist parallel to each other, and a connection with the non-physical world allows Synge a revelatory experience of the world of physical reality.

'Under Ether', therefore, dramatizes the tension between the physical and non-physical worlds, but it also implicitly presents us with a paradigm of Synge's perceived relationship between the spiritual and the social. A fragmentary typescript draft of 'Under Ether' held in the archives of Trinity College Dublin leaves much of an assumed original to the imagination; many of the pages are cut down into paragraph-sized pieces of text, which are then pinned together into a new sequence. In this way, the extant typescript version gestures in its format to a previous longer version, though what remains is (with a few exceptions) the text we find printed in Alan Price's edition of the *Collected Works*. One notable alteration, made in Synge's hand, is the title of the piece. The title of the typed version, 'A Surgical Idyll', is crossed out by Synge and replaced with the more familiar 'Under Ether: Personal Experiences During an Operation'.[24] The original title begs more questions than its replacement answers. The onus falls on the word 'idyll'. More usually associated with the picturesque, the idealized, and especially the pastoral, the word redirects our reactions to this short prose work. However, we must be careful not to conflate the idyll as a form with

---

[24] TCD MS 4357, f.1.

the pastoral subject (the idyll is, after all, distinct from the eclogue). Derived from the Greek εἰδύλλιον (*eidullion*), the diminutive of 'form' or 'picture', the idyll is characterized by simplicity of style and by its short form, rather than by the pastoral subject with which it is commonly associated. As one contemporary of Synge's suggested, 'an idyll is a picture of life as the human spirit wishes it to be.'[25]

If, as we know, 'Under Ether' was initially conceived by Synge as an idyll, we might ask whether it was the form or the content, or the interplay between the two, that first inspired the definition. The work itself is formally reminiscent of the idyll, giving as it does a single scene and 'picture'; however, rather than taking the ideal as its subject, it instead maps out a relationship between the real and the ideal. It works, in the mode of mystical experience, to reveal the ideal, though this process is fraught. Synge's experience in the surgery itself is far from idyllic, with his descriptions of the operating tools and the slightly demonic hospital staff serving to reinforce the narrator's discomfort with, even fear of, his setting. However, in this context, the induced world of the symbol, which Synge enters under anaesthetic, is made idyllic, releasing the narrator as it does from the hellish torment of the operating table. This reading would suggest that Synge conceives the idyll as something inherently non-physical, 'unreal' (which, of course, it must always be), and as something that is achieved only through separation from the material world. However, as we have already seen, the relationship between the physical and non-physical, between the spiritual and material worlds, is particularly strained in this piece, with each world taking turns to break through into the other, disrupting any sense of binary and creating the principal tension of the piece. The position of the narrator, who for the most part exists in a tortuous limbo between two modes of experience, indicates that for Synge there is always a necessary, if difficult, relationship between the world of the surgery and the world of the idyll, between what is painfully physical and what is dangerously or threateningly spiritual. In this way, the Romantic or pastoral idyll is modernized by Synge, and is asked to accommodate fractured and uncomfortable relationships. This uneasy transition between worlds is in part a dramatization of the struggle between the purely spiritual and the purely material, with the narrator both unwilling and unable to privilege one over the other.

[25] Martha Hale Shackford, 'A Definition of the Pastoral Idyll', *PMLA*, Vol. 19, No. 4 (1904), 583–92, pp. 586–7.

However, it is also representative of a transition between literary approaches, and dramatizes Synge's own place between movements. Here, he is working towards a modernist aesthetic while still operating within a largely Romanticist mode, reaching towards an idea of an external unity but finding himself continually thwarted, bringing into question the existence of a Romantic sublime.

The Romantic poets who ranked among Synge's lifelong literary models have received much critical attention for their use of opiates as a means of accessing non-physical worlds. Synge read the works of Shelley, Wordsworth, Coleridge, and Southey in the years 1895 to 1896, at the same time as his first encounters with theosophy and socialism.[26] However, his use of the trope of anaesthesia as a stimulant for mystical experience is subtly different to the Romantics' use of opiates. Coleridge and Southey used laudanum to open the 'doors of perception', and to effect both recreational and artistic freedom. Shelley, however, believed in the possibility of drugs to help with a move beyond the restraints of the physical world, and to reveal unities that had revolutionary political implications. In the world revealed by opiates, Shelley believed, the imagination could move beyond internalized sociopolitical structures and arrive at radical notions for social reform.[27] Synge, in this respect, is much closer to Shelley than to the other major Romantics in his conception of the effects of stimulants. His sense of a direct association between religious and political upheaval, detailed in the 'Autobiography', suggests that in turning to pantheism, theosophy, and occultism, Synge was drawing on the political implications of his spiritual exploration. However, he moves beyond the Romantic. Rather than being interested solely in the revelations of the non-physical world, Synge finds a meaningful tension in the battle between the physical and non-physical worlds where access to the symbol is frustrated and fractured. Although 'the old Romantic aspiration to overcome fragmentation' is still an impetus, the difficulty of this process becomes a key

---

[26] See Synge's notebook, TCD MS 4379, and his reading diaries, TCD MSS 4416–7. TCD suggest that MS 4379 was used between 1894 and 1895, but it was undoubtedly used until a later date. See the discussion of Synge's notes on socialism below.

[27] See Katherine Singer, 'Stoned Shelley: Revolutionary Tactics and Women Under the Influence', *Studies in Romanticism*, Vol. 48, No. 4 (Winter 2009), 687–707, pp. 687–9. Althea Hayter, in her *Opium and the Romantic Imagination* (London: Faber & Faber, 1968), distinguishes Shelley from the other Romantic poets for his construction of opium-inspired dreams as allegory, pp. 78–9.

concern.[28] Just as it is in the places where the 'old' and 'new' clash that Synge finds his greatest inspiration, so it is in the places where the physical and non-physical worlds compete that he focuses his writing. Where one temporality encroaches on another, and where the modern begins to compete with the pre-modern, 'authentic', or 'natural', access to the sublime becomes fraught with the tensions of competition.

In constructing his own history in his 'Autobiography' during the years 1896 to 1898, Synge insisted on a directly causal effect between the upheaval of his religious views and that of his politics. On first encountering Darwin's *On the Origin of Species* during his teenage years, Synge tells us, he experienced a quintessentially Victorian crisis of faith. He 'relinquished the Kingdom of God', and later gave up the charade of attending church in the winter of 1889, much to his mother's dismay.[29] This severance with his cultural and class background of Anglo-Irish Protestantism resulted directly in a reassessment of his politics, which 'went round from a vigorous and unreasoning loyalty to a temperate Nationalism. Everything Irish became sacred' (*CW* II, 13). Rather than becoming an atheist, as some critics and biographers suggest, Synge became interested in pantheism (via Spinoza and the Romantic poets), and eventually began a course of reading in theosophy and occultism. That he viewed his change in religious views as precipitating directly his shifting political temperament shows how deeply he associated orthodox Protestantism with his class background and with Unionism, and by extension how his shift away from dogmatic, organized religion was accompanied by a shift towards a socialist politics which was often at odds with the politics of his Protestant family. However, it would be too easy to assume that Synge's religious epiphany was a direct cause of this shift. Rather, Synge expressed his anger towards the activities of his Anglo-Irish family at an early stage, showing that his concern for social justice was present long before he rejected the Protestant Church outright in 1899. In 1885, for example, Synge's brother Edward began evicting tenants in Cavan, Mayo, and Wicklow. Synge, at the age of just 14, argued strongly with his mother about the rights of the tenants, until she asked him, 'What would become of us if our tenants in Galway stopped paying their rents?'[30] Synge posits the idea that Darwin was the indirect cause of his change in politics,

---

[28] Charles Taylor, *Sources of the Self: The Making of Modern Identity* (Cambridge: Cambridge University Press, 1989), p. 470.

[29] See Robin Skelton, *J. M. Synge and His World* (London: Thames & Hudson, 1971), pp. 22–4.

[30] Greene and Stephens, *J. M. Synge, 1871–1909*, p. 11.

though in fact he was geared towards matters of social justice long before his break from Protestantism. The fact that Synge chooses to link the religious and the political when writing his 'Autobiography', however, is revealing.

Writing in his 'Autobiography' that once rid of 'theological mysticism' he became more open to the 'profound mysteries of life', Synge tells us that in childhood he 'had even psychical adventures which throw perhaps an interesting light on some of the data of folklore' (CW II, 10). Though it is clear that he rejected his family's Protestantism years before he first encountered the modern theosophical and occultist movements, Synge rewrites his own history in order to plot a trajectory towards this moment of mystic discovery, positioning himself as a man instinctively receptive to supernatural experience. In relating one such incident, Synge again draws on his favourite image of the passage into a spiritual world (the mist), and his writing is again replete with Symbolist imagery through which time is collapsed:

> One evening when I was collecting [moths] on the brow of a long valley in County Wicklow wreaths of white mist began to rise from the narrow bogs beside the river. Before it was quite dark I looked round the edge of the field and saw two immense luminous eyes looking at me from the base of the valley. I dropped my net and caught hold of a gate in front of me. Behind the eyes there rose a black sinister forehead. I was fascinated. For a moment the eyes seemed to consume my personality, then the whole valley became filled with a pageant of movement and colour, and the opposite hillside covered itself with ancient doorways and spires and high turrets. I did not know where or when I was existing. At last someone spoke in the lane behind me—it was a man going home—and I came back to myself.
>
> (CW II, 10)

Synge inserts a connection between folklore, naturalist practice, and mystical experience, but he is also creating a trajectory for his own artistic life which leads right up to the period from 1896 to 1898, when his 'Autobiography', along with 'Under Ether', 'Étude Morbide', and early sections of The Aran Islands were composed.[31] Primarily, these experiences

---

[31] This connection between folklore and the occult is not unique to Synge. As Seamus Deane notes, 'Occultism as a set of doctrines that circulated in the urban worlds of London and Dublin was the ascendancy of folklore, the system of beliefs that circulated among the peasantry without any doctrinal formulation; occultism was the theory of which folklore was the

are described by Synge as episodes in which reason and time are lost to an unbound universe: turrets and ancient doorways exist on a hillside in contemporary Wicklow, and Synge is subsumed into the world around him, which reveals and displays itself in an almost psychedelic manner. Synge's writing often has recourse to such experiences in order to dramatize the potential to connect in new ways with a higher reality. It is interesting to note Edward Stephens's claim that Synge was not unique in his family unit regarding matters of psychical experience, which were apparently largely accepted as a commonplace for the Synges, with Stephens's father and his sisters claiming powers of second sight.[32] We need not, therefore, assume that Synge's interest in psychical phenomena stemmed solely from his engagement with theosophy and Symbolism; however, it is clear that the Symbolist aesthetic aided his ability to express such experiences.

Much work has already been done on Synge's primitivism and the influence on his thinking of anthropological tomes such as Frazer's *The Golden Bough* (1890), which he read in 1898, and works of evolutionary science.[33] However, Synge also read many pseudoscientific works on telepathy, hallucinations, and other phenomena.[34] Works such as *Phantasms of the Living* (1886), which he read in January 1899, asserted that telepathy was an undeniable fact in nature, basing its assertions on the depositions of over 2000 participants.[35] Others saw the decline of dogmatic religion as being evidence of a new spiritual dawn. For example, Laurence Oliphant's 1888 work *Scientific Religion* (also read by Synge in January 1899) assessed hysteria and hallucinations as being indicative of a growing propensity among people to experience psychical or mystical phenomena. Hailing the dawn of 'new vital impulses' (a phrase strikingly reminiscent of Synge's sense of a 'new creative force'), Oliphant suggests that the rise in people being treated for mental illnesses is due to an increased receptivity in those

---

embodied praxis.' *Strange Country: Modernity and Nationhood in Irish Writing since 1790* (Oxford: Clarendon Press, 1997), p. 112.

[32] Edward Stephens, *My Uncle John*, p. 68.
[33] See, for example, Castle, *Modernism and the Celtic Revival*; Mattar, *Primitivism, Science, and the Irish Revival*; James F. Knapp, 'Primitivism and Empire: John Synge and Paul Gauguin', *Comparative Literature*, Vol. 41, No. 1 (Winter 1989), 53–68; Toomey, 'Killing the da'.
[34] Between the years 1892 and 1903, Synge kept a regular diary of his reading. References to Synge's reading, therefore, are corroborated by his own evidence. After 1903, Synge's reading must be gleaned from references in letters, articles, and manuscripts. For his reading diaries, see TCD MSS 4413–22.
[35] Edmund Gurney, Frederic W. H. Myers, and Frank Podmore, *Phantasms of the Living*, Vol. I, Society for Psychical Research (London: Trübner & Co., 1886). See TCD MS 4420.

people to these new impulses, that 'a new light dawns upon them'.[36] Taking a turn of argument common to early evolutionary anthropologists like James Frazer and Andrew Lang, Oliphant suggests that 'savage' peoples are more receptive to psychical phenomena, though for him these phenomena are fact, not fiction. As in *Phantasms of the Living*, this is seen as attributable to the bent of modern thought since the Enlightenment, in which the intellectual and emotional aspects of the brain have been 'divorced'.[37] The 'savage', having not suffered such intellectual severing, has a holistic receptiveness to the supernatural. Revealingly, Oliphant (like Synge) chooses the image of the cloud to denote the contrast between the clear-sighted 'savage' and the myopic tendencies of modern, 'civilized' man:

What we call the beauties of nature are more or less concealed by what I can only describe as clouds, composed of living, sentient, perpetually moving atoms. The thickness of these clouds corresponds in density to the moral condition of the invisible human beings whose atoms compose them. Intermingled with them are the atomic forces of the animal creation, and in a lower stratum those of nature, which reveal themselves in a more or less distorted aspect, according to the medium through which they are seen. There are still portions of the globe where nature does not appear altogether unlovely. These are the regions sparsely inhabited by savage tribes, where the population is extremely thin, and which, excepting in the case of some rare explorer, are unknown to, and untouched by, civilisation. Here the atmosphere is comparatively clear, and nature relatively undefiled.[38]

It is not difficult to see how attractive an idea this might have been to Synge, nor is it difficult, in light of this discussion, to see how such theories played a vital role in his reception and representation of the Aran Islands and their inhabitants. The idea that the atmosphere is clearer in places 'untouched' by civilization, and that 'savage tribes' therefore live in a space which is more liminal, more prone to treating the natural and supernatural worlds as equally present, is one which underlies much of Synge's discussion of the

---

[36] Laurence Oliphant, *Scientific Religion: or, Higher Possibilities of Life and Practice through the Operation of Natural Forces*, 2nd edn. (Edinburgh and London: William Blackwood & Sons, 1888), p. 7. As discussed in the Introduction to this book, Synge posits a 'new creative force' as being behind the Irish Revival. See TCD MS 4393, f. 1r.

[37] Oliphant, *Scientific Religion*, p. 12; Gurney et al., *Phantasms of the Living*, p. lv.

[38] Oliphant, *Scientific Religion*, p. 117.

islands. Here, however, we also see Oliphant introducing another concern which is key for Synge: the encroachment of one culture onto another, the inevitable march of progress. Synge's social conscience exists side by side with his interests in mysticism: he keeps one eye on each world. It is worth noting, in fact, that one of the many abandoned projects that Synge began between 1896 and 1898 was a novel about nurses, a subject that creeps into 'Under Ether'.[39] However, even as he writes of symbolic flights through collapsed epochs, Synge never forgets his radical ideals. In the corner of one page of his abandoned draft for the novel, separate from the rest of the text, Synge wrote a single word: 'reform'.[40]

As Matthew Beaumont has suggested, socialism and occultism in the fin de siècle can be viewed as elective affinities.[41] 'Under Ether', as we have seen, draws out the implicit links between the social and spiritual in Synge's prose. For him, the competition between worlds occurs both between the physical and spiritual and between the economically modern and pre-modern. The clash between two economic systems, between the world of capitalist competition and a socialist world of cooperation or community, is an integral component in the clash between the spiritual and the physical, and between the rational and non-rational. Written largely over a period of five years, from 1898 to 1902, Synge's *The Aran Islands* is ostensibly an account of his experiences living amongst the islanders during a period in which the modernization schemes of the Congested Districts Board for Ireland (CBD), alongside more general economic pressures, were effecting cultural and social change on the islands. Variously defined as documentary, quasi-documentary, utopian study, fictionalized confessional autobiography, and 'a reliable picture of how things were', *The Aran Islands* is part spiritual autobiography (as both Robin Skelton and John Wilson Foster have termed it) and part 'portrait of the artist'.[42] Rather than being a critical sourcebook for the plays or a veracious account of island life (which it is not), *The Aran*

---

[39] The opening pages for Synge's novel about nurses are found in TCD MS 4382, ff. 2–5.

[40] TCD MS 4382, f.2v.

[41] Matthew Beaumont, 'Socialism and Occultism at the Fin de Siècle: Elective Affinities', *Victorian Review*, Vol. 36, No. 1 (Spring 2010), 217–32.

[42] Donna Gerstenberger, *John Millington Synge* (Boston: Twayne, 1990), p. 8; Watson, *Irish Identity and the Literary Revival*, p. 45; Adele M. Dalsimer, '"The Irish Peasant Had All His Heart": J. M. Synge in The Country Shop', in Adele M. Dalsimer, ed., *Visualising Ireland: National Identity and the Pictorial Tradition* (Winchester, MA: Faber & Faber, 1993), 201–30, p. 204; Mary C. King, *The Drama of J. M. Synge* (New York: Syracuse University Press, 1985), p. 19; Thornton, *J. M. Synge and the Western Mind*, p. 59; Robin Skelton, *Celtic Contraries* (Syracuse, NY: Syracuse University Press, 1990), p. 36; John Wilson Foster, *Fictions of the Irish Literary Revival: A Changeling Art* (Syracuse, NY: Syracuse University Press, 1987), p. 112.

Islands shows how Synge's primary concerns were elicited by an engagement with a modernizing community, and how his writing style became more modernist in a bid to accommodate the tense dynamics of a transitioning world.

Many critics have discussed Synge's Aran Islands as representing a socialist or even anarchist commune, or what Elizabeth Gilmartin has called an 'idealized, naturally socialist community'.[43] However, the idea of the islands as what Sinéad Garrigan Mattar has called an 'air-locked Arcadia' continues to be questioned and dismantled in criticism.[44] The argument that Synge's Aran Islands are somehow a 'timeless space', an 'oblivion to histor-ical process', is still levelled in criticism, but this is gradually giving way to a more nuanced understanding of Synge's work which recognizes it as 'a radically innovative engagement with Ireland's modernity'.[45] Likewise, mis-conceptions of *The Aran Islands* as a work 'analogous to documentary', with Synge characterized as 'invisible, perceiving, objective, and amoral', have been countered by a recognition of the narrative as a form of 'spiritual autobiography'.[46] In the light of this, and of the above discussion of Synge's focus, it is necessary to direct our attention to the places, both textual and cultural, where the socialist ideal meets with the world of commerce, the places where the 'air-locked Arcadia' is threatened, in both its physical and non-physical forms, by an interaction with the modern. The binary between the modern and the 'primitive' does not simply exist for Synge as a reference point between the islands and the mainland used to highlight the pre-modern elements of Aran; it also exists *within* the island community. The modern, by the time of Synge's visit, had already begun to weave itself into the everyday life of the island. It was no longer a distinct category, but rather

---

[43] Elizabeth Gilmartin, '"Magnificent Words and Gestures": Defining the Primitive in *Synge's The Aran Islands*', in Maria McGarrity and Claire A. Culleton, eds., *Irish Modernism and the Global Primitive* (New York: Palgrave Macmillan, 2009), 63–79, p. 71. See also Kiberd, *Inventing Ireland*, p. 490.

[44] Mattar, *Primitivism, Science and the Irish Revival*, p. 143.

[45] Oona Frawley, *Irish Pastoral: Nostalgia and Twentieth-Century Irish Literature* (Dublin and Portland, OR: Irish Academic Press, 2005), p. 82; Parsons, *The Ordnance Survey and Modern Irish Literature*, p. 122. Justin Carville, for example, argues that 'All sense of progress, of change, of modernity is removed from Synge's imaginative geography', and Weldon Thornton claims that 'we can safely say that the Aran Islands, especially the smaller two, were in Synge's day as uninfluenced by modern communication, transportation, and technology as any part of Europe, and that they differed little from what they had been a thousand years before.' Justin Carville, 'Visible Others: Photography and Romantic Ethnography in Ireland', in McGarrity and Culleton, eds., *Irish Modernism and the Global Primitive*, 93–115, p. 101; Thornton, *J. M. Synge and the Western Mind*, p. 60.

[46] Gerstenberger, *John Millington Synge*, p. 8; Skelton, *Celtic Contraries*, p. 8.

it was an intrinsic element, making the tension between the modern and the 'pre-modern' more complex and undoubtedly more interesting for Synge's study of competing worlds. The binary, rather than being external, had moved into the internal spaces of the islands and the islanders.

Robin Skelton has accurately observed that 'Synge saw the virtues of Aran life through spectacles provided in part by William Morris'; however, Synge did not have Morris's faith in planned society.[47] For Synge, the ruptures and tensions of Irish life gave a necessary vitality that was missing in the pristine utopia of texts like *News from Nowhere* (1890). Synge read Morris's socialist works around the same time that he first arrived in Paris (1894–5), and he made brief notes on them.[48] During this period, he also read the works of Marx, including his and Engels's *The Communist Manifesto* (1848), but it is clear that Morris's brand of aesthetic socialism was the greater influence. In reading Marx, as Declan Kiberd notes, Synge focused particularly on the passages outlining the division of labour and the working day (both clear influences on *The Aran Islands*).[49] However, Morris's influence is much more pervasive, and is interwoven with Synge's theosophical and occult thinking in a way which is subtle but perhaps more natural, given Morris's aestheticism.[50] In his notebook, unsurprisingly, Synge focused on Morris's thoughts on the 'primitive' society, particularly on 'the love of savages for ornament' and the special prominence given to beauty in these societies.[51] In *The Aran Islands*, Synge takes these ideas, alongside the ideals of Morris's Arts and Crafts Movement, in using ornament as a sign of opposition to capitalism. However, Synge does not stop there, and instead continues to extrapolate past this association, linking ornament and 'rarity' with access to a spiritual world.

In fact, the notebook used by Synge for his notes on socialism is itself a curiosity, and the dating it has been given by Trinity College Dublin is undoubtedly incorrect. TCD suggests that the notebook was in use between 1894 and 1895, based perhaps on the inclusion of notes in German and Synge's reading of the socialists, whose works he encountered in Paris.

---

[47] Robin Skelton, 'The Politics of J. M. Synge', p. 11.   [48] TCD MS 4379.

[49] Kiberd, *Inventing Ireland*, p. 489. Skelton suggests that Synge's views on the division of labour could also have come from Morris, via *The Aims of Art* (1887). See Skelton, *Celtic Contraries*, p. 49.

[50] See Beaumont, 'Socialism and Occultism at the Fin de Siècle', p. 220. For more on the relationship between the early Revival and the English Arts and Crafts Movement, see Nicola Gordon Bowe, 'Preserving the Relics of Heroic Time: Visualizing the Celtic Revival in Early Twentieth-Century Ireland', Cliff and Grene, eds., *Synge and Edwardian Ireland*, 58–83, p. 59.

[51] TCD MS 4379, f. 76r.

Interestingly, the manuscript also contains notes on Annie Besant's *The Ancient Wisdom*, which was first published in 1897. In fact, Synge (who kept a record of the books he was reading at any time in his diaries) does not note reading Besant's work until 1899. The notebook, therefore, was in use until at least 1897, but more probably until 1899. Hence, it appears that Synge revisited this notebook when he came to read more protractedly in occultism and theosophy, despite making use of other notebooks through the years 1895 to 1899. The fact that Synge revisited this particular notebook, which was dedicated originally to notes on socialism, when he came to make notes on occultist and theosophical texts suggests that he himself saw a connection between his socialism and his interest in occult theory and practice. Throughout *The Aran Islands*, particularly in the draft versions, this connection is invoked and explored by Synge as a method of framing his 'study of the onset of modernity'.[52]

The connection made here between socialism and occultism is not unique to Synge; in fact, it is made explicit throughout the history of the occultist and theosophical movements. When Helena Blavatsky and Henry Olcott founded the Theosophical Society in New York in 1875, thus beginning the modern theosophical movement, the first objective of the new society—'to form a nucleus of the Universal Brotherhood of Humanity without distinction of race, creed, sex, caste, or color'—was based on openly socialist principles.[53] In fact, as Peter Kuch notes, Blavatsky's synthesis attempted to solve the major problems introduced by nineteenth-century debates on science, religion, and philosophy. Modern theosophy promised harmony and equality, an ideal based on ancient spiritual connections rather than on factions or differences.[54] By incorporating evolutionary theory and modern scientific developments in areas such as thermodynamics and electromagnetism into a work of theology, Blavatsky offered a total world view in which the split between science and religion, and between social discords, could be reconciled. That Synge saw fit to use the language and theory of the occult, which offered a total world view, in places where the fractures between worlds were most apparent, shows a logical if subconscious application of

---

[52] Declan Kiberd, *Irish Classics* (London: Granta, 2000), p. 423.

[53] Demetres P. Tryphonopoulos, 'The History of the Occult Movement', in Leon Surette and Demetres Tryphonopoulos, eds., *Literary Modernism and the Occult Tradition* (Maine: The National Poetry Foundation, 1996), 19–50, pp. 44–5.

[54] Peter Kuch, *Yeats and A.E.: 'The antagonism that unites Dear Friends'* (Gerrards Cross: Colin Smythe, 1986), p. 9.

his reading, but also demonstrates the internalization of occultism into Synge's socialism and his engagement with the modernizing process.

Turning to Synge's drafts for *The Aran Islands*, we can see that this connection between modernization and occultism (and, by extension, between socialism and occultism) is more explicit in earlier versions. In fact, Synge edited out many of the key markers of modernization from the text, resulting in a series of undercurrents that, though not hidden by the author, remain (as one critic has noted) 'sotto voce'.[55] Though he ignored Lady Gregory and W. B. Yeats's advice to emulate George Borrow's popular travelogues by removing specific place names (which, Gregory commented, give 'a curious dreaminess to [Borrow's] work'), Synge may have been influenced by the two older writers in their suggestions to remove some of the book's historical specificities.[56] For example, one of the more obvious references to the modernization of the islands under the Congested Districts Board is given in the introduction to the published text, but an earlier draft shows that Synge was initially much more open about the changes being effected on the islands:

> Kilronan, the principal village in the north island, has been so much changed by the fishing industry developed there by the Congested Districts Board, that it has now very little to distinguish it from any fishing village on the mainland west coast. The other islands are much more primitive, but even they are changing every day. Thus since the earlier of the following pages were written, a trained nurse has come to live on them, a post-office has been put on Inishmaan, a telephone to Inishere, with various other changes have been made [*sic*] that it was not worth while to deal with in the text.[57]

In the typescript draft of this paragraph, Synge deletes all but the first sentence, thereby removing any sense of temporal distance between the book's conception and its publication. Rather than keeping an introductory section that would fossilize *The Aran Islands* as an already outdated text, Synge chooses to remove the passage of time and, in doing so, works to keep in abeyance the key tension of the narrative. It is clear from the

[55] David Fitzpatrick, 'Synge and Modernity in *The Aran Islands*', in Cliff and Grene, eds., *Synge and Edwardian Ireland*, 121–58, p. 150.

[56] Letter from Lady Gregory to J. M. Synge, quoted in Greene and Stephens, *J. M. Synge, 1871–1909*, pp. 120–1. No date given.

[57] TCD MS 4344, ff.5–6.

typescript draft, however, that the binary between the modern and the universal or spiritual is heightened in earlier drafts of the text, again suggesting that this binary underpinned the structure of the narrative, perhaps as a sort of scaffold that could be removed piecemeal in later drafts while a more nuanced narrative was perfected beneath. Rather than opting for a binary representation of the modern versus the unmodernized, Synge creates a pervasive spiritual atmosphere in his vision of the islands that reacts in certain places with the world of commerce and technology, of 'railroads and inland cities' (*CW* II, 108). The result is a text that avoids didacticism or polemic by subtly interweaving occult and socialist theory in a series of localized oppositions to encroaching capitalism.

When discussing the influence of Morris on Synge's text, critics usually turn to a passage in *The Aran Islands* which signals the most explicit point of contact. In this passage, Synge invokes the 'rarity' of the old as an example of the craft and beauty given to each individual object associated with the islanders' lives.[58]

> Every article on these islands has an almost personal character, which gives this simple life, where all art is unknown, something of the artistic beauty of mediaeval life. The curaghs and spinning-wheels, the tiny wooden barrels that are still much used in the place of earthenware, the home-made cradles, churns, and baskets, are all full of individuality, and being made from materials that are common here, yet to some extent peculiar to the island, they seem to exist as a natural link between the people and the world that is about them.   (*CW* II, 58–9)

The connection made between the life on the Aran Islands and 'mediaeval life' is quintessentially Morrisian, as is the focus on the crafted technologies of the pre-modern society. In his essay on 'The Lesser Arts', for example, Morris suggests that handcrafted objects were full of 'mystery and wonder': 'in the English country, in the days when people cared about such things, was there a full sympathy between the works of man and the land they were

---

[58] Nicholas Daly suggests that Synge's association of the primitive with a certain mode of production allows him to see the modernist text as an anti-commodity, thus linking individuality and uniqueness with personal style. See *Modernism, Romance and the Fin de Siècle* (Cambridge: Cambridge University Press, 1999), p. 134.

made for.'[59] Robert Volpicelli has argued that this passage in *The Aran Islands* shows that, for Synge, the way that these objects act as a 'natural link' between the islanders and their home 'reinforces a sense of belonging' that might be disrupted by imperialism and mass production.[60] 'Modernity', Paige Reynolds remarks, 'removes the intimacy between person and object, but this primitive Aran culture laudably reinstalls that bond or, more accurately, never relinquishes that connection.'[61] The focus on a 'natural link' between the people and the 'world that is about them' is a key concern throughout Synge's writings, and the disruption of this link through modernization becomes the fundamental basis for his opposition to systematic schemes of 'improvement.' If we look deeper into *The Aran Islands* via Synge's drafts, we find that Synge's focus on craft and rareness is linked implicitly to theosophy and opposes capitalism on those grounds. This complicates Malcolm Kelsall's assertion that Synge used a 'stock-in-trade' Morrisian Romanticism with little social concern for the islanders.[62]

In a passage from the typescript draft for *The Aran Islands* which is redrafted many times before being axed altogether, Synge uses his trained naturalist's eye to express the opposition of the natural landscape of Aran to 'the world of commerce'. Describing the view from the cliffs, he observes some choughs with 'aristocratic bills', commenting that 'everything on Aran has a certain rarity or distinction'. This rarity is, in his view, the key to the island's opposition to 'civilization' as he knows it. Continuing with his description, Synge writes, 'This absence of the...things—nettles, rats, and sparrows—that have collected by some affinity on the brink of civilization, seems to emphasise while I am here my remoteness from the world of commerce.' The isolation of the islands geographically is signified by the absence of 'common' plant and animal species, which come to symbolize the mass production of the commercial world. However, on further reflection, Synge (in a sway of pantheistic theosophical thought that provokes a rare moment of anti-scientism) goes on to discuss the features of some seabirds, suggesting that their striking colouration links them with universal law in a way that the theories of modern evolutionism do not accommodate:

[59] William Morris, *The Political Writings of William Morris*, edited with an introduction by A. L. Morton (London: Lawrence & Wishart, 1979), pp. 37, 46.

[60] Robert A. Volpicelli, 'Bare Ontology: Synge, Beckett, and the Phenomenology of Imperialism', in *New Hibernia Review*, Vol. 17, No. 4 (Winter 2013), 110–29, p. 119.

[61] Paige Reynolds, 'Synge's Things: Material Culture in the Writings of Synge', in Lonergan, ed., *Synge and His Influences*, 73–92, p. 76.

[62] Malcolm Kelsall, 'Synge in Aran', *Irish University Review*, Vol. 5, No. 2 (Autumn 1975), 254–70, p. 255.

What has marked these sea fowl with broad primitive colours stocking the
cliffs with snowy gull and pitch black cormorants while blue broken sky
would have afforded treble concealment?

Will new science explain their likeness to the white and black colour of the
boats as a new imitation…whereas a deeper truth knows that nature's
harmonies are otherwise assorted?[63]

It is perhaps unfair to hold Synge to this draft passage, which seems to have
been written hastily and quickly removed from the draft; however, it again
attests to the link Synge observed between rarity, the 'primitive', and a
universal, spiritual order, and how he elucidates this in opposition to the
commercial, scientific modernity of the mainland. What is perhaps most
interesting about this passage is the initial question, 'What has marked these
sea fowl…?', which suggests that even at this stage Synge was uncertain
about his spiritual beliefs and was committed neither to science nor to
theology. Searching for an underlying order in the manner of theosophy,
Synge is confident of a 'deeper truth' but is unable to name or define what
this might be. In whatever form or definition, however, it is clear that Synge
sees it as opposing modernity, and sees the conflict of modernization as
being not solely a conflict of economics or culture but also a conflict between
spirituality and scientific rationalism. His own biographical conflict between
belief systems, we can see, is read into the modernization process on Aran,
and by extension becomes translated into a literary conflict. The conflict of
modernization is a social conflict that also becomes a conflict between
spirituality and rationalism, between rarity and commercialism, and
between Romanticism and modernism.

In *The Aran Islands*, a vignette originally published as 'A Dream of
Inishmaan' shares in part the aesthetic of 'Under Ether' and signals how
Synge's engagement with occultism began to become an internalized aspect
of his approach to modernization. Throughout *The Aran Islands*, Synge's
narrator figure is concerned with separation and describes a sense of being
uninitiated into the cultural and spiritual world of the 'natives'. However, in
'A Dream of Inishmaan' the assumed distance of the narrator figure
becomes frighteningly uncertain. The title 'A Dream of Inishmaan', rather
than 'A Dream *on* Inishmaan', is significant in creating a sense of influence,

---

[63] TCD MS 4344, f. 293.

of a force actively affecting the dreamer. Rather than being simply a dream experienced *on* the island, the title indicates that this is a dream affected by the island, and one that comes to reveal the island in new and startling ways. Synge opens,

> Some dreams I have had in a cottage near the Dun of Conchubar, on the middle Island of Aran, seem to give strength to the opinion that there is a psychic memory attached to certain neighbourhoods.

> One night after moving among buildings with strangely intense light upon them, I heard a faint rhythm of music beginning far away from me on some stringed instrument.[64]

In this dream, Synge achieves a middle ground between being a completely passive and an active mystic, and this is figured in a similar way to 'Under Ether': the dislocation from the physical world is painful, and the lapse into the 'primitive' from the modern is unwilled. 'A Dream of Inishmaan' dramatizes the permeation of the islanders' minds by the island ('Their minds...have been coloured by endless suggestions from the sea and sky'), and the narrator begins reluctantly to *become*, via a supernatural initiation rite, an islander.[65] His reluctance is a fear of letting go of the self and losing contact with the modern world, but his desire to become initiated is fierce.

This is a meticulously invented dramatic scene, and we should be careful not to assume its authority as truth. In a draft version, Synge was more explicit about the associations between occultist mysticism and the global primitive in his dream sequence. In the following version of the opening lines of the dream, taken from Synge's typescript draft of *The Aran Islands*, the narrator explains the phenomenon in terms of a primitive dance, perhaps inspired by dervishes:

> Some dreams I have had since I have been in this cottage seem to corroborate the theory of the mystics, that there is a psychic memory attached to certain neighbourhoods....In many old religions the supreme

---

[64] *The Gael*, March 1904, p. 93. 'A Dream of Inishmaan' was reprinted in *The Gael* in 1904, but was originally published in the second issue (May 1903) of Pamela Colman Smith's magazine, *The Green Sheaf*, alongside a number of other accounts of dreams by writers such as Cecil French, W. B. Yeats and Colman Smith herself.

[65] TCD MS 4344, f. 93.

moment of ecstasy was reached in a whirl of incontrollable dancing, and a
few evenings ago when I began to sleep....[66]

This later typescript draft reveals that 'A Dream of Inishmaan' is a construct
designed to exemplify the reading in occultist and anthropological works
that Synge had been engaged in during the late 1890s. The dance, and the
seductive power of the island, are seen as being made possible and believable
by occultist and anthropological theory, and Synge depicts himself as par-
taking in this supernatural 'moment of ecstasy' as a way of demonstrating
the influence of the island, from which he has otherwise been painfully
separated. Rather than being acted upon, here Synge is acting; he is taking
part in a dance in order to promote mystic experience. He enters the world
of the idyll in terms strongly reminiscent of 'Under Ether': the same language, the same ideas of scientific laws being subverted, all appear in 'A
Dream of Inishmaan'.

> I could not distinguish any more between the instruments and the rhythm,
> and my own person or consciousness.
>
> For a while it seemed an excitement that was filled with joy; then it grew
> into an ecstasy where all existence was lost in a vortex of movement. I could
> not think that there had ever been a life beyond the whirling of the dance.
>
> At last, with a sudden movement, the ecstasy returned to an agony and
> rage. I struggled to free myself, but seemed only to increase the passion of
> the steps I moved to. When I shrieked I could only echo the notes of the
> rhythm.[67]

This recalls strongly the sense of elation given by the visions in 'Under
Ether', the panic of the narrator in his attempts to regain volition, and the
powerful influence of the rhythm of the train, which reduces speech to a
fearful imitation. The narrator is privy to something ancient, something
supernatural, and something 'forgotten' by the modern world, which the
island itself remembers psychically. The communion with the island is
figured in terms of religious ecstasy, but it is also figured in terms of a
cultural shock. It is more modernist than Romanticist because it functions

---

[66] TCD MS 4344, f. 347.   [67] *The Gael*, March 1904, p. 93.

on the spiritual moment as problematic rather than redemptive; it is the product of dislocation, of difference and competition, rather than being a moment of fluid harmony. In this way Synge complicates the progression from 'fractured self' to 'spiritual wholeness' that was typical of many narratives of theosophical conversion, foregrounding instead the particular social tensions from which conversions to occultism often sprang.[68] The communal, initiatory nature of the dance echoes Yeats's more overtly occult depiction in his 'Rosa Alchemica' (1897), in which his guide, Michael Robartes, tells the speaker that he must learn an 'exceedingly antique dance' in order to join an occult order: 'before my initiation could be perfected I had to join three times in a magical dance, for rhythm was the wheel of Eternity, on which alone the transient and accidental could be broken, and the spirit set free.' The 'whirling', 'passionate' dance of 'Rosa Alchemica', like the dance in Synge's 'Dream', draws out the tension between passive and active participation in the symbolic world: in Yeats's sequence, 'a mysterious wave of passion, that seemed like the soul of the dance moving within our souls, took hold of me, and I was swept, neither consenting nor refusing, into the midst.'[69] The frightening energy of the unseen world is accessed via physical, rhythmic participation, and the loss of control, both in Synge and Yeats, is integral to occult initiation. As Susan Jones argues, 'literary intimations of conflict, dissonance, or physical aban-donment' are characteristic of textual invocations of dance in modernist literature: 'celebrations of the energy (or discord) association with technol-ogy and mechanical movement stimulated a lasting exchange between text and dance.'[70] Just as the narrator of 'Under Ether' loses physical control and becomes mechanized ('I screamed: "Oh, no, I won't!" "No, I won't!" ... using the sullen rhythm that forms in one's head during a railway journey' (*CW* II, 41)), so the narrator of *The Aran Islands* reveals his discordant presence on the island through his subjection to the rhythmic, otherworldly music. What makes Synge's dream sequence particularly terrifying is not that the world seems changed on the narrator's return, but that it is so completely tranquil and opposite to the world of the dream: 'I dragged myself, trembling, to the

[68] See Selina Guinness, '"Protestant Magic" Reappraised: Evangelicalism, Dissent, and Theosophy', *Irish University Review*, Vol. 33, No. 1, Special Issue: New Perspectives on the Irish Literary Revival (Spring/Summer 2003), 14–27, p. 15.
[69] W. B. Yeats, 'Rosa Alchemica' (1897), in *Mythologies* (London: Macmillan, 1959), 267–92, pp. 286–9.
[70] Susan Jones, *Literature, Modernism, and Dance* (Oxford: Oxford University Press, 2013), pp. 3–4.

window of the cottage and looked out. The moon was glittering across the bay, and there was no sound anywhere on the island' (*CW* II, 100). The apparent deception, and the complete contrast between the psychic memory of the island and its physical appearance, are quietly threatening. The island, as a geographical and spiritual entity, is possessed of immense power while still appearing calm and benign.

The dream sequence in *The Aran Islands* is, undoubtedly, a pivotal moment within the text. As Robert Welch astutely observes,

> The moment that concludes the episode, when he looks out of the window at the moon on the sea, with all its implications of change, re-establishes variation, difference, the activity of transfigured realism, which measures these separations and holds them up for the mind. The story of this dream is nothing less than a description of the making of Synge the artist.[71]

The Aran Islands can and should be seen in part as an account of Synge's own artistic development. The separation between the island and its inhabitants is key to this. As the narrator becomes more actively involved in island culture through occult mystical experience, we realize as readers that the island must be distinguished from the islanders. The islanders (and Synge, too) move between the commercial, modernizing world of their material life and the spiritual, atemporal world of the island as a geographical and mystical category. The differences and separations identified by Welch are important to address: as Synge returns from the dream to the material world of the island, a distinction is established between the psychical experience and the physical one. Synge, in this distinction, is able to assert his pragmatic approach to modernization without jeopardizing his association of the island with spirituality. He avoids Romantic atavism by distinguishing the spiritual idyll from the physical world.

Throughout the published 1907 text and the earlier typescript draft, Synge reinforces an association between spirituality and non-physicality, and between material necessity and the modernizing world. The women of the island, who are seen in some ways as being 'the great conservative force' in the community due to their lack of travel to the mainland, are noted as having a 'singularly spiritual expression' (*CW* II, 54). While Maurteen tells him a fairy story, Synge writes,

---

[71] Robert Welch, *Changing States: Transformations in Modern Irish Writing* (London and New York: Routledge, 1993), p. 86.

> I seem to understand that the women needed and acquired a halo of supernatural interest to lift them from the mere routines of life in which they seem to move all their lives as in a mysterious atmosphere of dreams.[72]

Synge's association of women with spirituality is hardly unique, and may well have been influenced by his reading of Maurice Maeterlinck's collection of mystical essays, *Le Trésor des Humbles* (1896), which Synge took with him to the Aran Islands, and which contains an essay, 'Sur les femmes', that suggests that women are more primitive than men and thus have a 'communication with the unknown' from which men are denied.[73] The material or commercial world is seen by Synge as a necessary shield for the women, and indeed the men, to protect them from the sort of intense revelation that Synge himself recounts in 'A Dream of Inishmaan'. After the keening scene in Part I, for example, Synge observes that the women 'were still sobbing and shaken with grief, yet they were beginning to talk again of the daily trifles that veil them from the terror of the world' (*CW* II, 75).

Turning to the island's men, who are associated more explicitly with commerce and the effects of modernization, Synge is frustrated though pragmatic in observing their focus on the necessities of mainland economics. He writes,

> it is only in the intonation of a few sentences or some old fragment of melody that I can catch the real spirit of the island, for in general the men sit together and talk with endless iteration of the tides and fish, and of the price of kelp in Connemara.   (*CW* II, 74)

This frustration of Synge's desire to see 'the real spirit of the island', from which he feels barred and to which the men appear reluctant to grant him access, is indicative of his perceived distinction between the spiritual, 'real' world of the island, and the commercial, modernizing world in which its inhabitants must play a role. However, this participation in an increasingly globalized world is not condemned by Synge, who has a more accepting

---

[72] TCD MS 4344, f.359.
[73] Maurice Maeterlinck, *The Treasure of the Humble*, trans. Alfred Sutro (London: George Allen, 1903), p. 88.

stance than claims of his anti-modern ideology would suggest.[74] In one passage, Synge photographs a boy whose choice of dress marks him out as one of the more modern islanders, and thus as a sign of modernization. If we look at the typescript version rather than the printed text, Synge offers an insight into his perception of the relationship between modernity, commerce, and the spirituality of the island:

> We nearly quarrelled because he wanted me to take his photograph in his Sunday clothes from Galway, instead of his native home-spuns that become him far better. ~~He is half-consciously ambitious to free himself from the local distinction of the island, as well as from its weakness.~~[75]

In addition to the first sentence, which we find printed in the 1907 text, Synge suggests that the boy is attempting to remove himself from the 'local distinction' of the island. Again, the word 'distinction' is used, echoing Synge's Morrisian description of the islanders' tools and crockery alongside his observations of 'distinction' as contrary to commerce, which is 'common'. In wearing his Galway clothes, the boy is freed into the world of mass production, and is not so intimately tied with the insular traditions of the island. Commerce, as Synge understands, gives the boy a licence to liberate himself from an isolating culture. The idyllic world of the artisanal island, associated as it is with a different spiritual order, is necessarily distinct from the commercial and physical worlds. Synge does not stigmatize the boy for his willingness to partake in modernity; rather, he understands the urge for liberation that the modern life, just like the spiritual life, can offer.

In many ways, Synge's early work sets him apart from current notions of Revivalism: there is a sense of inevitable and even welcome progress, but also an emphasis on cultural, temporal shock, which belongs both to the islanders and to Synge as narrator and observer. Over the course of his visits to the Aran Islands, Synge's writing internalizes occultism and socialist theory as a way of exploring modernity in its scientific, technological, imperialist, and economic manifestations. Synge's attempt to dramatize the clash of old and new results in a visceral and strained transition between worlds, which is complex and fractured in its response to a world that resists idealization.

---

[74] Luke Gibbons, for example, refers to Synge memorably as a 'latter-day Canute, attempting to hold back the "filthy modern tide"', in *Transformations in Irish Culture* (Cork: Cork University Press, 1996), p. 23.

[75] TCD MS 4344, f.143.

This is at the heart of the book's experimental form, which employs a 'fragmented, episodic, sometimes cyclical narrative' in order to adequately address the pressures of modernity.[76] Over time, access to the idyll of the spiritual world becomes rationalized against the necessities of economics, and Synge pragmatically presents the two worlds, as James Knapp has written, as 'contrary but not alternative'.[77] The contest is never resolved, nor does its process signal to us a place for Synge in the critical binary of 'modern' or 'anti-modern'. Open to flux, to change, to tension, Synge's early prose is an intricate reaction not just to modernity or to the primitive but to the process of modernization which creates a necessary though uncomfortable dialectic between the two.

---

[76] Parsons, *The Ordnance Survey and Modern Irish Literature*, p. 121.
[77] Knapp, 'Primitivism and Empire: John Synge and Paul Gauguin', p. 64.

2

The Wicklow Essays

Science, Nature, and the Re-enchanted World

In a letter of 1888, Synge's evangelical mother, Kathleen, showed a deep concern for her son's religious well-being: 'I can see no sign of spiritual life in my poor Johnnie.'[1] Although the first chapter of this book has explored an array of spiritual interests in Synge's early work, examining his use of esoteric discourses, Synge's sense of the importance of spirituality, and especially a spiritual connection to the natural world, was much more wide-ranging. Synge's mother, however, was not alone in assuming that her son was 'a stranger to God'.[2] Indeed, Synge's own narrative of the religious doubt which resulted from his reading of Darwin's *On the Origin of Species* has for a long time been taken as evidence of his 'flight from religious belief'.[3] It has been seen as an archetypal late-Victorian crisis of faith that prompted the writer to 'replace' religiosity with a 'natural community' of peasants. Synge's *The Aran Islands*, one critic maintains, is an effort to 'replace an absent center, the death of a transcendental God'.[4] Others have differentiated between a rejection of Christianity, especially the evangelical Protestantism of Synge's mother, and the wholesale rejection of spiritual belief. Daniel Casey, in a short biographical sketch of the writer, argues correctly that Synge's 'sense of religion was pantheistic—encompassing a divine scheme promoting uniformity and cosmic harmony in nature'.[5] The relationship to nature, and the transference of faith from Christianity into the natural world, are central to Synge's reaction to evolutionary theory, and form an essential component in his idealization of harmonious (and 'primitive') relationships to nature. Rather than fleeing from religious belief,

[1] TCD SSMS 6220, f. 15. Kathleen Synge to Robert Anthony Synge, 16 April 1888.
[2] Letter from Kathleen Synge to Robert Anthony Synge, quoted in Greene and Stephens, *J. M. Synge, 1871–1909*, p. 19. No date given.
[3] Toomey, 'Killing the Da', p. 157.
[4] Edward Hirsch, 'The Imaginary Irish Peasant', *PMLA*, Vol. 106, No. 5 (October 1991), 1116–33, p. 1126.
[5] Daniel J. Casey, 'John Millington Synge: A Life Apart', in Edward A. Kopper, Jr., ed., *A J. M. Synge Literary Companion* (New York and London: Greenwood Press, 1988), 1–13, p. 12.

J. M. Synge: Nature, Politics, Modernism. Seán Hewitt, Oxford University Press (2021). © Seán Hewitt.
DOI: 10.1093/oso/9780198862093.003.0003

Synge harnessed the disorientating effects of his Darwinian encounter by using science as a way of resacralizing, or re-enchanting, the world around him. In this way his work enacts a migration of the spiritual, transferring religious awe from a distinct Christian deity and back into the natural world.

In his 'Autobiography', Synge recounts times in his childhood spent with his neighbour and friend Florence Ross. He tells us, 'We were always primitive', and that 'if we had been allowed...we would have evolved a pantheistic scheme like that of all barbarians' (*CW* II, 7). Monotheistic religion, for Synge, seems 'foreign to the real genius of childhood' (*CW* II, 7). Monotheism, therefore, is set in opposition to both the pantheist and to the 'primitive'; however, throughout his 'Autobiography' Synge traces his development as an artist through an increasing attainment of both states through the practice of natural history. As he grew older, he tells us, he became 'more interested in definite life', developing a naturalist's eye, crouching in bushes to watch 'the mere movements of the birds' (*CW* II, 7). Of his moth-collecting hobby, he writes that 'it gave me a great fondness for the eerie and night and encouraged a lonely temperament which was beginning to take possession of me' (*CW* II, 9). Although, he tells us, he eventually 'lost almost completely' his interest in natural science, he is keen to emphasize that the link with nature itself remained potent: 'the beauty of nature influenced me more than ever' (*CW* II, 9). His abilities as a writer are associated directly with his reading of Darwin. Natural history, rather than enforcing the shock of modernity, is thus reworked and made commensurable with the aspiration to regain the 'primitive', harmonious, and spiritual connection to nature central to Synge's artistic philosophy.

Synge's perception of the 'eeriness' of naturalist practice, of an imminent spirituality in nature, is not as idiosyncratic as it might seem. Alfred Russel Wallace, who conceived the theory of evolution through natural selection independently of Darwin, published a short book on *Spiritualism* (1892), arguing for spiritualism as a positivist science, and many contemporaneous works on magic and occultism foregrounded evolutionary science in their understanding of a spiritual plane.[6] Synge read Wallace's book in 1897, alongside a number of works on mysticism, magic, and the supernatural, such as Jules Bois's *Le Satanisme et le Magie* (1895), Catherine Crowe's

---

[6] See Alfred Russel Wallace, *Spiritualism* (Philadelphia: J.B. Lippincott, 1892), p. 3. For more on Wallace's reconciliation of science and spiritualism, see Janet Oppenheim, *The Other World: Spiritualism and Psychical Research in England, 1850–1914* (Cambridge: Cambridge University Press, 1985), pp. 296–325.

The Night-Side of Nature; or, Ghosts and Ghost Seers (1848), and Frédéric Paulhan's *Le nouveau mysticisme* (1891).[7] In many of these works, writers attempted to reconcile material science with new spiritual movements such as theosophy. Charles Leland, like Synge, saw that 'men of science' and 'theosophists, spiritualists, Folk-lorists' were all working towards 'a grand solution of the unknown'.[8] However, there was a notable antagonism towards materialist positivism. The French writer Édouard Schuré, for example, whose work Synge read repeatedly throughout 1898, argued that the positivist philosophies of Comte and Spencer had led to an intellectual untruth: 'A force de matérialisme, de positivisme et de scepticisme, cette fin de siècle en est arrivée à une fausse idée de la Vérité et du Progrès.'[9] However, he also suggested that science and religion were reconcilable through a recognition of their kindred projects: 'La Religion répond aux besoins du cœur, de là sa magie éternelle; la Science à ceux de l'esprit de là sa force invincible.'[10] What Terry Eagleton terms 'a kind of mystical positivism' at the fin de siècle, therefore, is common throughout Synge's reading, though it is given more definite theorization in his own prose works.[11]

Jason Willwerscheid has suggested that Synge's experience of religious trauma in reading *On the Origin of Species* was not merely a theological but also an aesthetic crisis, seeing in the 'Autobiography' a 'dying out of poetry' when faced with the natural world as a material rather than spiritual presence.[12] However, such an argument conflates the physical, page-by-page chronology of the 'Autobiography' with the chronology asserted by Synge himself. According to the 'Autobiography', Synge first encountered Darwin at the age of 14 (*CW* II, 10), and this does indeed precipitate the often-quoted 'agony of doubt'.[13] However, earlier in the text, recounting his

---

[7] See TCD MS 4418.

[8] Charles Godfrey Leland, *Gypsy Sorcery and Fortune Telling* (London: Fisher Unwin, 1891), p. v. Synge read Leland's book between 1898 and 1899. See TCD MS 4378, f. 71v.

[9] Édouard Schuré, *Les Grands Initiés: Equisse de l'histoire secrète des religions* (Paris: Perrin, 1922), pp. x–xi. 'By dint of materialism, positivism and scepticism, this end of the century has come to a false idea of truth and progress.'

[10] Schuré, *Les Grands Initiés*, p. viii. 'Religion responds to the needs of the heart, hence its eternal magic; science responds to those of the spirit, hence its invincible force.'

[11] Terry Eagleton, 'The Flight to the Real', in Sally Ledger and Scott McCracken, eds., *Cultural Politics at the Fin de Siècle* (Cambridge: Cambridge University Press, 1995), 11–21, p. 15.

[12] Jason Willwerscheid, 'Migratory movements: evolutionary theory in the works of J. M. Synge', *Irish Studies Review*, Vol. 22, No. 2 (2014), 129–46, pp. 131–2.

[13] It is worth noting here that Synge's own chronology may be more narrative device than biographical truth. W. J. McCormack, for instance, thinks it more likely that Synge's crisis with Darwinism did not occur until his mid-twenties. See *Fool of the Family*, pp. 42–3.

'sixteenth year' (that is, after his reading of Darwin), Synge makes it clear
that his poetic apprehension of nature was not diminished but enhanced by
Darwin:

> Natural history did [much] for me ... To wander as I did for years through
> the dawn of night with every nerve stiff and strained with expectation gives
> one a singular acquaintance with the essences of the world. The obscure
> noises of the owls and rabbits, the heavy scent of the hemlock and the
> flowers of the elder, the silent flight of the moths I was in search of gave me
> a passionate and receptive mood like that of early [man]. The poet too
> often lets his intellect draw the curtain of connected thought between him
> and the glory that is round him. The forces which rid me of theological
> mysticism reinforced my innate feeling for the profound mysteries of life.
>
> (CW II, 9–10)

The heightened awareness, the 'passionate and receptive mood', is both
connected with natural science and with 'early man'; the figure of the
naturalist poet, freed from the obstructive 'curtain' of intellect which
Synge associates with other writers, is both modern and pre-modern. The
dualism associated with the project of Enlightenment, scientific positivism,
and modernity in general is avoided *through* natural history: the attentive
poet, newly acquainted with 'the essences of the world', is made alert to 'the
glory that is round him'. Furthermore, as suggested in Laurence Oliphant's
Scientific Religion, this focus on sensitivity, on receptiveness to the 'mysteries
of life', is figured as 'innate' rather than learned, as 'primitive' rather than
civilized.[14] This passage reworks the typical associations of materialist science and Enlightenment with 'the disenchantment of the world' by collapsing any neat vision of progress itself: the acquaintance with natural history
becomes an acquaintance with the 'eerie' mystery of nature, and the scientific modernity implicit in being 'rid of theological mysticism' becomes, in its
own way, a route to the 'profound mysteries of life.'[15] The critical misun-
derstanding that Synge's attempt at 'bridging the gap' between himself and
the natural world might constitute 'a way of denying Darwin' is the result of
a too-strict application of a binary of Enlightenment versus faith, or

---

[14] Oliphant's book is discussed in the first chapter of this book.
[15] 'The project of the Enlightenment was the disenchantment of the world.' Max Horkheimer
and Theodor Adorno, *Dialectic of Enlightenment*, trans. John Cumming (New York: Herder &
Herder, 1972), p. xv.

Romanticism versus science, which is not consonant with Synge's much more nuanced negotiation of these large-scale approaches to the natural world.[16]

Positivist and materialist science, which precipitated Synge's rejection of Protestantism, had a perhaps unexpected result in recalibrating his relationship to nature. Protestantism, as a concomitant process of wider Enlightenment upheavals, 'eradicat[ed] the traditional idea that spiritual power pervades the natural world, and is particularly present in sacred places and in spiritually charged material objects', and thus, alongside the projects of positivist science, is suggested to have led to a 'disenchantment' of the world. The movement of Protestantism, from the Reformation onwards, was in part to redress the transference of God to his creation, to emphasize the material world *as material* rather than as a spiritual, 'ensouled' world able to 'transmit any spiritual power in or of itself'.[17] During the nineteenth century, this narrative was compounded by materialist, positivist science. Narratives of disenchantment were not solely theorized by philosophers in the twentieth century. In fact, disenchantment was a common theme in much of Synge's reading. Thomas Huxley, for example, said that disenchantment 'weigh[ed] like a nightmare upon many of the best minds of these days'; the advance of material science, he commented, 'threatens to drown their souls'.[18] Synge, in being liberated from a disenchanted Protestantism by Darwin, uses Darwinian science in a process of re-enchantment. This is, in a way, the most complete rebellion against the restrictiveness of his Protestant upbringing.

Though not entirely aligned with the scientific Enlightenment, Protestantism shared many of its motivations. Jane Bennett, for example, summarizes the eighteenth-century Enlightenment as a project which

> sought to demystify the world according to faith, where nature was God's text, filled with divine signs, intrinsic meaning, and intelligible order. In the face of belief in an enchanted cosmos, the Enlightenment sought to push God to a more distant social location; in the face of unreflective allegiance

---

[16] Frawley, *Irish Pastoral*, pp. 85–6.

[17] Rupert Sheldrake, *The Rebirth of Nature: The Greening of Science and God* (London: Century, 1990), p. 20.

[18] Cited in James Ward, *Naturalism and Agnosticism: The Gifford Lectures Delivered before the University of Aberdeen in the years 1896–1898*, 2nd edn., Vol. I (London: Adam & Charles Black, 1903), p. 17. Synge read Ward's lectures in their year of publication (1899). See TCD MS 4420.

to tradition, it sought self-determination and self-conscious reason; in the face of a view of knowledge as mysterious divine hints, it sought a transparent, certain science; in the face of a sacralized nature, it sought a fund of useful natural resources.[19]

It is interesting, then, that the encounter with positivist and materialist science and philosophy (Comte, Darwin, and Huxley, in particular) led Synge to reject not only Christianity but also the very commonalities between Enlightenment thought and Protestantism. Rather than accepting a desacralized nature of immovable and predictable laws, Synge instead rejected the very project of disenchantment itself, using positivist science contra positivism, and contra Protestantism, in his vision of a mystical, sacralized, but also 'Christless' (*CW* I, 6) world view.

Writing his 'Autobiography', Synge drew links between his childhood self and his adult preoccupations. Referring to his early childhood, Synge writes that 'Even at this time I was a worshipper of nature' (*CW* II, 5). The ease with which he links religious and naturalist practice (he 'worships' nature) is indicative of the survival of pre-Darwinian, even Romantic, tendencies. In fact, the phrase itself is a direct echo of Wordsworth's 'Tintern Abbey', in which the older poet imagines his younger self, 'so long / A worshipper of Nature'.[20] W. B. Yeats, who described being 'deprived by Huxley and Tyndall...of the simple-minded religion of my childhood', claimed to have retaliated by creating 'a new religion' in the form of 'an infallible Church of poetic tradition'.[21] Synge, on the other hand, though Darwin may indeed have precipitated his loss of orthodox faith, did not feel 'deprived' in the same way, and turned not to a 'Church of poetic tradition' but rather deeper into the world of the naturalist. He remained a member of the Dublin Naturalists' Field Club until 1888, 'worked systematically at his hobby' of collecting butterflies, moths, and beetles, and kept detailed notebooks documenting his naturalist pursuits.[22]

In his early work 'Vita Vecchia', which explores many of the key themes of the 'Autobiography' in fictionalized form, Synge is careful to draw a distinction between occult mysticism and what he calls the 'mystery' of

---

[19] Jane Bennett, *Unthinking Faith and Enlightenment: Nature and the State in a Post-Hegelian Era* (New York and London: New York University Press, 1987), p. 7.

[20] William Wordsworth and Samuel Taylor Coleridge, *Lyrical Ballads, with a few other poems* (London: Penguin, 2006).

[21] Yeats, *Autobiographies*, pp. 115–16.

[22] Greene and Stephens, *J. M. Synge, 1871–1909*, p. 8.

nature. His rewriting of certain passages of *The Aran Islands* to obscure occult references (as discussed in Chapter 1) is reflective of a general progression in his prose works, which begin with explicit symbolism and occultism and move towards a mysticism based in moments of acute communion with the natural world. As in the 'Autobiography', there is an emphasis in 'Vita Vecchia' on the relationship between simplicity, associated by Synge and others with the 'primitive' (and, implicitly, the more 'natural') and receptiveness to a sort of secular mystical experience. Towards the end of the piece, there is an evocative description of the arrival of springtime in Ireland, full of striking detail and a sense of the uncanny. Woods 'grow purple with sap', birches stand 'like candlesticks', hazel trees come and '[hang] the woods with straight ear-rings of gold, till one morning after rain spectres of green and yellow and pink began to look out between the trees' (*CW* II, 23–4). Again, however, the mystical, other-worldly sense of the 'essences' of the world are tied by Synge not to a religious experience but rather to an intense and scientific observation:

> We do wrong to seek a foundation for ecstasy in philosophy or the hidden things of the spirit—if there is a spirit—for when life is at its simplest, with nothing beyond or before it, the mystery is greater than we can endure. Every leaf and flower [and] insect is full of deeper wonder than any sign the cabbalists have invented.   (*CW* II, 24)

Rather than meditating on any occult symbolism, Synge's narrator gives his attention to what the 'Autobiography' might call 'definite life'. Pitting himself against cabbalism, which exerts a strong influence on theosophical teachings, Synge asserts his own modern form of enchantment. The mystery does not come from anything 'beyond' nature but rather from a close and simple observation of physical nature itself. Where some other modernists have rejected scientific positivism as antagonistic to spirituality, Synge harnesses this knowledge and deploys it to emphasize the spiritual potential of a meeting between science and the artistic imagination.[23] In this way he

---

[23] For other modernist re-enchantments and discussions of the rejection of scientific positivism, see John Bramble, *Modernism and the Occult* (Basingstoke: Palgrave Macmillan, 2015), pp. 1–6; Randall Styers, *Making Magic: Religion, Magic, and Science in the Modern World* (New York: Oxford University Press, 2004), p. 212; Leigh Wilson, *Modernism and Magic: Experiments with Spiritualism, Theosophy and the Occult* (Edinburgh: Edinburgh University Press, 2013), pp. 28–30.

contributes to our understanding of an alternative reaction to modernity which complicates the 'secularization thesis', showing that (rather than modernization being coterminous with secularization) the sacred could be reinterpreted and made central to a number of modernist philosophies and literatures.[24] Rather than Darwin and the naturalists being seen as among the principal disenchanters of the world, Synge's nuanced exploration of ecological relationships suggests that a radical re-enchantment is made possible not by any practical occultism but by practical scientific observation. The techniques and principles of modern science are applied by the modern writer to suggest the potential of attaining a unity with nature exemplified in the perceived 'pre-modernity' of certain types of Irish peasantry.

Synge's reading in evolutionary science was not, of course, confined to Darwin. He read widely, exploring the works of Henry Drummond, T. H. Huxley, James Frazer, Herbert Spencer, and Benjamin Kidd.[25] Each of these writers used the basic tenets of evolutionism in new applications, from sociology and psychology to materialist science and even, in the case of Drummond, to reassert the truth of Christianity. As critics such as Sinéad Garrigan Mattar, Mary Burke, and Jason Willwerscheid have shown, Synge's use of evolutionary theory was by no means an unquestioning application of Darwinism but, rather, a selective and individual reaction to the works of a variety of theorists.[26] Protestant reactions to evolutionism are particularly revealing in the case of Synge's quest for a sacralized world, and there are many commonalities to be found between the writings of prominent Protestants and Synge himself. During the German Enlightenment, Protestants including Friedrich Oetinger searched for a positive alternative to mechanical theories of nature, affirming that 'there was a mystery to things *in* and *beyond* their natural properties' which were thus left untouched by natural science. In the early twentieth century, German biologist and philosopher Hans Adolf Driesch explored the concept of vitalism, of an entelechy operating alongside the visible natural order,

---

[24] For more work on the limits of the 'secularization thesis' in studies of literary modernism, see Pericles Lewis, *Religious Experience and the Modernist Novel* (Cambridge: Cambridge University Press, 2010), especially pp. 23–51.

[25] See TCD MSS 4416, 4419.

[26] See Willwerscheid, 'Migratory Movements'; Mary Burke, 'Evolutionary Theory: And the Search for Lost Innocence in the Writings of J. M. Synge', *The Canadian Journal of Irish Studies*, Vol. 30, No. 1 (Spring 2004), pp. 48–54; Mattar, *Science, Primitivism, and the Irish Revival*.

which would become central to later experimental modernisms through the work of Henri Bergson and others.[27]

Whereas many evangelical Protestants in Ireland refuted post-Darwinian concessions to science and textual criticism in religious circles, suggesting that they subverted scriptural authority and the concept of biblical inerrancy, others adapted their theology into different brands of Anglicanism which were made compatible with evolutionary (if not strictly Darwinian) thought.[28] In Synge's time, Henry Drummond, whose *The Ascent of Man* (1894) Synge read in 1895, asserted that evolution was the ultimate process by which divine love could be expressed on earth.[29] Drummond, a Scottish naturalist and Free Churchman, had experimented in mesmerism, and wrote a number of sermons and books which sought to uncover evidence of natural law in the spiritual world.[30] The key arguments of *The Ascent of Man* are that science and religion should use evolutionary theory as a point of harmony rather than difference, and that through the process of evolution aspects of the 'unseen' are assimilated into the 'seen', or that physical nature is moulded by and representative of some cosmic energy or 'higher influences'.[31] Drummond sees the theory of evolution not as 'the statement of a mathematical proposition which men are called upon to declare true or false', but as a new 'method of looking upon Nature' that is radically unifying. The evolutionist, in *The Ascent of Man*, is both a spiritual and pioneering figure: 'his understanding of his hourly shifting place in this always moving and ever more mysterious world, must be humble, tolerant, and undogmatic.'[32] For Drummond, as for Synge, the naturalist's approach results in an increased mystery, a recognition of their own contingency, and an attention to the continuing shifts in their relationship to the natural world. Synge's own conception of the relationship between positivism and

---

[27] John Dillenberger, *Protestant Thought and Natural Science: A Historical Interpretation* (Nashville and New York: Abingdon Press, 1960), pp. 193, 232–3. For more on vitalism and modernism, see Omri Moses, *Out of Character: Modernism, Vitalism, Psychic Life* (Stanford: Stanford University Press, 2014).

[28] See David Livingstone, 'Darwin in Belfast: The Evolution Debate', in John Wilson Foster and Helena C. G. Chesney, eds., *Nature in Ireland: A Scientific and Cultural History* (Dublin: Lilliput, 1997), 387–408, especially pp. 390–4.

[29] See TCD MS 4416.

[30] See James R. Moore, *The Post-Darwinian Controversies: A Study of the Protestant struggle to come to terms with Darwin in Great Britain and America, 1870–1900* (Cambridge: Cambridge University Press, 1979), p. 224.

[31] Henry Drummond, *The Ascent of Man* (London: Hodder & Stoughton, 1894), p. 415.

[32] Drummond, *Ascent*, pp. 11, 9.

spirituality in the study of nature is part of a wider attempt to disrupt the logical progression from science through to atheism, as Drummond attests:

> Though a positive religion, in the Comtian sense, is no religion, a religion that is not in some degree positive is an impossibility. And although religion must always rest upon faith, there is a reason for faith, and a reason not only in Reason, but in Nature herself. When Evolution comes to be worked out along its great natural lines, it may be found to provide for all that religion assumes, all that philosophy requires, and all that science proves.[33]

There was, therefore, certainly a precedent in Protestant reactions to positivist science that does not square with a binary view of Enlightenment and disenchantment.

Drummond's notion of a positive religion, referencing Comte, hints towards what Terry Eagleton has called a trend for 'mystical positivism' at the fin de siècle.[34] Synge read and made notes on Comte's *Course in Positive Philosophy* in 1896. In this work, Comte outlined three fundamental 'theoretical conditions' through which the development of human intelligence passed over the ages.[35] These were the theological (or 'fictitious') stage, the metaphysical (or 'abstract') stage, and the scientific (or 'positive') stage.[36] Comte asserts that, in the nineteenth century, the progression through to the positivistic stage was almost complete. However, in microcosm, Comte suggested that each individual might also 'look back upon his own history' and see that 'he was a theologian in his childhood, a metaphysician in his youth, and a natural philosopher in his manhood'.[37] Synge's early prose writings are all, in part, attempts at plotting the growth of the artist from a theologian to a positivist and back to a stage of metaphysics, an oddity that might be explained by his simultaneous reading of Comte alongside Blavatsky, Nietzsche, and Hegel.[38] The 'Autobiography' asserts that the theological stage was ousted by the arguments of scientific evidence; however, rather than completing this progression towards positivism, Synge's

---

[33] Drummond, *Ascent*, pp. 69–70.   [34] Eagleton, 'The Flight to the Real', p. 15.

[35] See TCD MSS 4379, 4417. It is likely that Synge read Comte in Harriet Martineau's condensed, translated edition, which offered Comte's six-volume *Course in Positive Philosophy* (1830–42) in a two-volume edition published in 1853.

[36] Auguste Comte, *The Positive Philosophy of Auguste Comte*, trans. Harriet Martineau, Vol. I (London: John Chapman, 1853), pp. 1–2.

[37] Comte, *Positive Philosophy*, p. 3.   [38] See TCD MSS 4379, 4417.

own plotting of his early experiences relocates the artist in the stage of heightened metaphysics, using scientific principles to access an understanding of the world unavailable to theological mysticism. Likewise, in the later 'Étude Morbide' (1899), the narrator claims that 'I am hearing many ghost-stories. Since I have come back to nature my rather crude materialism has begun to dissatisfy me. Nature is miraculous and my own dreams were something extra-human' (*CW* II, 33). The dissatisfaction with his 'rather crude materialism' suggests that this conception of positivist science has been limited by its inability to accommodate the ineffable and is thus untrue to nature itself. A more accurate science, therefore, would be required to encompass the 'miraculous' as well as the purely material.

An early draft of the 'Étude' was illustrated by Synge with 'drawings of insects, of a bird's wing compared to a human hand' and other 'Darwinian' figures as well as half-human, half-animal drawings and a sketch of an insect turning into a violin.[39] Elsewhere in the unpublished text is a passage in which Synge, like Drummond before him, works to reconcile science and the imagination, taking William Blake as his inspiration:

> Blake taught that true imagination was a view of the eternal symbols of Being, but who may know in his own mind or that of others these symbols from mere hallucinations. I am driven back on science—of all names the most abused. If science is a learning of truth, nature and imagination being a less immediate knowledge of the same, the two when perfect will collide. The law of evolution is only truly understood by an effort of the imagination and a few more such efforts and man will be as god. This then is the task of all who labour to work with transcendental imagination the data no sane instructed being may deny.[40]

The prophetic mode is understood as being further enhanced by science, and the imagination is given a vital role in achieving the 'learning of truth' which science, nature, and imagination strive towards. Synge distances the positivistic perception of symbolic truths from 'mere hallucinations', distinguishing them from the true 'data' available to the receptive, imaginative, and 'instructed' artist. In this way, he rejects a completely Blakean emphasis on the power of the imagination, suggesting that imagination must combine with positive knowledge to attain the most 'perfect' truth. In this passage,

---

[39] King, *The Drama of J. M. Synge*, p. 4.
[40] TCD MS 4350, f. 59v. Transcription given in King, *The Drama of J. M. Synge*, p. 4.

therefore, Synge understands the projects of science and the artistic imagination as coterminous, defending the former by showing its affinities with the latter. An imaginative vision of an enchanted world is not antithetical to science but part of a grand project of truth-seeking.

The sketches of insects becoming stringed instruments that surround this draft, and Synge's contemporaneous note-making on the works of Blake, Swedenborg, and a number of theosophists, reveal that his reading in Romanticism, mysticism, and theosophy was integral to his formulation of a vitalist principle in nature, his preoccupation with an unseen force or presence which is perpetually translated into physical reality. This incorrectly dated notebook (which, as argued in the first chapter of this book, was in use until at least 1899) contains notes on Besant's *The Ancient Wisdom* (1897), her *Esoteric Christianity* (1898), and Yeats and Ellis's edition of the works of Blake (1893), but also refers to a hierarchical system of being detailed in Besant's manual *Reincarnation* (1892), which Synge read in 1898.[41] Synge's notes on *The Ancient Wisdom* are separated from his notes on *Reincarnation* by some thoughts (in French) on Nietzsche's *Zarathustra* (ff. 47r–48v) and Blavatsky's *The Voice of Silence* (f. 35r), and are followed by attempts to summarize Yeats and Ellis's argument on Blake's theory of nature and art (ff. 50r–56v). From *Reincarnation*, Synge draws a hierarchical list from the 'physical body' through to 'âtma (the one self)' (f. 48r), and seems preoccupied with theosophy's view of the various planes of existence. In *Reincarnation*, Besant discusses the perpetual reincarnation principle and the cycle of the transmigration of life through astral doubles before theorizing the creation of mankind in terms of a growing potential of the mind to accommodate or react to the divine force:

Here were, we may say, the two poles of the evolving Life-manifestation: the Animal with all its potentialities on the lower plane, but necessarily mindless, consciousless, errant aimlessly over the earth, unconsciously tending onwards by reason of the impelling force within it that drove it ever forward; this force, the Divine, itself too lofty in its pure ethereal nature to reach consciousness on the lower planes, and so unable to bridge the gulf that stretched between it and the animal brain it vivified but could not illume. Such was the organism that was to become man, a creature of

---

[41] TCD MS 4379. Synge must have read the 1898 edition of Besant's lectures on *Esoteric Christianity* rather than the revised 1901 edition, since he notes reading the text in his diary of 1898. See TCD MS 4419.

marvellous potentialities, an instrument with strings all ready to break into music; where was the power that should make the potentialities actual, where the touch that should waken the melody and send it forth thrilling into space?[42]

The concept of the 'animal', full of 'marvellous potentialities', as 'an instrument with strings all ready to break into music', and the final question, which calls for a sort of divine musician, ready to 'play' the instrument into life, was clearly embedded in Synge's artistic mind. Not only was he a talented violinist, but during this period he was heavily concerned, as we can see in his thoughts on Blake's work, with the divine potential of the scientifically instructed artist. His sketches of fauna as stringed instruments in his drafts for 'Étude Morbide' are a clear invocation of this principle, whereby the 'instructed' artist is able to 'play' nature, or to bring it into a higher life via the divine potential of the imagination. Here, Synge comes close to the vision of artist as magician shared by Yeats, though he routes this through scientific rather than occult knowledge. Summarizing Yeats and Ellis's introduction to their works of Blake, Synge noted: 'B[lake] held that by laborious and slavish copy of nature as well as of the masters the language of art could be learnt. Once learned the artist's duty was to cultivate imagination till it became vision and draw from that' (f. 50v). The artistic imagination, once it is familiar with the forms of nature, is able to become visionary. Synge's theory of nature, bound as it is with spiritualism, mysticism, and scientific instruction, is a consistent attempt to emphasize the divine potential of the natural world and the artist's ability to connect with the immanent spirituality of the universe.

The particular and nuanced relationship that Synge elucidates throughout his Wicklow essays is the bedrock of his understanding of humanity's place in nature and of his theory of the imaginative power of the poet; it becomes key to his reactions to modernization as a process in which the delicate dynamics of both ecological and social systems are shifted, impacting both physically and psychologically on the natural world and our relationship to it. The Wicklow essays follow a dictum that is rooted in the evolutionary theory of the naturalists which Synge read during the 1890s, namely that a species will exhibit particular characteristics which make it suited to its environment and place within the ecosystem. This principle of

---

[42] Annie Besant, *Reincarnation* (London: Theosophical Publishing House, 1910), first published 1892, p. 10.

evolutionism, common to Darwin, Huxley, and Drummond, was variously conceived, with Drummond giving a predictably unique but compelling theory.[43] Synge's essays explore the various consequences of species adaptation and the effects of environment, drawing on the contemporary proliferation of social Darwinist thought. 'The Oppression of the Hills' (written between 1898 and 1902) begins with a general statement that is inflected throughout the essays: 'Among the cottages that are scattered through the hills of County Wicklow I have met with many people who show in a singular way the influence of a particular locality' (CW II, 209). However, in many ways Synge's essays are a testament to a sort of maladaptation: rather than being adapted to suit their environment, the people of Wicklow (with the exception of the tramp figures) are shown to be under its influence. The power (both psychic and physical) of the natural world constantly overcomes them. This is escaped, in Synge's thought, by the vagrants of the county, who exist outside the influence of local social and environmental influences, and thus are able to attain an uninterrupted spiritual unity with nature. If adverse socio-economic conditions have affected a form of degeneration and maladaptation among the settled peasantry, this is escaped through a life of vagrancy.

In the Wicklow essays, Synge's concept of the 'influence' of a locality is more in tune with Drummond's theory of involution than with the more traditional theory of species adaptation in Darwin and Huxley. 'Involution' is the crowning moment of Drummond's Ascent in that it clarifies his idea of evolution as a theory that can unite theologians and naturalists, attempting to explain the moral evolution of man through the unseen force of divine love. In the final chapter of the Ascent, Drummond concludes that:

> The secret of Evolution lies, in short, with the Environment. In the Environment, in that in which things live and move and have their being, is found the secret of their being, and especially of their becoming. And what is that in which things live and move and have their being? It is Nature, the world, the cosmos—and something more, some One more, an Infinite Intelligence and an Eternal Will. Everything that lives, lives in

---

[43] Synge read and made notes on Darwin's *The Descent of Man* (1871) and Henry Drummond's *The Ascent of Man* (1894) in 1895 (see TCD MS 4416), and was at least familiar with the work of Huxley, referring to his *Evidence as to Man's Place in Nature* (1863) in an essay on Anatole France which he drafted in 1904. See TCD MS 4393, ff. 24v–26v.

virtue of its correspondences with this Environment. Evolution is not to unfold from within; it is to infold from without.[44]

That the environment is both physical and 'something more', and that all life is the expression of both these seen and unseen factors, are unifying ideas, and their potential for Synge was immense. The idea of a folding, cyclical temporality in nature is found in 'Étude Morbide' in the narrator's experience of astral travel. Here, 'symphonies of colour...moved with musical recurrence round centres I could not understand', and his entire vision ends as 'all these things rolled themselves in a vortex and left a single lily in their wake' (CW II, 34).[45] The folding and unfolding of the unseen world into a physical production in Drummond's Ascent is echoed in Synge's characterization of the cyclical, unbound universe of the vision.

Drummond continues his theory of involution by widening the idea to encompass not only physical nature as an expression of cosmic nature but also the possibility that this 'cosmic' or 'unseen' nature might exert an intense 'possession' of physical nature:

Growth is no mere extension from a root but a taking possession of, or a being possessed by, an ever widening Environment, a continuous process of assimilation of the seen or Unseen, a ceaseless redistribution of energies flowing into the evolving organism from the Universe around it.[46]

The process of involution, as Drummond theorizes it, might involve both a 'possession of, or a being possessed by' the environment, either seen or unseen. Such a theorization has clear implications for a discussion of enchantment or 'mystery' in relation to the natural world. Synge's early formulation of a 'natural' art, in which all emotion is 'part of the sequence of existence' and the 'cosmic element' of the artist is in 'harmony' with 'the laws of the world' (CW II, 3) draws on a similar set of underlying ideas: that the 'cosmic' purpose or law might pass through into a process of creation and shape it into something definably 'natural'. It is easy to see, even on the level of artistic theory, how Drummond's ideas might have attracted a young Synge prone to the expression of pseudo-mystical statements about

[44] Drummond, Ascent, pp. 414–15.

[45] For more on occult conceptions of astral travel, particularly in relation to the Order of the Golden Dawn, see Owen, The Place of Enchantment, p. 130.

[46] Drummond, Ascent, p. 415.

the processes of creation. Synge's statement regarding the 'influence of a particular locality' is one of Drummondian involution rather than Darwinian evolution; the environment's 'energy' or 'unseen' presence is felt throughout and acts without warning on the local inhabitants. The problem with reading Synge's essays in terms of traditional Darwinian evolutionism is that the works themselves do not suggest any particular adaptation among the Wicklow people. In fact, the people of the Wicklow glens, rather than being 'in possession of', are more often than not 'being possessed by', the environment.

'The Oppression of the Hills' is the clearest example of the psychic effects of the natural world on the settled people of the glens. Synge opens by emphasizing the 'influence of a particular locality' on the people, and he describes a landscape in which the rain is constant throughout the year, continuing until 'the thatch drips with water stained to a dull chestnut and the floor of the cottages seems to be going back to the condition of the bogs near it' (*CW* II, 209). The built environment is returning slowly to a natural state, and the efforts of the people are insistently undone by the effects of the climate. The idea that the 'soul' of nature might be asserting itself through physical nature, and that the unnatural built environment might be undone by a process of involution, is made literal in this image. T. H. Huxley, with whose work Synge was familiar, emphasizes this idea of nature destroying the unnatural in his *Evolution and Ethics* (1894): 'nature is always tending to reclaim that which her child, man, has borrowed from her and has arranged in combinations which are not those favoured by the general cosmic process.'[47] Synge illustrates the return to a natural state at the very beginning of this first Wicklow essay not only as a way of suggesting the antagonism of the climate to the settled communities in the glens but also to introduce an implicit paradigm for a reorganized, 'natural' society.

The connection between the people and the weather is strong: when the sun rises, it has an 'almost supernatural radiance', and the men and women emerge from their cottages 'with the joy of children recovered from a fever' (*CW* II, 209). In such passages, Wicklow becomes contrary to the virtues of vitality and health that Synge prized in the peasantry:

---

[47] T. H. Huxley and Julian Huxley, *Evolution and Ethics, 1893–1943* (London: The Pilot Press, 1947), p. 40. Synge makes numerous references to Huxley's work in TCD MS 4393, particularly his *Evidence as to Man's Place in Nature* (1863). See ff. 25v–26v.

> This peculiar climate, acting on a population that is already lonely and dwindling, has caused or increased a tendency to nervous depression among the people, and every degree of sadness, from that of the man who is merely mournful to that of the man who has spent half his life in the madhouse, is common among these hills.   (*CW* II, 209)

The spectre of emigration and population decline is felt throughout, and is linked to an unhealthy relationship to nature prompted by social ills. An old man, remembering the Wicklow of his youth, tells Synge that 'you'd see forty boys and girls below there on a Sunday evening, playing ball and diverting themselves; but now all this country is gone lonesome and bewildered, and there's no man knows what ails it' (*CW* II, 210). The image of a vibrant population with 'a fine constitution' (*CW* II, 210) in comparison to the present 'lonesome' and 'ail[ing]' country is important context for Synge's essays, which link the socio-economic concerns of the Wicklow peasantry and the psychic effect of the environment in a relationship of mutual interdependence. The people depict the earth itself as ailing, and as such understand the effects of their climate (both natural and socio-economic) as nature's assertion of a sort of psychic retribution on mankind, as in the story of the man who was taken by 'some excitement', ran off into the hills naked, where his 'naked foot-marks' were found in the mud, and later his dead body, 'and it near eaten by crows' (*CW* II, 209–10). This is an image of a landscape feeding off humanity, enacting the very socio-economic violence done to it and to the peasantry, re-emphasizing the vulnerability of these isolated people to abstracted forces, whether natural, economic, political, or historical. This more political point is not merely inferred from the text. In an earlier version of the 'The Oppression of the Hills', Synge explicitly links ideas of congestion with the mental disorders suffered by the people of Wicklow. After meeting a woman who 'has lived by herself for fifteen years in a tiny hovel', Synge notes that she was 'troubled by neurasthenia and hysteria and vague terrors'. He comments, 'We hear every day of the horrors of overcrowding, yet these desolate dwellings on the hills here with an old widow dying far away from her friends...have perhaps a more utter, if higher sort of misery.'[48]

---

[48] This earlier version is given by Alan Price in a textual note. *CW* II, 210–11.

Synge's highly descriptive prose is attuned to the landscape's potential to reflect its 'unseen' presence, to the places in which what he calls, in 'Étude Morbide', the 'veil' (*CW* II, 34) between a purely physical and a more mystical experience of nature might be made possible by attentive observation of both the aesthetic and physical processes of the environment. In a remarkable passage in 'People and Places' (a composite of pieces written between 1898 and 1908), Synge explores the parallels between the 'seen' and the 'unseen', focusing on the landscape in a way that might allow him to access the points at which the process of involution is revealed:

> At the end of the Upper Lake at Glendalough one is quite shut off from the part that has been spoiled by civilization, and when one fishes there from dusk to midnight a feeling of isolation creeps over one that it would be hard to pass. A little wind is of use when one is fishing, but it is on perfectly still nights that the lake is most beautiful. The water catches and returns in a singular half-interpreting way the last light of the sky and the coloured depth and shadow of the cliffs. In some places a lip of white sand cuts off the real cliff from its double, but in other places the two are nearly unified. As the night comes on herons cry with a lonely desolate note that is echoed backwards and forwards among the hills, and stars begin to glitter in the sky and at one's feet in the water. One seems to be set on the side of a solitary cliff between two reaches of stars, yet in one's face [the] other cliff stands out with a purple density that is much more than darkness....
>
> (*CW* II, 195)

This passage, which stands alone in the published text, represents Synge's descriptive powers at their most acute. What is more, it is particularly concerned with how the landscape might expand, claim, and inhabit its own significance. The water's reflective surface suggests the cyclical quality of nature as it 'catches and returns' in a 'half-interpreting way' both the light of the sunset and the absence of light in the cliffs. The cliff, revealingly, has its 'double' in the water, and the two are 'nearly unified' in places. This observation, rather than simply being a description of the reflections in the lake, becomes a way of understanding the connections between the sky and the land, the places where the two might connect, and the way in which the lake allows one to stand, as Synge does at the end of the passage, *in* the sky: 'stars begin to glitter in the sky and at one's feet in the water'. This is a mystical observation rather than an instance of pathetic fallacy: Synge suggests that the natural world might be a portal to something beyond human experience, rather than being merely a repository of human emotion. These are not specified as the *reflections* of stars (though on one level, of course, we understand them as such) but rather as representative of the idea that a landscape can provide a connection to something beyond itself, and that a person standing in that landscape can become part of a cosmic system. The cliff has both a 'real' and non-physical presence; it has a 'double' in the non-physical realm which is revealed in the cyclical play of light on water. Here, Wicklow becomes a place of spiritual potential, a place replete with mystical possibilities. The Upper Lake, 'shut off from the part that has been spoiled by civilization', is a place in which a 'primitive' connection to nature can be reclaimed by the writer.

For Synge, receptivity to nature becomes a way of accessing a divine, or at least non-physical, world that is part of, rather than separate from, the physical phenomena that usually occupy the naturalist's attention. 'The People of the Glens', which is also a 'collection of impressions' written over many years, includes a similar descriptive passage which is used to explain the 'influence of a particular locality' on the mental state of the Wicklow people.[49] Passing through a narrow gap on a hill, Synge notices 'a handful of jagged sky with extraordinarily brilliant stars' and, when he reaches the top of the hill, the proximity of the stars creates an emotional response that, on recollection, seems to explain the tendency towards mental illness among the people:

> There was not light enough to show the mountains round me, and the earth seemed to have dwindled away into a mere platform where an astrologer might watch. Among these emotions of the night one cannot wonder that the madhouse is so often named in Wicklow.
>
> (*CW* II, 219)[50]

Again, there is a slip in the language. Just as the stars reflected in the Upper Lake at Glendalough were recognized *as* stars themselves, so the emotions of the narrator in the above extract *become* the 'emotions of the night'. As in the passage from 'People and Places', the physical landscape becomes a place in which something much more than the physical world is present. The

---

[49] Edward Stephens, in his private papers, describes the article (published in *The Shanachie* in spring 1907) as 'a collection of impressions of people seen at different times, perhaps years apart'. See *CW* II, 216.

[50] A different version of this passage is given in TCD MS 4396, ff. 32–3, dated 'Spring/ Summer 1907'.

earth, in its darkness, seems to have 'dwindled away', providing a platform from which the night sky can be observed. The 'emotions of the night' are related to a proximity to a non-physical or higher world, and Synge's description of the landscape again focuses on pinpointing why and how certain features of the natural world shape and influence the human mind.

These momentary glimpses of transcendence, where the landscape allows the human observer to experience, self-reflexively, points of confluence with the extra-human world, and their own involution from the environment, are also undercut by Synge through a recognition of difference felt by the 'modern' narrator. He describes being 'forced back to the so-called spiritual mood' (*CW* II, 199) by the onset of twilight. While the people of the glens, and especially the vagrants, 'unite in a rude way the old passions of the earth' (*CW* II, 199), Synge himself feels his own problematic relationship to the sublime. In a longer passage, in which he questions his emotional response to the twilight in the glens, Synge finds the source of his 'profound... remorse' (*CW* II, 200) in the moments when the 'diurnal temperament jar[s] against the impulses of perpetual beauty which is hidden somewhere in the fountain from whence all life has come' (*CW* II, 200). The secret source of life, which is perpetual, is contrasted to the time-bound physical world, and to Synge as narrator, as a way of explaining his emotional response. His close observation of nature, which is intimately linked with his reading of evolutionary theory, leads to a moment of supreme sadness in the recognition of the expansive and mysterious time of nature and his own fleeting experience of the world. A passage added in 1908, not long before his death, and certainly at a time when he knew he was dying, confirms this reading. After a dream in which he travels to all of the places he has visited, tying together his life's work in Connemara, Kerry, and Wicklow, he wakes with a dry throat, 'thinking in what a little while I would be in my grave and the whole world lost to me' (*CW* II, 201). The moment of imaginative freedom is cut short by a recognition of the human body. For Synge, the 'near feeling' (*CW* II, 201) to nature is the single most important experience: the sublime is not an experience outside nature but an experience of nature itself.

Synge's sublime is not 'involuntary secular' (in the sense that Thomas Weiskel describes in *The Romantic Sublime*) because its secularity is acknowledged as the very thing that allows it to accomplish the most complete re-enchantment of the natural world.[51] In the Wicklow essays,

---

[51] Thomas Weiskel, *The Romantic Sublime: Studies in the Structure and Psychology of Transcendence* (Baltimore and London: The John Hopkins University Press, 1976), p. 4.

the idea of what Yeats would call the 'great memory' of nature is felt through a close harmony with the 'divine unconsciousness' (*CW* II, 35), which is gained most fully through a varied and contingent relationship to the physical phenomena of the natural world.[52] The figure of the vagrant, in particular, is presented by Synge as having privileged access to an understanding of physical nature because of his proximity to it. The very act of motion, 'with its whole sensation of strange colours and of strange passages with voices that whisper in the dark' (*CW* II, 196), creates a sense of profound interconnectedness. The 'affections' of the vagrant, which build through continual movement, 'rest for a whole life time with the perfume of spring evenings or the first autumnal smoulder of leaves' (*CW* II, 196). As Alan Price has noted,

> In the Wicklow essays the tension between dream and actuality is mingled with the contrast between two ways of life; between the desolation of the people of the glens and the vigorous enterprise of the roaming tramps and tinkers. The people of the glens are oppressed by their surroundings, and find existence more of a nightmare than a dream.[53]

Though the dynamic between the people of the glens and their surroundings is much more subtle than Price suggests, making use of evolutionary theory and a mesh of sociopolitical issues, the binary holds. The vagrant, through an experience of nature in various states and places, is able to see the world as a repository not just of his own memory but of a more universal interrelatedness. Hearing the noises of the glen, he connects them to 'the chant of singers in dark chambers of Japan', to dancers in Algeria, and in the sound of trout in the river at his feet he 'forgets the purple moorland that is round him and hears waves that lap round a boat in some southern sea' (*CW* II, 196).[54] His access to the 'great memory' allows him to gain a transcendent understanding which moves beyond the local to encompass the global. He retains the very qualities that Synge assigns to his own experience of naturalist observation, recognizing the 'profound mysteries' of nature through a close observation that is as transportive as any occult practice.

---

[52] W. B. Yeats, 'Magic' (1901), in *Essays and Introductions*, 28–53, p. 28.

[53] Alan Price, *Synge and Anglo-Irish Drama* (London: Methuen, 1961), p. 92.

[54] This is a relatively early passage, found in TCD MS 4335, f. 4. E. M. Stephens has dated this version to 1898.

The transnational appeal of occultism is replicated for Synge in the vagrant's access to a universal consciousness, which stresses the potential of the 'primitive' to link psychically across temporal and geographical boundaries. Not only is 'the tinker constituted as an exemplary domestic exotic' in this text, but he is also linked with a pre-civilized temporal realm.[55] Synge's article 'The Last Fortress of the Celt', composed from various sections of *The Aran Islands* and published in the American magazine *The Gael*, was illustrated with a naked woman on a desert island. This simple drawing depicts a sandy island scene, with distant trees and a calm sea. In the foreground, the naked woman sits peaceably amongst some foliage, reclining her head against the border of the picture frame. This titular illustration brings a completely different set of aesthetic associations than Jack B. Yeats's later line drawings for *The Aran Islands*, and thus situates the 'primitive' in a global context, underlining Synge's primitivism as one which links the Irish peasantry to other international cultures being 'civilized' under imperialist expansion (see Figure 2.1, below).[56] It appears that Synge's is the only contribution to this issue of *The Gael* to carry an illustration like this: the style of the drawing does not match the house style, which opts for more heavily detailed and ornate illustration. The choice, therefore, is significant. The editor, and perhaps Synge himself (though there is no record of correspondence), have chosen here to suggest an idyll, an almost prelapsarian desert island which suggests timelessness and is so unlike the desolate 'mass of wet rock' described towards the end of 'The Last Fortress'. Thus, throughout Synge's articles, the primitive is codified as the occupier of a global space from which the 'civilized' observer is barred.[57] The Wicklow vagrant, through his constant travel, 'has preserved the inheritance of change and moves all his life among the fine pageants of the earth, growing familiar with what is most vital'.[58] Elsewhere, reflecting his privileging of harmony between mankind and the natural world, Synge

---

[55] Mary Burke, *'Tinkers': Synge and the Cultural History of the Irish Traveller* (Oxford: Oxford University Press 2009), p. 22.

[56] J. M. Synge, 'The Last Fortress of the Celt', *The Gael*, April 1901, 109–13. The illustration of the woman on the desert island sits above the title of the piece, and thus contextualizes the entire article in terms of the discourses of global primitivism. Although the illustrator is not credited in the pages of the magazine, the majority of the illustrations are done in a similar style, and so it is likely they were carried out by a house illustrator.

[57] For more on discourses of the global primitive in Revivalist culture, see Maria McGarrity and Claire A. Culleton, 'Introduction', in McGarrity and Culleton, eds., *Irish Modernism and the Global Primitive*, 1–16, and Joseph Lennon, 'Introduction', *Irish Orientalism: A Literary and Intellectual History* (New York: Syracuse University Press, 2004), xv–xxxi.

[58] TCD MS 4335, f. 1.

Figure 2.1 Illustration for J. M. Synge, 'The Last Fortress of the Celt', *The Gael* (April 1901), p. 109. Illustrator unknown. American Catholic Historical Society Collection. Digital Library, Villanova University.

writes that 'the tramp life [is] the only life that is really in unison with the country'.[59] The vagrant, through his travelling, escapes the involuting influence of any particular locality and is instead able to pass through an environment with a transcendent understanding of nature.

In the final essay of the Wicklow group, entitled 'Glencree', which was written in 1907 and first published in the fourth volume of the 1910 *Collected Works*, Synge completes his idealization of the vagrant figure in an image of holy union with nature. In this essay, Synge's blurring of the natural and supernatural is most intense. Mankind is largely absent from 'Glencree', and the psychic aspect of nature is given full prominence through extensive description in which the natural world is again transformed into something 'great and queer' (*CW* II, 235), taking on a striking sense of the uncanny. The description is moved into the present tense, increasing the effect of the disorientating images that move across the glen. Luminous clouds, which have always been a signal for Synge of the shift into an otherwise unseen world, move across the landscape and begin to distort his perspective.[60] The diffusion of light in the cloud, and the way in which shadows expand in size, is used to explore the difference between an 'actual' and unseen landscape:

> The little turfy ridges on each side of the road have the look of glens to me, and every block of stone has the size of a house. The cobwebs on the furze are like a silvery net, and the silence is so great and queer, even weasels run squealing past me.... Once in every minute I see the little mounds in their natural shapes that have been mountains for a week. I see wet cottages on the other side of the glen that I had forgotten. Then, as I walk on, I see out over a cloud to the tops of real mountains standing up into the sky.
>
> (*CW* II, 235)

The landscape becomes 'queer', a favourite word of Synge's. It is nonconforming and refuses to act according to the sensory logic of the observer. The cloud distorts shape, size, and any ability to distinguish between the 'real'

---

[59] TCD MS 4335, f. 8.

[60] In 'Under Ether', for example, 'clouds of luminous mist' swirl around the narrator as he passes into another world (*CW* II, 41), and the Aran Islands are approached through a 'dense shroud of mist' (*CW* II, 49), and are covered in 'grey luminous cloud' (II, 82). A similar trope occurs towards the end of Emily Lawless's *Grania* (1892), an early inspiration for Synge's *The Aran Islands*, in which a pervasive fog descends over the islands, so that 'reality and unreality had become one'. Lawless, *Grania*, p. 233.

and the unreal, between what is perceived and what exists physically. In a manuscript draft, a cloud above the lake is even more surreal: 'grey fingers are coming up and down, like a hand that is clasping and opening again.'[61] The natural and supernatural become blurred, and thus Wicklow becomes a place in which the writer can recover a form of primitive consciousness. Throughout the essay, this sensory distortion is tied back to the extreme psychic effects of the landscape: 'there is a strange depression in the cottage', an old woman is 'wandering in her mind', 'all one's senses are disturbed' (*CW* II, 235). There is a continual blurring of the line between physical nature and perceived nature in which the human is decentred and becomes lost in a natural world which works according to a 'queer' system. Nature's 'profound mystery' is reasserted, and the 'sense of enchantment' is given prominence. In fact, throughout the essay things appear to be passing in and out of nature, creating a radical realization of interconnectedness in which the animals and plants seem to translate a higher purpose. The way that the light acts on the bracken gives it 'a nearly painful green' (*CW* II, 235), and the 'enormous' figures of the sheep (which were made almost holy by the light in 'People and Places' (*CW* II, 195)) are 'passing in and out of the sky line' (*CW* II, 235). Likewise, standing at the cottage door, Synge notes that 'the little stream I do not see seems to roar out of the cloud' (*CW* II, 235). There is a constant passage in the natural world between a purely physical presence and something that appears to link the animals and features of the landscape with the sky, and with a mysterious, unseen dimension.

This descriptive style emphasizes Synge's reclamation of a primitive state as a writer. Edward Tylor, in his discussion of animism in *Primitive Culture* (1871), asserted that 'savage dream-theory', and the concept that the dream-self could act *in reality*, was symptomatic of a broader characteristic of 'primitive' humanity: 'Their imaginations become so lively that they can scarcely distinguish between their dreams and their waking thoughts, between the real and the ideal'.[62] Darwin, in *The Descent of Man*, refers to Tylor's remarks on dream theory before asserting that 'savages do not readily distinguish between subjective and objective impressions'.[63] Such assertions were commonplace in late Victorian anthropology. In fact, Synge himself closely paraphrases James Frazer's *The Golden Bough* (1890) in *The*

---

[61] TCD MS 4335, f. 96.

[62] Edward Tylor, *Primitive Culture: Researches in the Development of Mythology, Philosophy, Religion, Language, Art, and Custom*, Vol. I (London: John Murray, 1920), p. 445.

[63] Charles Darwin, *The Descent of Man, and Selection in Relation to Sex*, with an introduction by James Moore and Adrian Desmond (London: Penguin, 2004), p. 117.

Aran Islands when he notes that 'These people make no distinction between the natural and the supernatural' (*CW* II, 128).[64] This primitivist idea was particularly attractive to writers of the period and appears in the works of Hardy, Yeats, and others. The folklorist and anthropologist Edward Clodd observed to Hardy that 'your Dorset peasants represent the persistence of the same barbaric idea that confuses persons and things'. Hardy riposted that this 'confusion' is also 'common to the highest imaginative genius, that of the poet'.[65] Synge, if he had been asked, might have taken a similar tack.[66]

Physical nature, in 'Glencree' and throughout the Wicklow essays, is porous, and is a symbol of its own mystery. The 'queer' perspectives given throughout recognize both the ability of nature to transfigure itself, to act of its own accord, and to assert a powerful influence on both animal and human life. The natural world, through a process of involution, exerts itself through the physical landscape, and reveals in certain times and places how a close observation can lead to a fleeting experience of 'profound mystery'. In 'Glencree', Synge gives over the majority of the piece to a description of this psychic connection between seen and unseen nature; but the essay shifts in tone, tense, and focus in the final paragraphs, offering a juxtaposition in the figure of a wandering vagrant. On a much clearer Sunday in an autumnal Glencree, Synge is lying in the heather (a scene that recalls the 'Étude Morbide'—'Among heather I experience things that are divine' (*CW* II, 35)—and 'The Creed'—'The loneliness of heather breathes delight' (*CW* I, 6)), when he hears footsteps behind him. On this day the sky is 'covered with white radiant clouds', which break in places to reveal 'a blue sky of wonderful delicacy and clearness' (*CW* II, 235). Hearing a tramp approach a spring below him, Synge sees the man look round 'to see if anyone was watching him' (*CW* II, 236) before taking off his shirt and washing it in the pool. Synge is hidden among ferns, and so the tramp seems to act without self-consciousness. This scene of the tramp washing in a spring, overlooked by the hidden narrator, provides a clear image of intimacy and closeness to the natural world. It acts in a similar way to another famous scene of Synge-as-eavesdropper in his 'Preface' to

---

[64] 'A savage hardly conceives the distinction commonly drawn by more advanced peoples between the natural and the supernatural.' James Frazer, *The Golden Bough: A Study in Magic and Religion* (Hertfordshire: Wordsworth Editions, 1993), p. 10.

[65] Quoted in Gillian Beer, *Open Fields: Science in Cultural Encounter* (Oxford: Clarendon Press, 1996), pp. 42–3.

[66] Indeed, a little later, the idea that 'the faculty of discerning between the actual and imaginary is absent' in Irish-language literature was given as a defining characteristic. See Eleanor Hull, *The Poem-Book of the Gael* (London: Chatto & Windus, 1912), p. xxiv.

The Playboy of the Western World (*CW* IV, 53), though what the 'Preface' claims for authentic language, this scene in 'Glencree' claims for an intimate, healthy, and ultimately redemptive relationship to nature. This scene is the crux of Synge's theory of environment in the Wicklow essays in that it represents the observance of a pure relationship to the natural world, one which gives spiritual access to both physical and non-physical nature and which results in a serene, almost god-like, aura in the vagrant figure. The 'natural link', as in *The Aran Islands*, is conceived in terms of a porous world, a recognition of natural and supernatural wholeness, which allows the 'primitive' figure to connect transcendentally to the natural world.

This passage about the vagrant (as discussed above) is found under the title 'By the Waysides of Wicklow' in a manuscript dated to 1898 by E. M. Stephens, and the version of 'Glencree' published in the *Works* of 1910 ended here.[67] Alan Price, however, in his 1966 edition of Synge's prose, adds a final paragraph from another draft, which serves to comment on the significance of the scene described.[68] Here, Synge hears the first signs that the people are travelling back from Mass, and offers a comparison between the tramp and the cottage-dwellers of Wicklow:

> By his act of primitive cleanness this man seemed to have lifted himself also into the mood of the sky, and the indescribable half-plaintive atmosphere of the autumn Sundays of Wicklow. I could not pity him. The cottage men with their humour and simplicity and the grey farm-houses they live in have gained in a real sense—"Infinite riches in a little room", while the tramp has chosen a life of penury with a world for habitation.
>
> (*CW* II, 236)

Again, the vagrant's transnationalism is emphasized. Just as the stream and the sheep seem to pass in and out of the clouds in the first passage, so here the tramp, through this private and intimate act of communion with nature, 'seemed to have lifted himself... into the mood of the sky' and the atmosphere of Wicklow itself, expanding himself into a global rather than a local figure. Nomadic man, as Synge suggests throughout the Wicklow essays, does not suffer the psychic 'possession' of 'a locality' because his constant motion allows for a 'primitive' knowledge of the world. The cottage-dwellers,

---

[67] TCD MS 4335, ff. 12–13.

[68] This paragraph is found in TCD MS 4335, f. 22. This draft is marked 'to revise for the Manchester Guardian'; however, Synge never published the article here.

influenced by the landscape through their involution of it, are connected to their locality and are envied for this; however, the vagrant, who through his motion has bypassed the influence of any single place, has 'a world for habitation'. Not only this, but he becomes part of that world in a way unavailable to settled peoples. Synge's sense of ultimate literary value in the transnational, outlined in his critical works, finds a correlative in the global vision of the 'primitive'.[69]

It is not solely the vagrant's access to nature, however, that Synge venerates. Throughout his drafts, as in *The Aran Islands*, this access is linked to a form of labour which is pre-industrial. In an early version of this essay, Synge writes:

Vagrant tramps and beggars are still frequent ^common^ in every country where the labourer has ~~preserved~~ ^kept^ his vitality, and begets an occasional temperament of distinction.[70]

'Distinction', similarly to the 'individuality' and 'personal character' (*CW* II, 58–9) of the crafted tools discussed in *The Aran Islands*, is singled out, and is linked to a sort of 'vitality' which is displayed in the integrity of the vagrant life. The tramps have 'kept' (rather than 'preserved') this vitality, suggesting a sort of power retained in the face of change. For Synge, 'man is naturally a nomad', and 'all wanderers have finer intellectual and physical perceptions than men who are condemned to local habitations' (*CW* II, 195). Across these essays, Synge is formulating the theories of cultural and physical regeneration through connection to nature that he will elaborate on more fully in his articles 'From the Congested Districts' and *The Playboy of the Western World*. Elsewhere in the Wicklow essays, Synge pushes this idea further, suggesting that the life of the labourer, or anyone 'who works for recompense', is itself also inferior to that of the vagrant: 'for all our moments are divine and above all price though their sacrifice is paid with a measure of gold. Every industrious worker has sold his birthright for a mess of pottage, perhaps served him in chalices of gold' (*CW* II, 196). Synge praises the

---

[69] See, for example, Synge's review of the Irish Text Society's first volume of Geoffrey Keating's *Foras Feasa ar Éirinn* [*The History of Ireland*], edited by David Comyn and translated by Patrick Dinneen, in which Synge emphasizes his sense of the importance of international exchange in the Irish tradition, and clearly values in Keating what he sees as his own distinguishing qualities. Keating's 'foreign studies', and his time abroad, Synge writes, were 'of great use in correcting the narrowing influence of a simply Irish tradition' (*CW* II, 361).

[70] TCD MS 4335, f. 1.

vagrant for his insistence on living outside a system of paid labour, for his rejection of the unequal exchange of time and capital. In situating the vagrant outside this system, Synge suggests that this lifestyle allows one to escape the negative effects of modern social and economic forces. In 'The Vagrants of Wicklow', written in 1901–2, Synge observes:

> In the middle classes the gifted son of a family is always the poorest— usually a writer or artist with no sense for speculation—and in a family of peasants, where the average comfort is just over penury, the gifted son sinks also, and is soon a tramp on the roadside.   (*CW* II, 202)

Clearly identifying himself, as the poorest and most artistically gifted of his siblings, with the vagrant figure, Synge extends his vision of the ideal artist from one who is primitive and receptive to nature to one who is also transnational, who is able to retain a connectedness both to the local and to the global. He also, however, identifies himself with a certain contrariness towards the strictures of paid work, seeing creativity and connectedness to nature as forcing one outside of established society.

As ever, Synge's idealization of the vagrant is both political and artistic, as he makes clear at the end of 'The Vagrants of Wicklow'. There is 'a peculiar value', he suggests, in the life of the vagrant 'for those who look at life in Ireland with an eye that is aware of the arts also' (*CW* II, 208), and he expands the figure of the tramp into his vision of the ideal artist (associated implicitly with himself):

> In all the healthy movements of art, variations from the ordinary types of manhood are made interesting for the ordinary man, and in this way only the higher arts are universal. Besides this art, however, founded on the variations which are a condition and effect of all vigorous life, there is another art—sometimes confounded with it—founded on the freak of nature, in itself a mere sign of atavism or disease. This latter art, which is occupied with the antics of the freak, is of interest only to the variation from ordinary minds, and for this reason is never universal. To be quite plain, the tramp in real life, Hamlet and Faust in the arts, are variations; but the maniac in real life, and Des Esseintes and all his ugly crew in the arts, are freaks only.   (*CW* II, 208)

Synge's idealization of the vagrant is framed as the foundation of a 'healthy' art, posited in opposition to Decadence, and Huysmans's Jean Des Esseintes in particular. The protagonist of À Rebours (1884), an embodiment of ancestral degeneration combined with effete and often depraved tastes, is 'a mere sign of atavism and disease'.[71] Again, encoded here is the idea that progress is healthy, with 'atavism' as its opposite. Throughout his career, as Chapters 4 and 6 of this book demonstrate, Synge pitted his writing against the Decadent movement, invoking the evolutionary principle and seeing his work as combatting both literary and social degeneration. In establishing the vagrant figure, with his transcendent relationship to nature and the universal, as an artistic and social ideal, therefore, Synge lays the groundwork for future, more vigorous protestations against 'unhealthy' art.

Thus Synge first establishes an ideal relationship to nature, combining natural science and mystical experience, and then extends this to a more wide-ranging theory of life and art. In the final image of the tramp in 'Glencree', which concludes the Wicklow essays, Synge brings us full circle, using the same language and ideas that he first established in his 'Autobiography'; however, he expands the significance of his vision of harmony with nature, which comes to encompass certain relationships to capitalism, modernity, and social and political pressures. If, for the young Synge, his practising of natural science gave him 'a passionate and receptive mood like that of early [man]' (CW II, 10), the older writer works to recover that primitive, spiritual bond with nature through a literary re-enchantment of the natural world. In an early notebook, used between 1896 and 1898, Synge's thought is redolent with the theosophical teaching of correspondences: 'A human being finds a resting place only where he is in harmony with his surroundings, and is reminded that his soul and the soul of nature are of the same organisation.'[72] Elsewhere, this is extended to a view of artistic composition, with Synge arguing that 'All art that is not conceived by a soul in harmony with some mood of the earth is without value' (CW II, 35). In many ways, the 'Glencree' vagrant—freed from the effects of capitalism, depopulation, and land issues by his nomadism—is the apotheosis of this theory and thus represents the ideal connection to nature. In fact, the same language of connecting to 'some mood of the earth' is repeated in Synge's description of the vagrant washing: 'this man seemed to have lifted himself also into the mood of the sky' (CW II, 208).

---

[71] For more on Des Esseintes as a symbol of degeneration, see Daniel Pick, Faces of Degeneration: A European Disorder, c. 1848–c.1918 (Cambridge: Cambridge University Press, 1989), p. 74.

[72] Quoted in Skelton, Celtic Contraries, p. 37.

By connecting this human relationship to nature with an ideal of an art that is 'in harmony' with the earth, Synge bases his literary value system in a reclamation of this state. Natural history, we recall, and his moth-collecting, encouraged in Synge a sensitivity to nature which 'gives one a singular acquaintance with the essences of the world' (*CW* II, 9), and thus his practice is linked with the primitive, and his writing becomes a way of recovering a link to the natural world which forms the basis of all 'healthy' art. Rather than the experience of 'early man' remaining unattainable, Synge reconciles his modern scientific knowledge with his aim to reclaim a lost harmonious relationship to nature. His resacralization of the natural world in the face of personal crisis was not a process conceived contra science but was instead seen as coterminous with the scientific project; positivism, natural history, and evolutionary theories were harnessed as a way of recalibrating the relationship to the natural world and the position of the human observer within it. Hence, it is a specifically modern form of enchantment that seeks to expand the potential of the Romantic project by applying the principles of positivist science. In many ways, Synge's vision of the mystery of nature, and of the potential of returning to a pre-modern unity with the natural world, is akin to that of fin de siècle occultism, though for him it is openly consonant with, rather than a reaction against, the new world view ushered in by the proponents of natural history. Through science, and through a re-enchanted world view, Synge is able to attain, if only momentarily, the ideal spiritual relationship to nature enjoyed by 'early man', and represented most fully in the wandering figure of the vagrant.

3

'A Black Knot'

Temporalities in the One-act Plays

Making notes on the *First Principles* (1862) of the English polymath Herbert
Spencer, whose work encompassed sociology, political theory, anthropology,
and biology, Synge paid close attention to observations made on the relationship between space, time, and matter. Shortly after documenting
William Morris's theory on the structure of societies, the city, and the
evolution of the market, and Marx's work on communes and the division
of labour, Synge's notes on Spencer display a persistent interest in travel,
motion, and new conceptions of how space is perceived in relation to
temporality in a modernizing world. He summarized part of Spencer's thesis
as follows:

> We think in relations. Relations are of two orders, – of sequence and of co-
> existence; the one is original the other derivative. The abstract of all
> sequences is Time. The abstract of all co-existences is Space. Our con-
> sciousness of space is a consciousness of co-existent positions.[1]

The relationships between time and space, and the coexistences of time and
space in an unevenly developing country, are fundamental to Synge's literary
experiments, and are explored here just pages after noting the rapidity of
development in societal structures and economics.[2] Spatialized time, and the

---

[1] TCD MS 4379, ff. 93r. This notebook passage has been mistranscribed by Christopher
Collins to suggest that Synge was aware of a concept of 'space time': however, not only is such an
idea misleading with regards to Spencer's theories as put forward in *First Principles*, but it is also
anachronistic. Collins mistranscribes the passage by suggesting, through ellipsis, that two non-
consecutive clauses run on from each other, and by cutting the final part from the phrase
'conception of space time and matter' so that it appears 'conception of space time'. Christopher
Collins, '"The Cries of Pagan Desperation": Synge, Riders to the Sea and the Discontents of
Historical Time', *Irish Theatre International*, Vol. 3, No. 1 (2014), pp. 7–24, p. 8.

[2] For more on the importance of time/space in modernism, see Nicholas Daly, *Literature,
Technology, and Modernity, 1860–2000* (Cambridge: Cambridge University Press, 2004); Lloyd,
Irish Times; Chris Morash and Shaun Richards, *Mapping Irish Theatre: Theories of Space and
Place* (Cambridge: Cambridge University Press, 2013); Gerry Smyth, *Space and the Irish*

J. M. Synge: Nature, Politics, Modernism. Seán Hewitt, Oxford University Press (2021). © Seán Hewitt.
DOI: 10.1093/oso/9780198862093.003.0004

fluctuating and often tense relationship between different time-spaces and temporalities, underpin his move from prose into drama. The theatre, as a site where motion is staged and represented, becomes in the case of Synge's staged one-act plays a vehicle for exploring the changes in temporal and spatial relationships as a result of modernization. Synge quotes directly from Spencer in his notebook: 'The conception of motion as presented or represented in the developed consciousness involves the conception of space, of time, and of matter.'[3] For Synge, this observation, and a heightened awareness of temporal and spatial modernity, led to a formal crisis, or 'formal desperation', whereby the spatialization of time, and its apparent ability to run at different speeds, both structure and threaten to destabilize the prominent one-act form of the Irish Dramatic Revival.[4] His development of a hierarchy of spiritual and temporal experience in *The Aran Islands* and the Wicklow essays thus informs the structures and movements of his first staged plays, *Riders to the Sea* (1904) and *The Shadow of the Glen* (1903), set on Inishmaan and in Wicklow, respectively.

In a notebook used between 1900 and 1904, the period during which he wrote these two plays, Synge was intent on expressing his sense of modernity in literature, and this is linked explicitly to historical and sociological factors observed both in writing and through travel and social observation. Drafting his article on 'The Old and New in Ireland', he focused on the necessity of literature's adaptation to its environment, on its responsibility to remain responsive to shifts in language, custom, and science.[5] In a variety of ways, his reading in evolutionary theory informs his understanding of literary tradition: to 'survive', he suggests, a literature must evolve according to the shifting pressures of its environment. Looking back over nineteenth-century Irish literature, he identifies a series of semi-conscious changes in both writers and readers, focusing notably on the Famine years as a period of social upheaval:

Cultural Imagination (Basingstoke: Palgrave Macmillan, 2001); Andrew Thacker, *Moving Through Modernity: Space and Geography in Modernism* (Manchester and New York: Manchester University Press, 2003).

[3] Herbert Spencer, *First Principles*, 6th edn. (London: Watts & Co., 1937), p. 154. Quoted by Synge in TCD MS 4379, f. 92v.

[4] The idea of 'formal desperation' is key to Frank Kermode's understanding of modernism's proximity to chaos. Quoted in Malcolm Bradbury and James MacFarlane, eds., *Modernism: A Guide to European Literature, 1890–1930* (London: Penguin, 1976), p. 26. See 'The Modern', in Frank Kermode, *Modern Essays* (London: Fontana, 1971), 39–70, p. 48.

[5] This article was published, without the draft sections quoted below, in *The Academy and Literature*, 6 September 1902.

... life was changing and had almost changed but the newer conditions had not begun to have an effect that was plain to everybody. The school of 48 and the writers like Lever and Lever [*recte* 'Lover'] were more beginning [*sic*] to lose hold on readers but very few knew why they had wearied of them.[6]

A consciousness of different coexistent temporalities is mapped by Synge onto literary history. Literature, he suggests, loses its currency when it loses touch with changing social conditions. He also applied this theory to language itself, arguing for a 'cycle of life' for words and the idea that words might lose currency and then be repurposed or re-energized.[7] This stance directly advocates literature as responsive to cultural changes, as an art that must adapt in form and content to 'newer conditions'.

Synge, who was still engaging with processes of modernization on the Aran Islands, also made notes on how distinct forms of modernity were encroaching on the communities of his native Wicklow, drafting an unpublished article on social and cultural change amongst the rural inhabitants of the county. Unlike in his Wicklow essays, which focus on poor economic and social conditions in relation to a connection with nature, this essay discusses forms of cultural change in fashion and aesthetics. Proximity to the urban areas of Dublin was resulting, he suggests, in a 'revolution in dress and architecture' in the rural areas of Co. Wicklow. Here, the tone is one of nostalgia for a disappearing set of customs, with outward appearances signalling a more pervasive interior modernization of consciousness:

> In a few years, in fifteen or twenty at the most, the generation of old women who still look out in admirably picturesque clothes from the doors of many cottages will have passed away. The round bonnet with white frills that frame the face, with frilled-in-shawls, the old world....[8]

---

[6] TCD MS 4393, f. 3r. Another draft of this article is found in TCD MS 4356.

[7] See Padraic Colum, 'My Memories of John Synge', in Mikhail, ed., *J. M. Synge: Interviews and Recollections*, 62–9, p. 66. Edward Stephens suggests that such an idea may have come from Synge's reading of Archbishop Trench's lectures, *English Past and Present*, in which Trench argues that words 'wear out, become unserviceable', until 'A time arrives for a language when... its own local and provincial dialects are almost the only sources from which it can obtain acquisitions such as shall readily constitute an increase in wealth.' See Stephens, *My Uncle John*, p. 46, and Richard Chenevix Trench, *English Past and Present* (New York: Redfield, 1855), Lecture II, pp. 40–84.

[8] TCD MS 4393, f. 11v.

This lamentation of the casualties of 'progress' is seen through the visible signs of costume and architecture, and the gradual replacement of apparently authentic clothing with what Synge later calls 'cheap and ill-fitting dress' is representative of the deeper cultural effects of mass production. As in the incident in *The Aran Islands*, where Synge asks to photograph the young man in his 'native home-spuns' but is rebuked, changing fashions are here seen as correlating to changes in consciousness.[9] However, Synge also suggests that contemporary discussions of the possibility of reintroducing 'Irish dress' were 'rather fanciful'.[10] His view of modernization always accommodates a firm understanding and belief in evolutionary theory: going backwards is not an option, and progress is inevitable.

This is in tune with another article in the same notebook, a draft review of Anatole France's *Histoire Comique* (1903) that was never published. Here, Synge further embellishes his theory of literature's duty to respond to, and evolve with, changing social conditions. Near the beginning of this draft, Synge leaves a note for himself to consider: 'Rate at which scientific theories are absorbed into literature.' Later he elaborates, suggesting that 'A not uninteresting study might be made to show how long an idea takes, in the average . . . from its . . . first limited scene of life on to the harder plain where it is used by writers who seek art rather than reason.' It would appear that this is understood by Synge largely as a structural, formal, and aesthetic change caused by changing world views within both artist and audience. He argues that, 'In the work of Anatole France, it would not be easy to find a passage that is out of harmony [with the] rigorous science of . . . Huxley,' suggesting that the fundamental changes in reason and world view caused by evolutionary theory and other developments had inevitably resulted in, and required, a new literature:

> Can it be doubted that a view of life such as is seen in Huxley's 'place of Man in Nature' will tend to change the root notes [?] of literature nearly as thoroughly as ~~Christianity changed~~ ecclesiastical ideas changed pagan ideas of antiquity . . . .[11]

---

[9] This is an observation not uncommon in sociological theories of modernization, in which the modernization of dress and accessories are seen as signifiers for the modernization of the wearer: 'They are the outward, visible signs of an inward transformation of consciousness. They express the collisions, the conflicts and even the rituals brought about by the intrusions of modernity into traditional social life.' Peter L. Berger, Brigitte Berger, and Hansfried Kellner, *The Homeless Mind: Modernization and Consciousness* (Harmondsworth: Penguin, 1973), p. 130.

[10] TCD MS 4393, f. 14v.   [11] TCD MS 4393, ff. 24v–26v.

The deletion of 'Christianity' in favour of 'ecclesiastical ideas' underlines Synge's rebellion as pitting itself against doctrinal or 'theological' strictures rather than against Christianity or spirituality in general. 'Christianity', not specified as 'ecclesiastical', might be seen to continue many 'pagan ideas'; doctrinal, organized religion, on the other hand, is posited as a more definite break from the past. The phrase 'root notes' echoes another used in his notebooks, where Synge connected his sense of modernity in literature to a 'chaos of root ideas', a common feature of early modernism.[12] In this draft article, he returns to this phrase ('the root notes') to map the foundation of literature amongst changing social, cultural, and religious conditions, thereby tethering it, however uncertainly, to the experience of modernity. In a later (also unpublished) article on France's work, Synge notes the attention to 'the theory of cellular life' and the evolution of ideas, observing that 'these opinions are not, of course, dogmatically stated, but are interwoven gradually through the texture of the story'.[13] Eventually, he learnt the lesson of his earlier 'Étude Morbide' (1899) and *When the Moon Has Set* (1900–3), which were certainly dogmatic, and recognized the importance of attending to modernity in 'texture' rather than overt statement, of drama as a complex praxis rather than the staging of a binary argument.

Synge's notions of literature as a responsive art form reveal a deeply held commitment to the responsibility of the writer to adapt and react to social changes, taking from extensive reading in evolutionary theory and anthropology the core idea that without progress, and without degrees of modernization, literature would inevitably lose touch with its audience. The responsiveness of his work was a consciously held value. It would be wrong to assert, therefore, that a play like *Riders to the Sea*, as 'a drama of a house divided against itself by the pressures of history and time', is inflected by an understanding of the conflicts of modernization that Synge 'consciously denied'.[14] The sea change that Synge divines in modern literature penetrates right down to the 'root' of artistic production, and so must be conceived of as a total change encompassing not simply variations on

---

[12] 'How does modern literature exist in the chaos of root ideas?' TCD MS 4392, f. 2r. For explorations of chaos in modernist writings, see Pericles Lewis, *The Cambridge Introduction to Modernism* (Cambridge: Cambridge University Press, 2007), p. 7, and Malcolm Bradbury and James MacFarlane, 'The Name and Nature of Modernism', in Malcolm Bradbury and James MacFarlane, eds., *Modernism*, 19–56, pp. 26–7.

[13] TCD MS 4346, 'A Tale of Comedians', ff. 2–3.

[14] King, *The Drama of J. M. Synge*, p. 49; Judith Remy Leder, 'Synge's *Riders to the Sea*: Island as Cultural Battleground', *Twentieth-Century Literature*, Vol. 36, No. 2 (Summer 1990), 207–24, p. 222.

traditional plot and character but also on structure, form, and aesthetics. It therefore becomes essential to our reading of Synge's one-act plays to ask if, and how, his drama reacts to changing social conditions. If it is not an unconscious reaction, then how does Synge rework traditional or established dramatic forms and tropes (even in the limited context of the early Irish Literary Theatre) to create a drama that is, by his definition, responsive and 'modern'?

In recent years, interest in the temporalities of modernism has been complemented by increased study of the uses of space in modernist writings.[15] In Irish studies, Christopher Morash's work on 'mapping' the Irish theatre has shown how the staging of various domestic peasant dramas at the Abbey and other venues during the Revival era set the tone for the development of the theatre movement over the course of the century, working to embed a tradition of reworked plots and reused scenery. Beginning with Hyde's *Casadh an tSúgáin* (1901), Morash notes that, although the peasant cottage had been frequently staged in the Irish theatre, the writers and directors of the Revival movement were the first to confine drama (in many instances) to the cottage interior. By 1911, the Abbey company had reused more or less the same set sixteen times, and the trope of the 'stranger in the house' had become attached to the spatial restrictions of the stage.[16] Critics of Synge's one-act plays have demonstrated the importance of the cottage interior to his first staged works, and have explored the confluence of the financial and spatial limitations of the stage and Synge's own artistic purposes. A recurring issue in criticism has been that of the cottage door: the threshold between two worlds, between what is restrictively interior and what is frighteningly exterior, a key dramatic device in Symbolist theatre which was maintained in the Maeterlinckian theatre of Synge and Yeats.[17] In fact, this onstage reminder of the spatial limitations of the physical stage has been seen as pivotal to the 'major structural antithesis' of Synge's plays, the antithetic tension 'between the mimetic space (that which is made visible and represented on the stage) and the diegetic space (that which is referred to by the characters).'[18] This structural antithesis has

---

[15] Thacker, *Moving Through Modernity*, pp. 2–7.

[16] Christopher Morash, *A History of the Irish Theatre, 1601–2000* (Cambridge: Cambridge University Press, 2002), p. 121; see also Morash and Richards, *Mapping Irish Theatre*, pp. 36–8.

[17] Worth, *The Irish Drama of Europe*, p. 73. See especially W. B. Yeats's *The King's Threshold* (1905), Yeats and Gregory's *Cathleen Ni Houlihan* (1902). See also Aspasia Velissariou, 'The Dialectics of Space in Synge's *The Shadow of the Glen*', *Modern Drama*, Vol. 36, No. 3 (Fall 1993), 409–19.

[18] Velissariou, 'The Dialectics of Space in Synge's *The Shadow of the Glen*', p. 409.

been seen to reflect the tendencies of character and plot within Synge's drama. However, staging a cottage interior in the one-act form adds the pressure of time to the pressure of space, and Synge utilized this pressure to give a strained and ironic awareness to his use of the form that is missing from other one-act plays of the period. It is at the point that this structural antithesis leads to formal crisis, or to a significant complication of plot, that Synge departs from the established one-act play model of the early Revival, and it is at these points that he exhibits a potent concern with the effects of modernization on conceptions of time and space in both the communities in which he travelled and in the theatre itself.

In many ways, a study of character and plot cannot express the more radical dramatic differences between Synge's use of the one-act form and that of his contemporaries in the Revival movement. Judith Remy Leder, in her study of *Riders* as representative of a culture in a transitional stage of modernization, takes as given a common critical misconception of Synge already dealt with here in Chapter 1: that his Aran Islanders are presented as 'naive and charming primitives whose lives, while not Edenic, were largely and happily unspoiled by contact with the modern world'.[19] Despite the fact that this book has already unsettled the critical commonplace that Synge 'consciously denied' modernization, Leder's argument that Synge subconsciously developed 'modernizing' or 'transitional' characters cannot hold because it is based on the assumption that Synge's drama works contrary to his own aesthetic, political, and social concerns. Rather, Synge made explicit his concern with the processes of social modernization and its impact on the forms, structures, and subjects of modern literature.

Francis Mulhern, in *The Present Lasts a Long Time*, has shown how an increasing awareness of change has a temporalizing effect, defining modernity as 'a form of "temporalization"', an invariant production of present, past and future that "valorizes the new" and, by that very act, "produces the old"'.[20] In Ireland, as elsewhere, there was a sense in which time became spatialized, and became intimately linked with geography. For Revivalists, the places in which the Irish language was still used as a daily vernacular were figured as 'old', and journeys to the west in Revivalist literature generally have a sense of time travel. Whereas railways and telegrams had

---

[19] Leder, 'Synge's *Riders to the Sea*: Island as Cultural Battleground', p. 207.
[20] Francis Mulhern, *The Present Lasts a Long Time: Essays in Cultural Politics* (Cork: Cork University Press, 1998), p. 20. Mulhern's critique, in this passage, draws on Peter Osborne's *The Politics of Time: Modernity and the Avant-Garde* (London: Verso, 1995).

the effect of 'collapsing' time and distance in industrialized areas and areas connected by modern modes of transport and communication, temporalization in Ireland produced a spatialized time in which the west became associated with the 'old' (or, in some cases, the atemporal) and the east and north-east (generally) with the 'new'. The International Meridian Conference in 1884 led to the introduction of global standardized time zones, and 'railway time' was effected across Britain. Time, in this sense, became 'exploitable, suffused with the values of capital', and was technologized and transmitted from urban areas.[21] In his Wicklow essays and *The Aran Islands*, Synge was persistently concerned with two opposing temporalities, the one circular, repetitive, 'natural' (and so verging on the spiritual), and the other linear, regulated, and thus subject to, and reflective of, modernizing forces. In his staged one-act plays, the points at which modernity collides with the 'natural' community or its representatives become key to both plot and structure. Rather than being presented through a narrator figure who gains sporadic access to a transcendent world, these plays depict the introduction of the modern into the cottage interior as a method of dramatizing the collision of temporalities. In this way, Synge's early drama implicitly critiques and complicates the conception of a rural and western population that was 'not only geographically distinct [but] historically precedent to the rest of the country'.[22] Community traditions, ways of knowing, and connections to the natural world are disrupted by emblems of modernity that represent new forms of production, capital, and relationships to the locality.

This is not necessarily the case in *The Tinker's Wedding*, though the basic dynamic between two traditions is still present. *The Tinker's Wedding* is the least successful of Synge's 'peasant plays', and he had much difficulty in settling on a form for it. Originally written as a one-act play, it was developed into a two-act version over the course of numerous drafts between 1902 and 1907; however, even at the galley stage Synge was uncertain about how to describe its formal aspects, considering labelling it as a one-act comedy in two scenes (*CW* IV, 5). Whereas Synge's other one-act plays, *Riders to the Sea* and *The Shadow of the Glen*, are condensed into a single act and scene, *The Tinker's Wedding*, whether we consider it as a one-act, two-scene play or a two-act play, works under different temporal restrictions and allows for different narrative effects.

---

[21] Armstrong, *Modernism*, p. 7.   [22] Deane, *Strange Country*, pp. 52–3.

The key frustration in the one-act version of the play is the priest's reluctance to marry Michael and Sarah. There is no attempt to deceive the priest (as in the first two-act version), not to mention an attempt by Mary to deceive Sarah by replacing her tin can with some empty bottles (which is only added later in the drafting process). In fact, when the curtain falls on the one-act *Tinker's Wedding*, all that has really happened is that the priest has refused to marry the couple. The plot is very simple and has the effect of a light comedy, though it gestures towards the questions of assimilation, non-conformity, and Romantic individualism which are more thoroughly worked up in the published 1907 version. As Christopher Collins has shown, Synge's drafts foreground residual pre-Christian culture in the characters of the tinkers, and the priest (and the institution of Christian marriage) is clearly an emblem of a counternatural impulse in modernity.[23] As Mary Byrne says in draft B, when she hears that the priest has warned the tinkers to keep 'safe' from God,

Youl'd never see the Almighty doing a thing to the larks or to the swallows or to the swift birds do be crying out when the sun is set,... and what way would he be following us in the dark nights, when it's quiet and easy we are, and we never asking him a thing at all? (*CW* IV, 279)

This is a play in which the orthodox and unorthodox are in contest, and Sarah Casey acts as the dramatic contention, posing the question of conformity and its limits. In fact, it is only in the two-act (or two-scene) form that Synge is able to sufficiently complicate the play beyond a simple exposition. Formally, the play is a hybrid for Synge. It perhaps has more in common with *The Well of the Saints* than with Synge's one-act plays and with *Playboy*, which gain their spark from the entrance of a 'stranger' (or a strange package), though the violent outburst of its conclusion (in which the tinkers tie the priest up in a sack) certainly prefigures the shebeeners' attack on Christy Mahon, and its vision of the moralizing priest links both with the Saint of *The Well* and the priest of *Riders to the Sea*.

In Synge's drama, the 'stranger in the house' (a figure frequently used by Yeats, Gregory, and other Revivalist playwrights) disrupts the spatial and temporal arrangement of the setting as it exists before the play begins. This

[23] Christopher Collins, *Theatre and Residual Culture: J. M. Synge and Pre-Christian Ireland* (London: Palgrave Macmillan, 2016), p. 65.

common trope, in which a 'stranger' from the outside world enters and disrupts the life inside the onstage cottage, developed during the Revival as a confluence of the circumstances of a modest stage, an amateur company, and limited finances, all of which suited the simple dramaturgy of this onstage dynamic. As Nicholas Grene has noted, 'the dramatic motif of the stranger in the house brings into play axes of inner versus outer, the material against the spiritual, familial, domestic life opposed to a life of individually chosen destiny.'[24] For a burgeoning dramatic movement, especially one focused on defining a new national literature, the tension between worlds, and between different ways of life, is particularly resonant: whether allegorical or representative, the strangers' encroachment on the interior world of the onstage cottage, and their attempts to lure the characters offstage into another, more uncertain, world, were inevitably read in terms of nation-building. Broadly speaking, the 'strangers' of the early Irish Literary Theatre were female and came from worlds opposite in many ways to the domestic interior. Often, they came from the Otherworld, or were members of the traveller community. Most famous is the Cathleen Ni Houlihan figure of Yeats and Gregory, but the trope was pervasive, from Yeats's earlier *The Land of Heart's Desire* (1894) to Edward Martyn's *Maeve* (1900), P. T. McGinley's one-act drama *Eilís agus an Bhean Deirce* (1901), and many of Douglas Hyde's plays, such as *Casadh an tSúgáin* (1901) and *Pleugsadh na Bulgóide* (1903). This ubiquitous trope, as Grene suggests, lends itself to an exploration of binary oppositions that are often figured in terms of competing temporalities.

Synge's staged one-act plays complicate this common binary approach through an increased sensitivity to localized and personalized temporal crises. They are characterized by a multiplicity of immiscible temporalities that neither plot nor structure is able to resolve. As *The Aran Islands* attests, the effects of modernization were keenly felt on a local and individual level, meaning that communities which might previously have been more cohesive were now experiencing a stratification of their members along a spectrum of 'old' and 'new', whereby the more 'modernized' members (such as the boy Synge wishes to photograph in his 'native home-spuns') were becoming separated from relatives and community members still associated with more traditional ways of life. Sociological theories of modernization suggest that this is a common factor in modernizing communities, and that

---

[24] Nicholas Grene, *The Politics of Irish Drama: Plays in Context from Boucicault to Friel* (Cambridge: Cambridge University Press, 1999), p. 53.

whereas unmodernized societies evince a high degree of integration, modern communities tend towards a 'pluralization of social life-worlds' and a high degree of segmentation, so that the more 'modern' members of a modernizing community, who have internalized new social structures, feel a sense of 'homelessness'.[25] In postcolonial theory, too, a sense of 'unhomeliness' is seen to characterize the colonized experience, meaning that such an estrangement is doubly compounded in the Irish context.[26] The 'natural link' becomes more tenuous, even broken. The regularization of time, the association of time with production and capital, 'spiritual' time versus 'material' time, circular time versus linear time: all are given focused attention by Synge, and his one-act plays display a high degree of pluralization. Morash has suggested that Synge's use of a camera on the Aran Islands, as a new technology of perception, made it possible for him to 'experience events in time in ways that were entirely new'.[27] The temporalizing effects of modernity are felt on both a local and a national level: time becomes spatialized, communities move towards segmentation, and there is, within the community and within the nation, 'layerings of different times, the coevality of different relations to time normatively distributed on the axis of tradition and modernity'.[28] In *Shadow* and *Riders*, a conception of plural lifeworlds and spatialized temporalities begins to strain against both form and plot, creating a sense of crisis that functions not only through an 'old/new' binary, or a 'past/present/future' relationship, but between multiple personal and communal temporalities which disrupt the potential of formal completion. In Synge's reaction to what Cóilín Parsons has termed the 'overlapping and discrepant scales and times' of modernizing Ireland, these one-act plays mark a definite trajectory into modernism and place Synge as a Revivalist modernist, a writer who took the plots, settings, and structures of the one-act plays already typical in the Revival movement and began to subject them to the formal and structural correlatives of social modernization.[29]

---

[25] Berger et al., *The Homeless Mind*, pp. 62–3, 113.

[26] See, for example, Homi K. Bhabha, *The Location of Culture* (New York: Routledge, 1994), p. 13; Leela Gandhi, *Postcolonial Theory: A Critical Introduction* (New York: Columbia University Press, 1998), p. 132.

[27] Chris Morash, 'Synge's Typewriter', in Cliff and Grene, eds., *Synge and Edwardian Ireland*, 21–33, p. 29. Morash draws on the exploration of these new technologies (camera, cinema, etc.) in Mary Ann Doane's *The Emergence of Cinematic Time: Modernity, Contingency, the Archive* (Cambridge, MA: Harvard University Press, 2002).

[28] Lloyd, *Irish Times*, p. 6.

[29] Parsons, *The Ordnance Survey and Modern Irish Literature*, p. 39.

To best illustrate Synge's modifications of the typical one-act 'stranger in the house' play of his contemporaries, we should first examine the way time and space function in plays that utilize the trope. The temporalities of Yeats's early one-act plays, including *The Land of Heart's Desire* (1894), and his collaborations with Lady Gregory, *Cathleen Ni Houlihan* (1902) and *The Pot of Broth* (1904), are illustrative of common codings of the interior and exterior worlds in the cottage plays of the Revival movement. The eponymous world of *The Land of Heart's Desire* is figured in direct temporal opposition to the cottage interior, and the opening stage directions state both the unknowability and temporal uncertainty of the spiritual land outside the onstage door:

> There is an open door facing the audience to the left, and to the left of this a bench. Through the door one can see the forest. It is night, but the moon or a late sunset glimmers through the trees and carries the eye far off into a vague, mysterious world.[30]

The liminal time in the 'vague, mysterious world', caught somewhere between evening and night-time, is further characterized, by the Faery child, as a place 'Where beauty has no ebb, decay no flood, / But joy is wisdom, time an endless song' (*VPl*, 205). Mary Bruin, reading her book and neglecting the housework, stands so that 'if she looks up she can see through the door into the wood' (*VPl*, 181), and is thus connected immediately in the mind of the audience with the timeless world of the forest. Hence, though she is taken by the Faery child in the final moments of the play, the sense that she belongs to, or at least longs for, the atemporal world is established early on, and the conclusion is a simple fulfilment of a conflict that is never complicated during the play. The action of *The Land of Heart's Desire* is a simple push-and-pull between two temporal worlds, and the audience is aware of the likelihood that Mary will be tempted by the forest before the Faery child even appears. There is no point at which the clash of temporalities is made problematic: one is established as the more powerful, and more alluring, at the very opening of the play, and this remains the case in the concluding episode. In *Cathleen Ni Houlihan*, Michael becomes almost

---

[30] W. B. Yeats, *The Variorum Edition of the Plays of W. B. Yeats*, ed. Russell K. Alspach (London: Macmillan, 1966), p. 180. All future quotations from Yeats's plays will be referenced from this edition and given in the body of the text using by the abbreviation *VPl* and page number in brackets.

hypnotized ('he has the look of a man that has got the touch' (*VPl*, 229)) by the other-worldly figure of Cathleen, who also signifies and promises the eternal agelessness of the exterior temporal world. In both plays, the stranger functions to remove a character from one, more restricted, temporal world into a world that is effectively atemporal and filled with promise. The same simple binary structure, which oscillates between two 'worlds' and finally settles on the more powerful, is found in Synge's early play *When the Moon Has Set*, in which the principal tension is derived from argument, or from what Robin Skelton has called a 'will she, won't she?' plot structure, leading to the marriage of Colm to the nun, Eileen.[31]

In comedic one-act plays such as Yeats and Gregory's *The Pot of Broth* and Gregory's *Twenty-Five*, which also utilize the 'stranger' motif, the comedy is in part provided by the stranger's deftness in accomplishing his or her task within the time frame proposed by the play itself. Though there is little opposition between two temporal zones, as in *Cathleen* or *The Land of Heart's Desire*, there is an opposition between two time structures. *The Pot of Broth* is a short sketch in which a tramp, seeking food in the house of the notoriously tight-fisted Sibby and her husband John, pretends to have a stone endowed with the power to make broth from only boiling water. Distracting the couple with conversation, the tramp adds various ingredients from the cottage kitchen to the pot, making a broth whilst keeping up the pretence that the stone has magical powers. By the end of the play, the couple are eager to have the stone, and the tramp exchanges it with them for some food and whiskey. At various points in the play, the tramp seems to exert a magical power over Sibby ('Well, he has the poor woman bewitched' (*VPl*, 249)), and thus belongs to the type established in the earlier 'stranger' plays. However, we know throughout the play that the priest, who is due to come to dinner, will interrupt the scheme and find out the tramp's trickery, and the tramp reminds us of this fact: 'I'd best not be stopping to bargain, the priest might be coming in on me' (*VPl*, 251). Completing his deception just in time, the tramp leaves the cottage with his food and drink just before the priest arrives for dinner. John, the husband, follows him up the path:

SIBBY   Where were you, John?
JOHN   I just went to shake him by the hand. He's a very gifted man.

---

[31]   Skelton, *The Writings of J. M. Synge*, p. 19.

SIBBY   He is so indeed.

JOHN   And the priest's at the top of the boreen coming for his dinner. Maybe you'd best put the stone on the pot again. (*VPl*, 252–3)

The sole purpose of John's going up the path after the tramp is to make the audience aware that, like an escape artist, the tramp has set up the time frame for his trick and then completed it just in time. Of course, the joke persists after the tramp has left with John's comment about putting the stone on the pot again: the feat has been completed effectively and within the allotted time and, aside from some dramatic tension, there have been no significant complications between what we might loosely term the exposition and dénouement. A similar structure is employed in Hyde's *Casadh an tSúgáin*, where the aim of getting the poet Hanrahan out of the door is proposed and completed with little complication, and in Lady Gregory's *Twenty-Five*, where the returned emigrant Christie Henderson arrives at his old lover's cottage the night before she will be forced to sell it, completing his objective of giving her £50 through a contrived card game just in time for the sale to be called off, and just before he must return to America.

The time structures of these plays, though functioning on the simple binary clash of two temporalities, do not often dwell on the more problematic results of competing worlds because, amongst other reasons, the time frame of the stranger is endowed with a greater power from the outset. The early one-act plays of Yeats, Gregory, and Hyde are characterized by a minimal spatialization of time, and function primarily through a simple interior/exterior opposition. The plays follow a simple narrative arc, which is made obvious to the audience at the beginning and does not meet any significant complicating factors, even predicating the success of the plot on its ability to work within the temporal constraints of the one-act form. The competition, in other words, is minimal, because the argument is effectively one-sided, and the plays work to confirm the superiority of one time frame over another.

The clash of worlds inherent in the 'stranger' trope, and more broadly in the cottage interior setting, is hardly unique to Synge; hence, his choice to utilize established conventions resulted in his plays being judged on the grounds established by their predecessors.[32] This was partly due to a

---

[32] See Ben Levitas, 'The Union of Sceptics, 1903–1906', in *The Theatre of Nation: Irish Drama and Cultural Nationalism, 1890–1916* (Oxford: Clarendon, 2002), pp. 75–114; Robert

problem of reception based on the allegorical nature of the established motif. Lauren Arrington has noted that 'realistic sets adorned with "authentic" artefacts contributed to the misinterpretation of the Abbey's style of naturalism as realism, provoking outrage from audiences who cried misrepresentation', and there was also the added problem of allegory, whereby figures on the stage began to be perceived as idealistic embodiments of Ireland.[33] In fact, on seeing *Riders to the Sea* for the first time, Joseph Holloway noted in his diary that 'Miss Honor Lavell as the half-demented, wholly-distracted old "Maurya" gave an uncanny rendering of the part, much suggestive of "Cathleen ni Houlihan," and was most impressive in the scene with her dead son.'[34]

It has often been suggested that *Cathleen Ni Houlihan* was a model for *Riders to the Sea*, and Lionel Pilkington has demonstrated how Synge's play might be read as the deliberate antithesis of Yeats and Gregory's.[35] A comparison with *Cathleen* illuminates some of the key ways in which Synge diverges from his models. In Yeats and Gregory's play, the son of the family (another Michael) is taken away by the eponymous character on the eve of his wedding to Delia, whose dowry is set to bring money into the family. Contrary to Synge's Michael and Bartley, the predicted death of the Michael of *Cathleen* promises eternal remembrance, significance, and life: 'They shall be remembered for ever, / They shall be alive forever' (*VPl*, 229). There is a basic difference in the effect of the exterior temporality on the male characters, resulting in a fundamental difference in the direction of the plot and tone.

Apart from the common forename given in *Riders* and *Cathleen*, there are other commonalities that point towards much more wide-ranging differences between the temporal configurations in the plays. At the beginning of

---

Welch, *The Abbey Theatre, 1899–1999: Form and Pressure* (Oxford: Oxford University Press, 1999), p. 26.

[33] Lauren Arrington, *W. B. Yeats, the Abbey Theatre, Censorship, and the Irish State: Adding the Half-Pence to the Pence* (Oxford and New York: Oxford University Press, 2010), p. 5. The confusion of reading Synge as a realist is also noted in Adrian Frazier, *Behind the Scenes: Yeats, Horniman, and the Struggle for the Abbey Theatre* (California: University of California Press, 1990), p. 86, and Richard Fallis, 'Art as Collaboration: Literary Influences on J. M. Synge', in Kopper, ed., *A J. M. Synge Literary Companion*, 145–60, p. 145.

[34] Robert Hogan and Michael J. O'Neill, eds., *Joseph Holloway's Abbey theatre: A Selection from his Unpublished Journal: Impressions of a Dublin Playgoer*, with a preface by Harry T. Moore (Carbondale: Southern Illinois University Press, 1967), p. 35.

[35] Lionel Pilkington, *Theatre and the State in Twentieth-Century Ireland: Cultivating the People* (London and New York: Routledge, 2001), p. 51. See also Robin Skelton, *The Writings of J. M. Synge* (London: Thames & Hudson, 1971), p. 42; Levitas, *The Theatre of Nation*, p. 88.

both *Cathleen* and *Riders*, a parcel is presented onstage: both parcels contain the clothes of a character named Michael, and both take centre stage as a key device in introducing the audience to the setting. In the case of *Cathleen*, the parcel contains a wedding suit, alerting the audience to the nuptials about to be interrupted; in *Riders*, the parcel contains the clothes that will identify the drowned body of Michael. The parcel of clothes in *Riders* finds its antithesis in the parcel Bridget is opening at the beginning of *Cathleen*. Whereas in *Cathleen* the parcel is opened easily, readily identified as Michael's wedding clothes, and given significance as a sign of wealth ('those are grand clothes, indeed' (*VPl*, 215)), the bundle in *Riders* proves difficult to open, difficult to identify, and contains the clothes of a dead man, perished with salt.

In *Riders to the Sea*, time is spatialized on the axis of relative modernity. The interior and exterior places are given significance not simply through the characters' deictic language but through the fact that we are presented with a multiplicity of time zones. In both one-act plays, objects, characters, and places (both real and imagined) request that time runs at different speeds, and these speeds often overlap and compete against both form and plot. As in Synge's prose works, the temperament of each character both determines and is determined by their relative access to a spiritual world. One contemporary critic reacted to Synge's decision to bring Bartley's corpse into the cottage interior, his decision to cross the threshold, as 'a cheap trick of the Transpontine dramatists', used for melodramatic effect rather than considered dramatic purpose.[36] However, we can see this con-clusion as an inevitability if we read Synge's play in terms of temporalities. Many of the objects that are so important to Synge's one-act plays are also brought across the threshold, and they bring with them a set of temporal associations, penetrating the 'old' world of the cottage interior with the new, modernizing 'big world'. The 'black knot' of rope that Cathleen struggles to untie, Michael's clothes, and Bartley's body are all charged with temporal associations in the context of the play. All three of these objects frustrate the time pressures of the one-act form, drawing attention to the opposing temporalities of the interior and exterior worlds of the play, and are con-nected in various ways to the speeds at which time is given as running in the modernizing world of the Aran Islands.

The dialectic between the interior world of the cottage and the 'big world' outside is established in the opening pages of *Riders*, and is linked with both

---

[36] *The Irish Times*, 27 February 1904. Quoted in Robert Welch, *The Abbey Theatre*, p. 29.

the speed of time, its constraints, and the plot of the play. Nora, holding the bundle of clothes that might belong to Michael, says to Cathleen: 'We're to find out if it's Michael's they are, some time herself will be down looking by the sea' (*CW* III, 5). The task is to find out, before Maurya returns to the house, if the clothes belong to Michael. While appearing simple enough, these lines point to the outside world, the interior world, and the bundle of clothes that has been brought from the former to the latter. An initial timescale is given, but then interrupted and replaced by a new one. Bartley, relaying the news that he will go out to sea, tells the others: 'I'll have half an hour to go down, and you'll see me coming again in two days, or in three days, or maybe in four days if the wind is bad' (*CW* III, 10). Here, Bartley's projected timescale signifies to the audience that, if he leaves, it will be impossible for him to return within the limited scope and time frame of the one-act, one-scene play. Just so, when Dan Burke in *The Shadow of the Glen* tells his wife Nora to leave the cottage, we know she will not return: 'You'll walk out now from that door, Nora Burke, and it's not to-morrow, or the next day, or any day of your life, that you'll put your foot through it again' (*CW* III, 53).

In fact, the characters of both one-act plays constantly refer to futures that will never be realized onstage, thus drawing attention to the form of the play itself, which constrains the possibilities of plot and time span allowed to longer forms of drama, and even to one-act plays which comprise more than a single scene. Short plays with epic scope were not uncommon in the Revival: Adrian Frazier notes one play, *Tá na Francaighe ar an Muir* [*The French are on the Sea*], which, though it only took ten minutes to read, was presented in five acts, with five years elapsing between the fourth and fifth act.[37] On a more modest scale, James Cousins's *The Racing Lug* (1902), to which *Riders* has been compared, comprises two scenes set approximately four hours apart, though this still allows for an anticipation of change that the one-act, one-scene form of *Riders* does not.[38] When the father goes out fishing in a storm in *The Racing Lug*, the movement between scenes gives the hope of a conclusion other than death. In *Riders*, the form does not allow for a passage of time beyond that experience in a single scene, and so there is little hope of a resolution other than death when Bartley leaves the cottage.

---

[37] Frazier, *Behind the Scenes*, p. 90.
[38] Joseph Lennon sees *The Racing Lug* as a 'precursor' to *Riders*. Lennon, *Irish Orientalism*, p. 347. According to McCormack, Synge himself saw the play at the Camden Street Hall in 1902. See *Fool of the Family*, p. 244. The text of *The Racing Lug* is published in Robert Hogan and James Kilroy, eds., *Lost Plays of the Irish Renaissance* (California: Proscenium Press, 1970).

In the published version of *Riders*, the necessity of speed in determining the owner of the bundle of clothes is frustrated by modern mass production. Traditional ways of knowing are complicated by the intrusion of modernity. It is difficult for Nora and Cathleen to tell, initially, if the material belongs to Michael's clothes because there are 'great rolls of it in the shops of Galway, and isn't it many another man may have a shift of it as well as Michael himself?' (*CW* III, 15). Unlike the tools Synge notes on the Aran Islands, which 'have an almost personal character' (*CW* II, 58), Michael's clothes are made with mass-produced materials and so are indistinguishable aside from a few personal touches of stitching. This item, which comes to typify the 'tyranny of impersonal things' that Yeats saw Synge's language as opposing, disrupts the 'natural link' common to the artisanal objects of the Aran Islanders, and signals the disruptive nature of modernity.[39] McCormack suggests that the contrast between the mass-produced material and the home-stitched stockings 'indicates Synge's craft in dramatizing overlapping modes of production which touched even the most isolated households, shoreline and suburban'.[40] For Synge, these 'overlapping modes of production' are also overlapping temporalities, and the foreign, mass-produced object is insistently alien to the cottage interior and the two women.

This minor intrusion of the modern world of commerce into the interior world of the cottage is pitted against the time frame of the play: the mass-produced product makes the task of identifying the owner of the clothes increasingly difficult and scuppers the necessity for speed. There is a persisting popular myth, perpetuated by Bórd Fáilte and merchandise companies, that each Aran family had a distinctive knitting pattern which would allow the bodies of drowned fishermen to be identified, which was certainly made improbable by the mass-marketing of Aran sweaters in the 1930s as a result of local industry schemes from the Congested Districts Board and the Crafts Council of Ireland.[41] The choice to use a shirt and stocking, rather than a sweater that might be identified by a knitting pattern, therefore, may be significant in Synge's case as a method of highlighting the interference of mass-market production on subject–object relations in modernizing communities. Indeed, as Síle de Cléir notes, the economically beneficial influence of global fashion markets on

---

[39] W. B. Yeats, 'Preface to the First Edition of The Well of the Saints' (*CW* III, 65).
[40] W. J. McCormack, *Fool of the Family*, p. 246.
[41] See Siún Carden, 'Cable Crossings: The Aran Jumper as Myth and Merchandise', *Costume: Journal of the Costume Society*, Vol. 48, Issue 2 (2014), 260–75, pp. 260–2.

Irish 'cottage crafts', well established at the turn of the twentieth century, was in part achieved through the modernization of 'peasant dress' in reaction to international tastes.[42] Regardless, the subject–object crisis presented by the unidentifiable shirt in *Riders* means that time, if only in this small sense, is split by the bundle of clothes: its modernity frustrates the ability of the characters to resolve the problem presented at the beginning of the play. In an earlier draft version of the play, which is presented in two scenes, the parcel of clothes is not even opened onstage, and its contents are not so difficult to identify. Here, Cathleen simply says: 'Quick now take out Michael's shirt to see if it's his they've found.'[43] In both this draft and another manuscript version, there is no mention of the 'big shops in Galway', and the clothes are identified solely from the dropped stitches.[44] Hence, there is no initial confusion and no frustration of the time frame as a result of modernized production.

If we examine the scene in which Nora and Cathleen attempt to open and decipher the contents of the bundle in the published versions, we can see just how intricately ideas of time, distance, modernity, and commerce are intertwined by Synge, making one of the principal difficulties of the play that of operating amid conflicting time zones and modes of production.

CATHLEEN [*trying to open the bundle*].   Give me a knife, Nora, the string's perished with the salt water, and there's a black knot on it you wouldn't loosen in a week.

NORA [*giving her a knife*].   I've heard tell it was a long way to Donegal.

CATHLEEN [*cutting the string*].   It is surely. There was a man in here a while ago—the man sold us that knife—and he said if you set off walking from the rocks beyond, it would be seven days you'd be in Donegal.

NORA.   And what time would a man take, and he floating? (*CW* III, 15)

The 'black knot' that 'you wouldn't loosen in a week' resists the imperative of opening the bundle. The time frame proposed by the knot, we might say, is set against the time frame proposed by the one-act form and the time frame allowed to Nora and Cathleen before Maurya returns. As Nora passes the

---

[42] Síle de Cléir, 'Creativity in the Margins: Creativity and Locality in Ireland's Fashion Journey', *Fashion Theory: The Journal of Dress, Body & Culture*, Vol. 15, No. 2 (2011), 204–24, p. 206.

[43] TCD MS 4394, ff. 3–4.   [44] TCD MS 4348.

knife to Cathleen, she links the time frame of the knot with the distance between Aran and Donegal: 'I've heard tell it was a long way to Donegal.' In turn, Cathleen links the knife with an expression of time and distance. The fact that it was the man who sold them the knife who also told them the time/distance to Donegal is important because it links the knife, the knot, and the distance between Aran and Donegal as three expressions of time: the time taken to untie the knot, the time taken to cut the string, and the time taken to walk to Donegal. It is only when Nora asks 'And what time would a man take, and he floating?' that we understand the purpose of her first remark as an attempt to establish an understanding of the relationship between distance, time, and different modes of travelling (walking and floating).

In the published version of the play, the word 'floating' acquires a significance that it does not have in many of the drafts. The above dialogue features in another, shortened form in a draft manuscript, where 'M' is Cathleen:

M.   Give me a knife. The string's destroyed with the salt water and the knot's tightened on me, the Devil twist it.
[*NORA gives her a knife.*]
M.   Wherever it was it is a cruel way from this place [*pulling out a torn shirt and one sock.*] (CW III, 237)[45]

Here, the knot tightens as Cathleen tries to loosen it, showing its resistance to her efforts. The knot, which she curses, is linked again with the temporalized distance between 'here' and 'wherever it was', and becomes a temporal signifier. Both geographical distance and measurable time collude in their frustration of the daughters' time constraints. Just as something needs to be done quickly, the knot tightens, and geography lengthens into an unknowable, 'cruel' distance. Additionally, it is the condition of the clothing, rather than the received wisdom of the man who sold the knife, that signals the distance to Donegal; hence, a degree of separation is added in the later draft between Nora and the knowledge of the geography of the 'big world', further signalling her reliance on received information and her inability to comprehend the spatialized time zone of the 'big world'. The speed with which a body (either living or dead) might travel from Aran to Donegal gains

---

[45] In all the MS versions of the play, Maur(y)a is the elder daughter and the mother's name is Bride. See CW III, p. 3.

increased significance in later drafts of the play, finally becoming explicit in the published text. In the same draft quoted immediately above, Cathleen uses the word 'floating', but it is not linked explicitly with time or distance, as it is in the published text. If we compare the drafted and published versions, we can see that the act of floating is given heightened significance as the play evolves:

Draft: M.   God help him it was him surely and isn't it a sad thing to think of him ~~there~~ floating and tumbling on the sea with no one keening him or—what's that. (*CW* III, 237)

Published: CATHLEEN.   Ah, Nora, isn't it a bitter thing to think of him floating that way to the far north, and no one to keen him but the black hags that do be flying on the sea? (*CW* III, 17)

In the earlier draft, Cathleen is interrupted by a sudden refocusing on the threshold, as a noise is heard outside, reinforcing the time constraints on the women's task. Michael's body is imagined 'floating and tumbling on the sea with no one keening him'. However, in the later version, 'floating' is given added significance, being qualified by a measure of distance ('that way to the far north') and being used as much as an expression of time as it is as a verb. 'Floating and tumbling' gives little sense of movement away from Aran, and takes on the common cyclical, folding sense of Synge's 'natural' temporality; 'floating that way to the far north', however, also reveals the verb as denoting an increasing distance from the cottage interior. Rather than being left 'with no one keening him', Michael is left without *human* keeners, with only 'the black hags that do be flying on the sea'.[46] The use of the supernatural, here as elsewhere in the play, works to underline the 'outside' as unknown, as menacing, adding to the claustrophobia of the onstage cottage. The added focus on the act of floating, related as it is in the later draft to ideas of time, distance, and the supernatural, shows Synge's reworking of the dialogue to include a sense of spatialized time. On the sea, floating, Michael's body moves at unknown speeds and through unknown places, and the temporality of this other world can only be guessed at by Cathleen and Nora.

---

[46] 'Black hags', as Tim Robinson has noted, is a direct translation from the Irish for cormorant, *cailleach dhubh*, though it adds a sense of the supernatural for the English-speaking audience. J. M. Synge, *The Aran Islands*, edited with an introduction by Tim Robinson (London: Penguin, 1992), p. xxx.

Through an insistence on multiple temporalities, and the difficulties of containing various proposed time frames within a one-act, one-scene play, *Riders to the Sea* demonstrates not only Synge's commitment to the portrayal of modernizing characters but also the way in which this portrayal leads to the modernization and complication of the literary form favoured by his contemporaries. In *The Shadow of the Glen*, time is a more explicit factor in the progression of both form and plot and, rather like the overlapping and competing time frames in *Riders*, each role in *Shadow* is characterized by a distinct temporality, and each vies for prominence and control in ways that are both willed and unwilled by the characters. The original setting of *Shadow* staged a stand-off between three different types of time, each brought in turn to the attention of the audience. Nora, the play's principal character, is the focus of these three temporalities and, as is usual in the 'stranger in the house' trope that Synge builds upon here, is the subject of the competition between worlds. The cottage interior of *Shadow* is defined in early drafts by a mechanized, linear time, and is later replaced by a temporal structure of counting, itself a linear activity symbolic of the accrual of material wealth, and this linear time is reinforced by Dan Burke. Nora Burke, on the other hand, trapped in her 'loveless marriage', experiences her own private temporality, which is repetitive, non-linear, and claustrophobic in the context of the isolated cottage interior. The Tramp, who is given the role of 'stranger' throughout, offers Nora another vision of time, based in the natural world outside the cottage, which is cyclical and eternal and in which her personal time has the potential to unify with 'natural' time. The action of *Shadow* (along with its form and structure) is based on the tensions arising from these three temporal worlds.

Only one of the temporalities in the play, the private and repetitive category, is personal to Nora, while the other two (the mechanized clock time of the cottage interior, and the circular and eternal time of the Tramp's outdoor world) are both presented and described by the male characters who vie, in different ways, to possess Nora and to direct her experience of time. In fact, even Nora's private temporal experience is the product and symbol of her loveless marriage to the materialistic and domineering Dan Burke, and so is, in this way, a symptom of male power.[47] The role of the stranger, in Synge's version of the trope as in the other stagings of the period,

---

[47] George Bernard Shaw's critique of marriage as a necessity of property rights follows a similar line. See George Bernard Shaw, *The Quintessence of Ibsenism* (London: Walter Scott, 1891), pp. 20–1.

is to introduce the idea of an alternative temporality; however, in *Shadow*, the Tramp's temporal vision is in competition not only with the temporal world of the cottage interior but also with the private temporal space of Nora Burke, who is isolated from the regulated, linear time of the cottage and her husband. Her personal, cyclical temporality, however, is aligned from the outset with that of the natural world.

In the opening stage directions of the version printed in the December 1904 issue of the Abbey's magazine, *Samhain*, Nora 'goes over and looks at a small clock near the chimney' before the dialogue begins (*CW* III, 32). Throughout the earlier drafts of the play, in both the *Samhain* and other typescript and manuscript versions, Nora returns continually to this time-piece: 'looks at a clock hanging on the wall'; 'looks at the clock again' (*CW* III, 38). In fact, in the version of the play Synge called 'Dead Man's Deputy', Michael Dara also draws our attention to mechanized time, sitting down and 'playing with his watch chain with his eyes on the dead man' (*CW* III, 256), linking Nora's confined life with men to the confines of linear time. The mechanized timepiece, whether clock or pocket watch, is continually referred to in these early versions of *Shadow*, and is one part of a persistent onstage tension between types, or conceptions, of time, one of which is momentary, or 'atomized', time, made up of innumerable discrete units, and the other of which might be referred to as fluid time, time conceived as flux. As Stephen Kern has noted, 'clocks produced audible reminders of the atomistic nature of time with each tick and visible representations of it with their calibrations. The modern electric clock with the sweeping fluid movement of its second hand was invented in 1916. Until then clocks could offer no model for time as a flux.'[48] In her study of narrative fictions of improvement, Helen O'Connell has noted that, in the Irish context of rural modernization, the peasant cottage was to be reformed in order to make it consonant with capitalist economics: 'The improved cottage would be shaped by the clock on the wall, instilling the necessary order and rationality of a modern economy.'[49] Synge's choice of prop draws exagger-ated attention to mechanized time: in an early typescript version of the play, the clock in the cottage is specified as 'a small clock hanging with a chain

[48] Stephen Kern, *The Culture of Time and Space, 1880–1918* (Cambridge, MA: Harvard University Press, 1983), p. 20.

[49] Helen O'Connell, *Ireland and the Fiction of Improvement* (Oxford: Oxford University Press, 2006), p. 24.

and weights near the chimney.'[50] This type of clock, often referred to as a 'wag-on-the-wall' clock, had a hanging pendulum weight which would swing back and forth to mark the passing of time, and would thus have made regulated time visible for the audience in a more exaggerated manner than a more discreet clock in which only the hands marked the movements of minutes and hours.[51]

The visible, mechanized time of the clock and pocket watch in the early versions of *Shadow* is contrasted with Nora's own private temporal space, itself visualized for the audience through her descriptions of the glen. Far from inhabiting the regulated, onward-marching time of the clock, Nora experiences a time which is repetitive, unchanging, and claustrophobic, picturing herself in a position of stasis:

NORA ...   I do be thinking in the long nights it was a big fool I was that time, Michael Dara, for what good is a bit of farm with cows on it, and sheep on the back hills, when you do be sitting, looking out from a door the like of that door, and seeing nothing but the mists rolling down the bog, and the mists again, and they rolling up the bog, and hearing nothing but the wind crying out in the bits of broken trees were left from the great storm, and the streams roaring with the rain? (*CW* III, 49)

NORA ...   Isn't it a long while I am sitting here in the winter, and the summer, and the fine spring, with the young growing behind me and the old passing, saying to myself one time, to look on Mary Brien who wasn't that height... and I a fine girl growing up, and there she is now with two children, and another coming on her in three months or four [*she pauses*]. (*CW* III, 49–51)

The way that time passes outside the cottage is repetitive, inexact, and circular ('the mists rolling down the bog, and the mists again, and they rolling up the bog'). Likewise, in the second example, though the seasons change outside, marking the temporal movement through the year, Nora herself seems caught in an unageing time zone, 'with the young growing behind [her] and the old passing'. The second speech makes it clear that this ageless time zone is private rather than universal, with Nora seeing herself as its sole inhabitant, 'sitting alone, and hearing the winds crying' (*CW* III, 41). In the regulated time of the cottage, Nora's cyclical time (which is 'natural')

---

[51] A 'wag-on-the-wall' clock is also a specified prop in James Cousins's *The Racing Lug*, which may have inspired Synge's use of this sort of timepiece for theatrical purposes.

becomes a sign of her isolation from the exterior world. As in the Wicklow essays and *The Aran Islands*, the mist in the first extract is associated with a non-regulated temporality, and the way it 'roll[s] down the bog' and 'up the bog' attests to its association with circularity and repetition. Nora, sitting on the threshold of the cottage, is separated from this temporality through her domestic confinement, but she is also connected to it. At the end of the play, Dan rebukes her for 'all the talk you have... of the mist coming up or going down' (*CW* III, 53). Nora's potential to access the natural/supernatural temporality is checked by her domestic life, which is strictly regulated and judged by its relative rationality. This is not just a reproach of the time taken for Nora to tell the Tramp and Michael Dara of her situation (thus prolonging her husband's 'death'); it is also a reproach of her private temporal world and her apparent introspection. Nora's potentially spiritual temporality is opposed to the regulated, linear temporality of mechanized time, and is different again to the temporal freedom offered to her by the Tramp.[52]

In later drafts and in the *Collected Works* edition of the play, the clock is removed by Synge, and the mechanized time it represents is replaced by a different sort of counting: the counting of coins on the kitchen table. Throughout her speeches, Nora continues to count her money, and the scene is structured not through constant referral to the clock but through constant referral to an increasing pile of coins (*CW* III, 49–51). Nora, it is clear, is unenthusiastic about her wealth (Michael, on the other hand, is quite excited), and we can see through these drafts that Synge's use of the clock, and the counting of coins, is underpinned by a sense of Nora's opposition to the regulated, materialist, 'modern' time of her married life, replaced but also implicitly symbolized by the counting of material wealth. Synge's localized opposition to encroaching capitalism in *The Aran Islands*, and his development of an alternative natural temporality outside capitalist economics in the Wicklow essays, begin here as an explicit association between regulated, linear time and materialism. In this change from counting time to counting coins, Synge's association between temporal modes and opposing world views is first explicit and then implicit: the dominant materialism of the cottage interior is represented by its linear temporality, and Nora's more natural, cyclical temporality becomes opposed to both

---

[52] For more on gendered relationships to time, and the relationship between 'female subjectivity' and time in the later modernist works of H.D., Virginia Woolf, and Gertrude Stein, see Bryony Randall, *Modernism, Daily Time and Everyday Life* (Cambridge: Cambridge University Press, 2007), pp. 22–5.

regulated time and to the accumulation of capital. Hence, what the Tramp offers to Nora is not simply an escape from a loveless marriage, or from the confines of materialism, but also an escape from both the mechanized, linear temporal world and from her own private experience of cyclical time, which, far from being a retreat from materialism, is merely another restrictive dimension of her isolation in a mechanized, male world.

Though her husband warns Nora that, when she leaves, she will experience age in a way she has previously been protected from, the Tramp suggests a different temporality. The following two descriptions of the temporal world outside the cottage show a distinct contrast:

DAN ... Walk out now, Nora Burke, and it's soon you'll be getting old with that life, I'm telling you; it's soon your teeth'll be falling and your head'll be the like of a bush where the sheep do be leaping a gap. (*CW* III, 53–5)

TRAMP You'll not be getting your death with myself, lady of the house, and I knowing all the ways a man can put food in his mouth ... We'll be going now, I'm telling you, and the time you'll be feeling the cold and the frost, and the great rain, and the sun again, and the south wind blowing in the glens, you'll not be sitting up on a wet ditch the way you're after sitting in this place, making yourself old with looking on each day and it passing you by. You'll be saying one time, 'It's a grand evening by the grace of God,' and another time, 'It's a wild night, God help us, but it'll pass surely.' (*CW* III, 57)

Dan warns that Nora's leaving will lead to certain death, to a triumph of linear time, whereas the Tramp offers a circular temporality, based on seasons and weather patterns, at once diverting and apparently eternal ('you'll not be getting your death with myself, lady of the house'). The cyclical patterns of the Tramp's speech ('and the great rain, and the sun again') echo Nora's own laments and suggest a new potential to merge her personal temporal experience with the 'natural' temporality of the exterior world. Both men frame the word 'old' differently: for Dan, age is a physical condition resulting in death; for the Tramp, age is the result of Nora's private, claustrophobic, repetitive time ('making yourself old with looking on each day and it passing you by'). In the Tramp's definition, it is the lack of participation that makes Nora 'old', whereas in Dan's it is participation itself which will result in the bodily degeneration of age. Mary King argues that 'The Tramp's diagnosis of Nora's situation suggests a condition of potential activity frozen in a state of conditional inactivity, of contact *not* made with the realities of time and place.'[53] Synge, on the other hand, insists that there can be no 'realities of time and place', emphasizing the subjectivity of these two entities most prominently in the way that modern, mechanized, and linear time disrupts the flowing movement of time in the outside world, but also in the setting of the cottage itself, where Nora, Dan, Michael, and the Tramp all abide by, and promote, different temporalities.

In 'People and Places', one of the Wicklow essays discussed in the previous chapter, Synge identifies the 'profound... remorse' (*CW* II, 200) which he feels in Wicklow in terms of the dissociation between his own temporal experience and the cyclical time of the natural world. The 'diurnal temperament jar[s] against the impulses of perpetual beauty which is hidden somewhere in the fountain from whence all life has come' (*CW* II, 200). In *Shadow*, Nora's emancipatory exit from the cottage suggests the potential to merge with the 'perpetual' time of nature, even if this merging is found, in the offstage future, to be incomplete or imaginary. Coming close to the 'fountain' of life is, for Synge, achieved through a natural communion which allows the personal time of the lonely, spiritually inclined Nora to be reconfigured in tune with the temporality of the world outside the cottage. The transcendent, atemporal experience which figured as a sort of mysticism in *The Aran Islands* and in the vagrant figures of the Wicklow essays is thus deployed in the language of the one-act plays to mark a separation between two distinct modes of being within the world, privileging the triumph of a spiritual and natural (over a mechanized or linear) temporality.

In *The Aran Islands*, as we have seen, Synge worked actively to register the disruptions of modernization on both the primitivist and Romanticist gaze, and his Wicklow essays established a distinct hierarchy of access to a natural, spiritual, cyclical temporal experience. His one-act plays continue this focus on the fractures of modernization by tending towards a pluralized temporal configuration which works against the idea that time in Ireland was stratified solely on a national geographical level. Again, the focus is on the local and personal, and on the much more complex effects of a multiplicity of coexistent temporalities, meaning that the pluralizing effects of modernization are embodied in the forms, structures, plots, and characters of Synge's staged one-act plays. The tendency towards a pluralization of temporality in Synge's work sets his early plays apart from those of his contemporaries as insistent responses to changing social relations. In turn, reading *Riders to the*

---

[53] King, *The Drama of J. M. Synge*, p. 72.

Sea and *The Shadow of the Glen* in this way forces a reconsideration of Synge's own relationship to social commentary, modernization, and to forms of literary modernism, which was not solely a relationship based on conscious consideration of changing social conditions and relations but one which Synge worked to embody in his drama through formal and structural modification of established tropes. Fractured communal relations are figured as fractures in the time frames of the drama, and the overlapping of temporalities and levels of modernization find their correlatives in the constant and unresolved competition for dominance from any one conception of time. These plays, far from being isolated from the concerns of modernization, or from reverting to a solely Romanticized vision of the peasantry, in fact register a sense of formal instability as a result of their fraught and multiple conceptions of time and space. The simple binary geographies and temporalities of the 'stranger in the house' trope become strained in Synge's work, and his consciousness of the sociological implications of unstable relationships to time (and, by extension, modernity) is translated into the plots and structures of the one-act plays.

4

Dialectics, Irony, and *The Well of the Saints*

Amongst Synge's papers in the archives of Trinity College Dublin is the earliest extant example of the writer's dramatic work. Pieced together by Synge himself from a longer (but now lost) version, *A Rabelaisian Rhapsody* (1898–1900) affords us a unique and often overlooked insight into the structures and key concerns of Synge's entire dramatic oeuvre.[1] This small dialogue is an act of synthesis whereby his reading in Christian mysticism and medieval literature is dramatized through the voices of key literary and religious figures. The main characters are two of Synge's lifelong influences, François Rabelais and Thomas à Kempis, though these are supported by cameo appearances from seventeenth-century German mystic Jacob Boehme and Fra Cosimo da Castelfranco, an Italian painter and Capuchin whose visionary religious paintings stemmed from various interests in esotericism, alchemy, and mysticism. Other appearances were planned from Petrarch and Laura, Nicolette (from the early thirteenth-century French chantefable *Aucassin et Nicolette*), Manon, the title character of Massenet's tragic *opéra comique* (1884), and the sixteenth-century Swiss-German alchemist and occultist Paracelsus, though these parts were either never written or were excised from the surviving text. The use of the term 'rhapsody', in fact, might refer not only to Synge's admiration for Rabelais but also to the piecemeal nature of the extant manuscript.

In *A Rabelaisian Rhapsody*, the characters debate the various merits of their literary styles and, by implication, establish rivalling theologies. Although the name of Rabelais features often in studies of Synge, no attention has yet been paid to Synge's association of a Rabelaisian style with a particular theology, nor have Synge's attempts to justify Rabelaisian

---

[1] The dialogue is not discussed in any of the major monographs on Synge, though Rabelais is sometimes referred to. See, for example, Mary C. King, *The Drama of J. M. Synge* (New York: Syracuse University Press, 1985), pp. 12, 59, 170; Thornton, *J. M. Synge and the Western Mind*, p. 28. Only Toni O'Brien Johnson refers to the *Rhapsody* in any detail. See *Synge: The Medieval and the Grotesque* (Gerrards Cross, 1982), pp. 18–19.

J. M. Synge: Nature, Politics, Modernism. Seán Hewitt, Oxford University Press (2021). © Seán Hewitt.
DOI: 10.1093/oso/9780198862093.003.0005

humour through religious means ever been explored.[2] *A Rabelaisian Rhapsody* reveals, firstly, Synge's early conceptions and ideals of drama as a form; secondly, the dialogue is used to express his more wide-ranging philosophy of aesthetic, moral, and spiritual value in different literary approaches; thirdly, it links both of these to particular modes of theological thought, thereby illustrating how the structures, forms, and textures of Synge's later drama are rooted in a pressing desire to anchor literary expression to spiritual well-being. As this book argues, the formulation of an artistic creed, so important to contemporaries such as Yeats and AE, is also fundamental to Synge's development, though his philosophy was never systematized. Unlike Yeats, he left no detailed expression of such a creed, though he nevertheless began his literary career with attempts to define his vision as an artist. Again, in contrast to Yeats, Synge's mature works rarely feature outright statements of moral or aesthetic principles. By tracing the evolution of his drama back to *A Rabelaisian Rhapsody*, however, it becomes clear that an implicit spiritual code is behind each of his later developments, and that the germs of the dialectical and ironical structures of *The Well of the Saints* (1905) are central to even Synge's very earliest work.

Synge experimented with a variety of forms previous to his turn to drama, writing poetry, journalism, and drafting a novel. As critics such as Mary King, Declan Kiberd, and Harry White have shown, Synge's early interests were linguistic and musical rather than theatrical, and these primary interests drive the structures and movements of his drama.[3] In fact, Synge records only two visits to the theatre in his 1890s diaries, one in September 1892 to see Beerbohm Tree's *Hamlet* in Dublin, and another in March 1898 to see Ibsen's *Ghosts* at Paris's Théâtre Antoine.[4] In 1894 he planned a play in German, though he never wrote more than a short scene-by-scene synopsis of the plot.[5] *A Rabelaisian Rhapsody* was drafted in the same notebook as his 'Étude Morbide' (1899) and, though it differs significantly in form, there are many commonalities between the two works. 'Étude Morbide', which Synge

---

[2] See, for example, the 'Introduction' of Toni O'Brien Johnson's *Synge: The Medieval and the Grotesque*, pp. 1–28; James F. Knapp, 'Primitivism and Empire: John Synge and Paul Gauguin'.

[3] King, *The Drama of J. M. Synge*, 'Origins are as emblematic as the results themselves', 1–17; Harry White, *Music and the Irish Literary Imagination* (Oxford: Oxford University Press, 2008), 'Why Synge Abandoned Music', 110–32; Declan Kiberd, *Synge and the Irish Language* (London and Basingstoke: Macmillan, 1979), pp. 19–53.

[4] See *CW* II, p. xii. Maurice Bourgeois also suggests that Synge also saw some Viennese farces and a few realist plays during his European travels. See *John Millington Synge and the Irish Theatre*, p. 17.

[5] TCD MS 4360, ff. 12–12v.

categorizes as a 'monodramatic study', lacks the dialogic structure of *A Rabelaisian Rhapsody* and is given instead in the form of a fictionalized diary. However, its arc from decadent solitude to rapturous pantheism, from a lonely bedsit in Paris to a life among the 'primitive' peasantry at Finisterre, mirrors the debate of the *Rhapsody*, which pits saintly asceticism and restraint against the vital exuberance of Rabelais. Both, in this way, are attempts to trace the development of the artist.

As with the majority of Synge's early writings, 'Étude Morbide' is generically unstable, and its autobiographical basis is thinly veiled. The use of the fictionalized diary, of the mad lover, the suicidal protagonist, and the 'primitive peasantry' illustrates the mixture of both Gothic and Decadent convention with which Synge was working in this early period.[6] It is also characteristic of Synge's early writings in that it struggles to conceal its influences: Thomas à Kempis, Herbert Spencer, Spinoza, Dante, and Wordsworth are all mentioned in the reading matter of the protagonist. However, as with his first play, *When the Moon Has Set*, there is no evidence in 'Étude Morbide' of Synge's satirical streak: in fact, *A Rabelaisian Rhapsody* is not only Synge's earliest extant dramatic dialogue but also our first evidence of his talent for irony. In the 'Étude', Synge enacts his own rejection of Decadence both in terms of generic convention and subject matter in favour of an art 'conceived by a soul in harmony with some mood of the earth' (*CW* II, 35). A similar progression is outlined in an earlier scenario for a play, written in German, in which the poet protagonist, 'who is fed up with the vanity of London life', eventually comes to consider, through dialogue with his two brothers, a 'broader view of mankind' (*CW* III, 181–2). The young protagonist of 'Étude Morbide' suggests that 'there is much that is similar in the saint's life and in the artist's', referring specifically to 'the same joy of progress, the same joy in infinitely exact manipulation' (*CW* II, 31). The saint's daily ritual of prayer and meditation, as D. S. Neff has noted, suggests to the young man that asceticism 'will increase his sensitivity to beauty'.[7] However, his reading of Thomas à Kempis results in the protagonist's mental state becoming increasingly morbid: his lover, on recognizing this, suggests that 'he read Spinoza as a change from the saints' (*CW* II, 32). On doing so, the narrator leaves for Finisterre, where he finds

---

[6] W. J. McCormack, for example, listed Synge's *When the Moon Has Set* under the category of 'Irish Gothic' in *The Field Day Anthology of Irish Writing*. See Seamus Deane, ed., *The Field Day Anthology of Irish Writing*, Vol. II (Derry: Field Day Publications, 1991), pp. 898–914.

[7] Neff, 'Synge, Spinoza, and *The Well of the Saints*', p. 139.

a community of peasants closely connected with nature and a sense of joy in all that is opposite to the saint's self-control and self-denial. Finally, the young man rejects Thomas à Kempis altogether with a series of grandiose statements:

> I am sick of the ascetic twaddle of the saints. I will not deny my masculine existence nor rise, if I can rise, by facile abnegation. I despise the hermit and the monk and pity only the adulterer and the drunkard. There is one world of souls and no flesh and no devil.   (*CW* II, 34)

The denial of the devil, the refutation of asceticism, and the emphasis on an ensouled world gives a theological backing to Synge's developing literary vision. The prominence of Spinoza in Synge's early works is, as Neff has astutely observed, an indication of his centrality to Synge's philosophy.[8] The only quotation from Spinoza's *Ethics* anywhere in Synge's oeuvre is found in 'Étude Morbide': 'Laetitia est hominis transitio a minore ad majorem per-fectionem', or 'Pleasure is the transition of a man from a less to a greater perfection' (quoted in *CW* II, 32).[9] As Neff glosses, 'pleasure results from a reasonable movement on the part of the organism towards a greater under-standing of the metaphysical, psychological, and ethical dimensions of pantheism, while sorrow results from an unreasonable movement on the part of an organism away from such an understanding.'[10] The choice of this maxim marks a revealing development in Synge's privileging of the joyous and vital over the restraint and self-denial emphasized in Christian dogma, and offers a key to understanding not only the arc of 'Étude Morbide' but also the logic behind the imaginary cast of *A Rabelaisian Rhapsody*.

Our dating of the *Rhapsody* is based on the fact that portions of its dialogue were later incorporated into *When the Moon Has Set*, but also on the fact that the majority of the figures dramatized in the fragment feature in Synge's reading and cultural activities between the years 1896 and 1898.[11]

---

[8]   Neff, 'Synge, Spinoza, and *The Well of the Saints*', p. 140.

[9]   This is also one of only three of Spinoza's definitions that Synge copies into his notebooks. All three are noted in Latin in TCD MS 4379, f. 66r.

[10]   Translation quoted in Neff, p. 140, from Spinoza, *On the Improvement of the Understanding, The Ethics, and Correspondence*, p. 174.

[11]   Synge most probably encountered *Aucassin et Nicolette* in 1895 while studying in Paris under Louis Petit de Julleville. See Alex Davis, 'J. M. Synge's *Vita Vecchia* and *Aucassin et Nicolette*', *Notes & Queries*, Vol. 58, No. 1 (March 2011), 125–7, p. 125. It is likely that Synge also encountered *Manon* in the city, as it was performed in every year of the 1890s except 1891 at the Opéra Comique. See Archives de l'Opéra Comique. https://dezede.org/oeuvres/manon/ [accessed 15 Nov 2016].

It is most likely, therefore, that the dialogue dates from between 1898 and 1900. Synge's choice of characters in the *Rhapsody* aligns him much more closely with Yeats and the movement of fin de siècle mysticism than previously supposed, and his association of various forms of spiritual experience with different literary styles illustrates how fundamental this period of experimentation was to his later association between style and forms of spirituality.[12] Not only this, but the form of the dialogue, which takes its cues from the Ossianic tales of early Irish literature, is a recurring feature in Synge's drama, and one which prepared him for his encounters with systematic modernization in the Congested Districts. His view of the pious modernizer seeking to convert a contrary population into a standardized and conforming community begins here as a literary debate, and later takes on a greater significance as his aesthetic theory is used to back up a political and sociological argument in favour of nonconformity.

In the *Rhapsody*, both Rabelais and Thomas à Kempis seek a mystical connection with the divine and a literary style that is the truest expression of God's will on earth. This apparently lofty subject matter is consistently undercut by Synge's satirical streak, which works to subvert à Kempis's piety. To begin with, Rabelais and à Kempis discuss their book sales in heaven and hell, and it is quickly established that Rabelais's pentalogy of novels, *Gargantua and Pantagruel* (c.1532–64), is more popular in both domains. There is 'no demand in Hell' for *The Imitation of Christ*, and *Pantagruel* is more widely read among the angels than Thomas à Kempis's devotional text (*CW* III, 183). The argument is weighted in favour of Rabelais, who expresses a Spinoza-inflected pantheism and works to emphasize the arc towards the justification of pleasure as a divine and evolutionary imperative that also structures 'Étude Morbide':

RABELAIS: In my book there is health and laughter and activity, the true worship of the Almighty.

THOMAS: Your book is as a great flood that bears along with it dead dogs, and swine and dunghills, to cast them out in the end like carrion on the wayside. My book is like a well of water, with ferns round it and the fragrance of the earth.

---

[12] For more on the critical history of Synge in relation to forms of fin de siècle mysticism, occultism, and spiritualism, see the first chapter of this book.

RABELAIS: My book is like the great sea that will drink up all the ordures of the world, and remain yet with clean lips and pure jubilant voice. Your book is a puddle, and marred forever but did an innocent cow look backward over it.

THOMAS: You cannot drink of the sea.

RABELAIS: Nor wash in your pool. If the weather be but hot enough, you will find there a cake of mud with frogs that breed about the centre. (*CW* III, 184)

Synge's reading of Nietzsche during this period is evident here: in *Thus Spoke Zarathustra* contempt for the body is depicted as the symptom of a sick soul.[13] Here, Zarathustra's call for the people to 'go under' into the *Übermensch* (or 'overman') is couched in the imagery of water: 'Truly, mankind is a polluted stream. One has to be a sea to take in a polluted stream without becoming unclean. Behold, I teach you the overman: he is the sea, in him your great contempt can go under.'[14] Rabelais's book is described in similar terms, being both of the body and yet able to wash away pollutants. The pristine 'well' of *The Imitation of Christ* is easily fouled, whereas Rabelais's book 'is like the great sea that will drink up all the ordures of the world'. Elsewhere, Synge would employ the same metaphor to discuss the difference between the Irish and English languages: 'If a well is made foul no one can approach it, but the sea is indifferent to everything and in a certain [way] the English language is like the sea which goes round the world as it does.'[15] Here, the transnationalism of English is preferred as a medium for literature because it allows for experiment and is adaptable, whereas Irish is susceptible to damage when exposed to new conditions. Likewise, *The Imitation* is pure but not purifying, whereas *Gargantua and Pantagruel* is expansive and is able to take in 'dead dogs, and swine and dunghills' and 'remain yet with clean lips and pure jubilant voice'. The form and style of each literary work is thus intimately connected with a particular theology, and Synge establishes the Rabelaisian as that which, though superficially

---

[13] Synge first notes reading Nietzsche, alongside Hegel, Spinoza, Comte, and Blavatsky, in the years 1894–5 (see TCD MS 4379). He read *Thus Spoke Zarathustra* in 1897 (see TCD MS 4418) and continued to make notes on Nietzschean philosophy in the early years of the twentieth century (see TCD MS 4393).

[14] Friedrich Nietzsche, *Thus Spoke Zarathustra: A Book for All and None*, ed. Adrian Del Caro and Robert B. Pippin, trans. Adrian Del Caro (Cambridge: Cambridge University Press, 2006), p. 6.

[15] Draft of the article 'The Old and New in Ireland', TCD MS 4393, f. 9v.

contaminated by 'the ordures of the world', is most full of 'health and laughter and activity'. Here, Synge takes his tenets directly from Rabelais, echoing the French author's 'advice to readers', which states that his book 'contains no foul infection / Yet teaches you no great perfection / But lessons in the mirthful art'.[16] This will be no surprise to readers familiar with Synge's mature drama; however, the centrality of mystical experience to this literary mode is instructive. The spiritual becomes implicated in the aesthetic, and thus when the grounds of the aesthetic are challenged by forms of standardizing modernity, the spiritual is also under threat. The significance of this formulation for the development of Synge's work cannot be overstated. Each change in style, and each new insistence on the Rabelaisian, acts as a form of protest against the perceived threat of modernization. The principles established in this short dramatic fragment are the anchor to which Synge's work clings through the various shocks of his career. The natural, the spiritual, that which is full of 'health and laughter and activity': all will become more important as the aesthetic and spiritual become implicated in a political vision for the peasantry and an ideal, self-governing Ireland.

In a handwritten section of the *Rhapsody*, Synge expands on his theory of the opposition between Rabelais and à Kempis, invoking a Kantian idea of the synthetic in order to express the potential unity inherent in different forms of experience:

T[HOMAS]. The many understand yet when the limbs lie asleep and the soul creeps out ^{like a white blouse} to the sound of harmonies that no reveller could conceive of we feel the universal synthetic mood near which all others are partial and of small importance.

R[ABELAIS]. At a fair also with good ale and the sound of fiddles and dances and the laughter of fat women the soul is moved to an ecstasy which is perfection and not partial.[17]

Both seek the synthetic, that product of the imagination which gives unity to the manifold, through their writings; hence, both are conceived as mystical. The key difference is that Rabelais's synthetic mood is characterized by 'ecstasy'. This is backed up by a note from Synge, left alongside the

---

[16] François Rabelais, *The Histories of Gargantua and Pantagruel*, translated with an introduction by J. M. Cohen (Harmondsworth: Penguin, 1986), p. 36.
[17] TCD MS 4354, f. 8.

manuscript after his death: 'I believe in gaiety which is surely a divine impulse peculiar to humanity and I think Rabelais is equal to any of the saints' (*CW* III, 182). Comedy, the expression of 'gaiety', is for Synge inherently divine. Restraint, asceticism, and that which denies the 'ordures of the world' by creating a 'well' of unsullied life are, conversely, seen as untrue or artificial. Elsewhere, Synge refers to the 'cosmic faith' of Rabelais, comparing his work to 'the magnificent Kermesse of Rubens', which 'expresses the final frenzy of existence'. Rubens's painting, itself full of 'dances and the laughter of fat women', attains a mystical essence in this description.[18] We can assume from the extant fragments of the *Rhapsody* that this dialectic between forms of mystical experience and their literary counterparts was the key function of the text, and that the various characters lined up by Synge were chosen for their ability to complicate and expand his own theory of visionary art.

Aside from Rabelais and á Kempis, Synge assigns another speaking role to Jacob Boehme, and his notes show that he also planned to include Paracelsus. Both of these figures featured heavily in the esoteric writings of Yeats and Blavatsky, and it is probable that Synge encountered them here, though it is also likely that he read Robert Browning's *Paracelsus* (1835) in the same year as he read *The Imitation of Christ*.[19] Boehme is discussed at length in Hegel's works, which Synge studied between 1896 and 1897, where he is assigned the position of the 'first German philosopher'.[20] Synge also read some of Boehme's *Aurora* in October and November 1897, at the same time as reading Yeats's introduction to Blake's poems, and made brief biographical notes on the mystic.[21] In Blavatsky's writings, Paracelsus is

---

[18] Quoted in King, *The Drama of J. M. Synge*, p. 170. From the two-act version of *When the Moon Has Set*, TCD MS 4351, f. 20.

[19] Synge notes reading Browning's *Dramatis Personae* (1864) in his diary for 1894, but also read Browning again in 1896, the same year as he notes reading *The Imitation of Christ*. See TCD MS 4415 and TCD MS 4417.

[20] Quoted in Elizabeth S. Haldane, 'Jacob Böhme and his Relation to Hegel', *The Philosophical Review*, Vol. 6, No. 2 (March 1897), 146–61, p. 146. For more on Hegel's use of Boehme, see Glenn Alexander Magee, 'Hegel and Mysticism', in Frederick C. Beiser, ed., *The Cambridge Companion to Hegel and Nineteenth-Century Philosophy* (Cambridge: Cambridge University Press, 2008), 253–80. Hegel dedicates a lengthy chapter in his *Lectures on the History of Philosophy* to Boehme. See *Lectures on the History of Philosophy*, trans. Elizabeth S. Haldane and Frances H. Simpson, 3 vols., Vol. III (London: Kegan Paul, Trench & Trübner, 1896), pp. 188–216. For Synge's brief notes on Hegel, see TCD MS 4379, ff. 1r–1v. Synge notes reading Hegel's works in his diaries for 1896 and 1897. See TCD MS 4417 and 4418.

[21] TCD MS 4418, ff. 67r–69v. In another journal, Synge notes reading 'Boehme's works with notes' and gives a brief biographical sketch and an outline of Boehme's 'Three Principles of the Divine' (i.e. sulphur, mercury, and salt). See TCD MS 4379, f. 59r. He also gives a brief quotation

conceived as an early father of the Theosophical movement, and his theory of magnetism and the 'identical composition of the earth and all other planetary bodies and man's terrestrial body' is incorporated into contemporary hermetic thought, echoing her axiom 'as above, so below'.[22] Likewise, Blavatsky's 'Seven Principles of Man', which Synge copied into his notebook, were supposedly lifted from Paracelsus's 'Seven Principles of Man' as detailed in Franz Hartmann's life of Paracelsus (1887).[23] Jacob Boehme is also heavily referenced in the work of Blavatsky and in Yeats's esoteric writings, particularly his 'master-key' to the symbolic system of William Blake, published in the first volume of his and Edwin Ellis's edition of *The Works of William Blake* (1893), which Synge read and made notes on in the same notebook as that used for his notes on Blavatsky, Spinoza, Nietzsche, and Hegel.[24]

As Ken Monteith notes, Yeats's contribution to the first volume, 'The Symbolic System', treats Blake's prophetic books as mysticism rather than myth, using the figures of Paracelsus and Boehme to authorize his own view of Blake's symbolism.[25] Since Synge read Yeats's *Works of William Blake* during the same month as he read Boehme's works, it is probable that his understanding of Boehme is coloured, in part, by Yeats's own representation of the mystic. The speaking part assigned to Boehme in *A Rabelaisian Rhapsody*, combined with Synge's own notes on the Yeats–Ellis edition of Blake's works, afford an insight into the particular aspects of Boehmean mysticism that Synge was attracted to. Not only this, it also gives further evidence of Synge's

---

from Boehme on f. 58r. The 'three principles' do not feature in Boehme's *Aurora*, suggesting that Synge read more widely in the mystic's work.

[22] H. P. Blavatsky, *Isis Unveiled: A Master-Key to the Mysteries of Ancient and Modern Science and Technology, Vol. I: Science* (London: Bernard Quaritch, 1877), p. 168. Paracelsus is referenced throughout the two volumes of this work, and also in the two volumes of Blavatsky's *The Secret Doctrine: The Synthesis of Science, Religion, and Philosophy* (London: Swan Sonnenschein & Co., 1888).

[23] See Arthur Lillie, *Madame Blavatsky and Her 'Theosophy'* (London, 1895), pp. 49–50, in which Lillie argues that it is 'quite certain' that Blavatsky lifted Paracelsus's principles into her own work, suggesting that Franz Hartmann's *Life and the Doctrines of Philippus Theophrastus Bombast of Hohenheim Known as Paracelsus* (1887) was the source text. It is clear that Synge is copying Blavatsky's 'Seven Principles' rather than Paracelsus's from the notebook, since he lists the principles under 'Mrs. B'. See TCD MS 4379, f. 48r.

[24] See TCD MS 4379, ff. 50r–56v.

[25] See Ken Monteith, *Yeats and Theosophy* (London and New York: Routledge, 2008), pp. 115–33.

attempt to debate in dramatic form the basis of his own aesthetic and spiritual system.

[JACOB BOEHME passes talking to himself.]

BOEHME. Some men love the devil who is nature and animals and children and women; these are the poets, for the poet sees the idea of God within the forms of the world. Some men love God and the angels and men; these are the philosophers who see the forms of the world within the Lord. Life is a chain;

God

The Angels

Men

Women

Children

Animals

Nature.

And woman is the link between the earthly and the divine. She laughs and weeps continually, and in the one the godly comes down to earth and in the other the earthly goes up to God. [*Exit.*] (*CW* III, 184–5)

In Yeats's explication of Blake's 'Symbolic System', Boehme is seen as more constricted by 'the language of the Churches', delivering his mystic message 'for an age of dogma'.[26] Blake's work, in contrast, is the prime exemplar of a literary–historical moment when 'the language of spiritual utterance ceases to be theological and becomes literary and poetical'; hence, the poet is seen as the supreme version of the mystic for a new age.[27] Synge's version of Boehme, however, is used as a mouthpiece for a vision of the poet-figure akin to Yeats's depiction of Blake. A commonality is drawn between Boehmean and Blakean mysticism in the idea of the 'looking-glass' or

---

[26] W. B. Yeats and Edwin John Ellis, eds., *The Works of William Blake: Poetic, Symbolic, and Critical, edited with lithographs of the illustrated 'Prophetic Books' and a Memoir and Interpretation*, Vol. I (London: Bernard Quaritch, 1893), p. xi.

[27] Yeats and Ellis, eds., *The Works of William Blake*, Vol. I, p. xi.

'vegetable glass' of nature, on which God meditates and 'beholds...His love for His own unity'.[28] Looking into this mirror, God 'enters on that eternal meditation about Himself which is called the Holy Spirit'.[29] The relationship between the imagination and nature is explored in the thought of the two mystics in a way that is replicated in Boehme's speech in the *Rhapsody*. The 'Preface' to the Yeats–Ellis *Works* explains the formulation as such:

> In imagination only we find a Human Faculty that touches nature at one side, and spirit on the other. Imagination may be described as that which is sent bringing spirit to nature, entering into nature, and seemingly losing its spirit, that nature being revealed as symbol may lose the power to delude.
>
> Imagination is thus the philosophic name of the Saviour, whose symbolic name is Christ, just as Nature is the philosophic name of Satan and Adam. In saying that Christ redeems Adam (and Eve) from becoming Satan, we say that Imagination redeems Reason (and Passion) from becoming delusion, – or Nature.[30]

The confluence of Boehmean and Blakean mysticism in the Yeats–Ellis explanation is thus assimilated into Synge's work: the poet, whose act of imagination works on seeing 'the idea of God in the forms of the world', is essentially based in a conception of nature as symbol. By 'constantly using symbolism', therefore, the poet 'reminds us that nature itself is a symbol' and thus is 'redeemed' from the 'delusion' of nature itself.[31] Just as Yeats makes recourse to elaborate charts in detailing Blake's symbolism, so Synge's own depiction of the 'chain' of life shows a similar tendency in explaining Boehme's typically early modern cosmology through diagrammatic means. In a note written in 1908, possibly as a draft for the preface to his own *Poems*, Synge's conception of literature likewise mirrors Yeats and Ellis's statement regarding imagination 'touch[ing] nature at one side, and spirit on the other'. Synge writes, 'what is highest in poetry is always reached where the dreamer is reaching out to reality, or where the man of real life is lifted out of it' (*CW* II, 347).

---

[28] Yeats and Ellis, eds., *The Works of William Blake*, Vol. I, p. 247.   [29] Ibid.

[30] Yeats and Ellis, eds., *The Works of William Blake*, Vol. I, pp. xxi–xiii.   [31] Ibid.

Paracelsus, whose part in the *Rhapsody* is either lost or remained unwritten at the time of Synge's death, likewise emphasized the integral role of sensuous nature in mysticism. The alchemist's doctrine of 'signatures', where 'the purpose (or "virtue") of all creation was darkly inscribed on its outward form', led him to read nature 'by means of the careful naturalist observation and laboratory experiment that he called magic and the scholarly tradition of divination and interpretation that he called the cabala'.[32] Synge's early prose, as seen in Chapter 2 of this book, shows the young writer dismissing cabbalist interpretations of nature for something more akin to contemporary naturalist field practice (*CW* II, 24); however, for both Boehme and Paracelsus, as the dramatist knew, the immanence of God in nature was paramount. In working out through dialogue the specifics of various mystical approaches and Christian cosmologies, therefore, we can witness the younger Synge arriving at his own conception of a mystical literature.

A Rabelaisian Rhapsody does not simply show, in Yeats's words, 'the language of spiritual utterance ceasing to be theological and becoming literary and poetical'; rather, it functions as the working out of a philosophical basis for Synge's own drama. The concern with a 'partial' or unified reading of the world, voiced in the dialogue between Rabelais and à Kempis in their opposing criteria of mystical literature, is tied up in the final speech from Fra Cosimo, who asserts that 'All is relative except the All', thereby unifying the 'tranquility' of à Kempis with the 'ecstasy' of Rabelais (*CW* III, 185). For Fra Cosimo,

> No one has understood motion therefore no one has understood the condition of life, for life is motion and sorrow and turmoil are the condition of life as are joy and tranquility their opposites whom they create and by which they are themselves created.   (*CW* III, 185)

It is in this view that we find the exposition of a philosophy closest to Synge's own.

In a final addition to the manuscript, composed later than the original dialogue, Synge pens a short conversation between 'C' and 'D', in which he brings the debate to a tentative conclusion. 'C' suggests that 'The gaiety of life is the friction of the animal and the divine', and 'D', playing devil's

---

[32] Jane Bennett, *The Enchantment of Modern Life: Attachments, Crossings, and Ethics* (Princeton and Oxford: Princeton University Press, 2001), p. 35 and note 7 to p. 35, p. 182.

advocate, argues that there is 'an antimony also in the idealist between his life that remains human and his exaltation'. The debate is moved forward again by 'C', who states that 'Ordinary life grows up into some mysticism as roots grow into a tree. Gaiety and pity are essentially in coexistent conflict.' 'D' simply responds, 'I suppose you are right...' (*CW* III, 186). The dialectical structuring of this dialogue, in which resolution is not achieved by either 'C' or 'D' but by their working together, is typical of Synge's dramatic writings. There is no clear-cut unifying vision of Synge's aesthetic and spiritual philosophy in the *Rhapsody*: 'C' (which, of course, precedes 'D' alphabetically) offers an answer, which 'D' at once affirms and questions. The word 'suppose' allows room for doubt: the constant back and forth between the characters is mirrored in the content of their debate, in the theory of 'coexistent conflict', of persistent dialectical relationships. We see here that the image of the roots and tree (used later in Synge's preface to his *Poems* (*CW* I, xxxvi)) is invoked to suggest that the progression from the 'ordinary' to the mystical is natural, and that one must be 'rooted' in the ordinary in order to achieve mystical experience. The tension between Rabelais and à Kempis, between 'gaiety and pity', is essential to the 'motion' of life emphasized in Fra Cosimo's speech. The coexistence of gaiety and pity is characteristic of Synge's work, as is the conflict between the two. The idea that the 'animal and the divine' must coexist to produce that essentially human characteristic, 'gaiety', is again both a mystical and literary ideal; in fact, as *A Rabelaisian Rhapsody* illustrates, the two categories are inseparable in Synge's aesthetic.

Much as the Spinozan philosophy of pantheistic pleasure countered à Kempis's *Imitation of Christ* in the 'Étude Morbide', so Synge's vision of Rabelaisian 'gaiety' counters à Kempis in the *Rhapsody*. This progression distils the concept of 'pleasure' or 'gaiety' into a literary as well as a philosophical concern, linking it with a certain form, style, and subject matter. Through the dramatization of various theological and philosophical approaches to mysticism, Synge's *Rhapsody* posits an ideal mysticism based in the 'ordinary', in the world of sensuous nature ('nature and animals and children and women') rather than in 'God and the angels and men' (*CW* III, 184–5). Synge's primitivist vision, which associates children and women more closely with nature (illustrated in *The Aran Islands*), privileges that which is grounded in the 'roots' of 'ordinary life'. 'Gaiety' is divine because it is both earthly and unifying, and because it avoids denying the pleasures of the body and the 'animal' while simultaneously allowing a uniquely human expression of spirituality. The use of Rabelais as a cipher for vitality is found again in early drafts of Synge's *When the Moon Has Set*, in which the character Colm (clearly a version of Synge himself, and also named after a saint) is found reading Rabelais and Boccaccio.[33] Rabelais, Colm admits, is 'brutal', a quality that Synge would later champion as the potential saviour of modern verse in the 1908 preface to his *Poems*.[34] His opposition to, and eventual 'conversion' of, the apparently frigid and pious Sister Eileen is based on Colm's appreciation for the natural world, which he reads in pantheistic, pseudo-pagan tones. Although Sister Eileen prefers 'Dante and Fra Angelico and Palestrina and Bach' to Rabelais and Boccaccio, Colm retorts that her chosen figures exhibit a 'pallid ecstasy [that] is a compromise with death and sterility'. After this, the play moves towards the dominance of his primitivist, vitalist, and pantheistic vision.[35] This dialectic is central to the structure of Synge's mature work in *The Well of the Saints*.

Through all of Synge's early dialogues, the opposition between spiritual and aesthetic value systems is key to the progression of the play, and in each case the particular mode of pantheism and brutalism suggested by the names of Spinoza and Rabelais is contrasted with the 'sterile' images of à Kempis and other, 'calmer' Christian figures.[36] In Yeats's *Where There is Nothing* (1903), à Kempis is also used as an example of an alternative 'happiness' that is disconnected from the earth, represented by the vital life of the tinkers, who hear 'the music of Paradise' when they sleep outside and experience a spiritual connection which is beyond orthodox Christian theology.[37] In this play, the main character Paul Ruttledge, an Anglo-Irishman associated with a large estate, defects to vagrant life to the shock of his dogmatic and image-conscious friends and relatives, and finally causes anarchy in the village by providing unbridled festivities in honour of his marriage. The play concludes with Ruttledge calling for the foundation of a new religion which is stripped bare of all law and which must be initiated via the destruction of the Church. Towards the end of the first act, a friar, Father Jerome, accosts Ruttledge and questions his suitability to tinker life.

[33] TCD MS 4389, f. 1.

[34] TCD MS 4389, f. 5; 'before verse can be human again it must learn to be brutal' (*CW* I, xxxvi).

[35] TCD MS 4389, ff. 5–7; TCD MS 4351, f. 20.

[36] For Sister Eileen, the paintings of Pietro Perugino (1469–1523) and Fra Angelico (1395–1455) are supreme examples of 'the calm of faith' in art. TCD MS 4351, f. 20.

[37] W. B. Yeats, *Where There is Nothing: Being Volume One of Plays for an Irish Theatre* (London and New York: Macmillan, 1903), pp. 78–80.

PAUL RUTTLEDGE   I am happy. Do not your saints put all opponents to the rout by saying they alone of all mankind are happy?

JEROME   I suppose you will not compare the happiness of these people with the happiness of saints?

PAUL RUTTLEDGE   There are all sorts of happiness. Some find their happiness like Thomas à Kempis, with a little book and a cell.[38]

As in Synge, à Kempis is used here to express a sort of happiness detached from the vitality of 'ordinary life', exemplified in typical Revivalist fashion in the life of the tinker. The relativism of 'happiness' is invoked to suggest alternatives to orthodox mysticism, setting spiritual life in Ireland in the hands of the most apparently 'primitive' and 'pagan' populations. As Ruttledge tells the friar, 'I think, Father Jerome, you had better be getting home. This people never gave in to the preaching of S. Patrick.'[39] In Yeats's play, unlike in Synge's, there is no attempt to associate the spiritual philosophy with a literary style, though this is, of course, an aspect present in Yeats's other works, his poetry especially.[40] The association between a new mysticism based in the 'ordinary' and 'natural' and the recalcitrant peasant populations of rural Ireland, or what Yeats called 'the visionary melancholy of purely instinctive natures and of all animals', is common to both writers, though Synge also insisted on the potential for mystical ecstasy.[41] This association is particularly pertinent in Synge's case, where the figure of the missionary (and modernizing) saint is invoked as the representative of an orthodox religion which is placed in opposition to true mysticism. The dialectical structure of these plays, and later Synge's *The Well of the Saints*, pits the sterile spirituality of the likes of à Kempis against the vital, joyous mystical potential of the Rabelaisian, and in doing so draws on the tradition of Ireland's Ossianic literature, which was receiving renewed attention as the potential native foundation for the new dramatic movement.

As Christopher Morash has noted, the consensus that there was no tradition of theatre in medieval Ireland proved problematic for the writers of the Irish Literary Theatre, who could not, strictly speaking, 'revive' an

---

[38] Yeats, *Where There is Nothing*, p. 78.   [39] Yeats, *Where There is Nothing*, p. 85.

[40] For more on the links between Yeats's spiritual philosophy and literary style see, for example, his essay 'The Autumn of the Body', *Essays and Introductions*, 189–94.

[41] W. B. Yeats, *Mythologies*, p. 5.

ancient tradition of specifically Irish drama.[42] Douglas Hyde, however, whose works Synge read and referenced often in his published and drafted essays, suggested that an essentially dramatic element could be found in the Ossianic writings of the Old Irish tradition.[43] This idea seems to have had particular resonance with Synge, and gained traction in both the theorizing of the dramatic Revival and scholarly studies of Old Irish writings. One of Synge's favourite contemporary writers, Anatole Le Braz, for example, wrote in his *Essai sur l'histoire du Théâtre Celtique* (1904) that, though the Irish were the only 'Celtic' peoples not to have developed a theatrical tradition, their epic literature was essentially dramatic in nature.[44] Synge's *The Well of the Saints* is designed specifically as Ossianic, and thus draws not only on Synge's predilection for dialectical writing but also on the Revivalist concern to tie the modern movement to a definably native tradition. This was not simply a passing phase for Synge: as late as 1906, he was sketching out a dramatic scenario, the 'Comedy of Kings', which he hoped would include 'ossianic dialogue' in which 'servants on pagan grounds hoot at monk' (*CW* III, 230).

As Ann Saddlemyer notes, Synge's letters to his German translator, Max Meyerfeld, specifically identify the words of the Saint in *The Well of the Saints* as originating in the words of a popular Old Irish prayer, 'St Patrick's Breastplate'.[45] What is not noted in Saddlemyer's edition of the plays is that scribbled on the back of one of the manuscripts for *The Well of the Saints* is Synge's own attempt at translating the prayer.[46] Synge's familiarity with the prayer, though it might indeed have come from one of the sources Saddlemyer suggests, was not primarily an engagement with a translated version but with the original, which was printed on the front page of a 1902 edition of *All Ireland Review* and in Whitley Stokes and John Strachan's *Thesaurus Palaeohibernicus* (1903).[47] It is probable that Synge had access to a recently printed version of the original prayer in making his translation, and that the decision to model his Saint on St Patrick was spurred on by the

---

[42] Christopher Morash, 'Irish Theatre', in Cleary and Connolly, eds., *The Cambridge Companion to Modern Irish Culture*, 332–8, p. 323.

[43] Douglas Hyde, *A Literary History of Ireland from the Earliest Times to the Present Day* (London: Ernest Benn, 1967), p. 511.

[44] Quoted and translated in Kiberd, *Synge and the Irish Language*, pp. 46–7.

[45] *CW* III, p. 90, n.5. For Synge's letter to Meyerfeld, dated 12 August 1905, see *CL* I, pp. 121–2.

[46] See TCD MS 4338, f. 150.

[47] Standish O'Grady, ed., *All Ireland Review*, Vol. 3, No. 2 (15 March 1902), p. 1; Whitley Stokes and John Strachan, eds., *Thesaurus Paleohibernicus: A Collection of Old-Irish Glosses, Scholia, Prose and Verse*, Vol. II (Cambridge, 1903), pp. 354–8.

contemporary enthusiasm for the saint and for Ossianic poetry in both scholarly and literary circles, alongside his growing sense of the vitality and the overlooked 'brutality' of Old Irish texts.[48]

In Hyde's *A Literary History of Ireland* (1897), which, as Declan Kiberd has shown, Synge read in its year of publication, the chapter on 'The Ossianic Poems' (dialogues between Ossian, son of Finn mac Cúmhail, and St Patrick) characterizes the figure of St Patrick in the poems as one who speaks with 'exaggerated episcopal severity' and 'denounces with all the rigour of a new reformer'.[49] By contrast, Ossian counters Patrick's theology with a vision of the Fenians as a poetic race who are fiercely loyal and 'impressionable to the moods of nature'.[50] In fact, the characterization of the Ossianic dialogues in Celticist writings and later studies was highly influential. In Ernest Renan's essay 'La poésie des races celtiques' (1854), which Synge read as part of his studies in the Irish language and folklore, the Ossianic dialogues are seen as typical of a wider divide in Irish history between the pagan and Christian impulses, or what Renan characterizes as the transition from the 'mâles sentiments de l'héroïsme' ('the masculine sentiments of heroism') to 'le sentiment féminin' ('the feminine sentiment'):

> Ce qui exaspère, en effet, les vieux représentants de la société celtique, c'est le triomphe exclusif de l'esprit pacifique, ce sont les hommes vêtus de lin et chantant des psaumes, dont la voix est triste, qui prêchant le jeûne et ne connaissent plus les héros.[51]

> What, in fact, exasperates the old representatives of Celtic society are the exclusive triumph of the pacific spirit and the men, clad in linen and chanting psalms, whose voice is sad, who preach asceticism, and know the heroes no more.[52]

The dialogues between Ossian and St Patrick, in which the Irish imagine the debate between 'les deux représentants de sa vie profane et religieuse' ('the

---

[48] See Kiberd, *Synge and the Irish Language*, p. 56. For more on the possible Ossianic sources for Synge's drama, see David Krause, ' "The Rageous Ossean": Patron-Hero of Synge and O'Casey', *Modern Drama*, Vol. 4, No. 3 (Fall 1961), 268–91; Anthony Roche, 'The Two Worlds of Synge's *The Well of the Saints*', in Ronald Schleifer, ed., *The Genres of the Irish Literary Revival* (Dublin: Wolfhound Press, 1980), 27–38.

[49] Hyde, *Literary History*, p. 501.   [50] Hyde, *Literary History*, pp. 503, 506.

[51] Ernest Renan, *Essais de Morale et de Critique* (Paris, 1860), pp. 432–3.

[52] Ernest Renan, *Poetry of the Celtic Races, and other essays*, trans. William G. Hutchinson (London: Walter Scott Publishing Co., 1896), p. 43.

two representatives of her profane and religious life'), are seen here as a conflict between a vigorous, perhaps violent, 'masculine' society, and the morose, ascetic society of Christian orthodoxy.[53] This is echoed in Synge's 'Étude Morbide', in the terms with which the protagonist rejects à Kempis: 'I am sick of the ascetic twaddle of the Saints. I will not deny my masculine existence' (CW II, 34). The translation given above, by William Hutchinson, chooses 'asceticism' for Renan's 'le jeûne'; however, 'fasting' might be more accurate, and it is 'fasting' which becomes a key point of criticism in The Well of the Saints when Martin Doul ironizes the Saint's moralizing. Although Synge's studies in Old Irish literature would certainly have revealed Renan's rather dilettante approach to the subject, in which the image of an idealized, pure, timid, and reserved Celtic race was put forward, the stark contrast which Renan observed in Old Irish dialogue poetry was harnessed by the dramatist.[54]

In modelling The Well of the Saints and other plays on a form of 'Ossianic dialogue', therefore, Synge is not solely invoking a specifically Irish form of drama: in fact, this form and its associated argument set up a sense of cultural, aesthetic, and social interface, whereby the 'reformer' (an orthodox and pallid type) is contrasted with the vigorous, humorous, and pagan community he attempts to 'improve'. The dialogues between Thomas à Kempis and Rabelais, between Ossian and St Patrick, and between the Saint and the Douls in The Well of the Saints are illustrative of a continuing formal preoccupation for Synge, in which a set of positive values is ascertained through dialogue. This image of the orthodox reformer, cultivated over many years in Synge's drama, ultimately prepared his vision of the systematic modernization of the Congested Districts, as the next chapter of this book demonstrates. Whereas David Krause asserts that Synge's use of the Ossianic dialogue is 'not so much concerned with the settlement of national issues as with the individual liberation of his tramps and playboys', terming Synge a 'pure' rather than 'political' artist, Synge's use of this dialectical form was mobilized by the dramatist for political as well as aesthetic ends.[55] As Skelton suggests, 'If . . . the figure of the Saint, travelling Ireland, curing ills, and preaching his truth, is also that of the political reformer, then The Well of the Saints can be regarded as politically loaded.'[56]

---

[53] Renan, Essais, p. 433.

[54] For more on Renan's relationship to later Celtic Studies scholars, and the implications on the Revival, see the first chapter of Mattar, Primitivism, Science, and the Irish Revival, 'The Rise of Celtology', pp. 41–82.

[55] David Krause, '"The Rageous Ossean"', p. 282.   [56] Skelton, Celtic Contraries, p. 55.

What Mary King has described as Synge's 'dialogic imagination' is illustrated by his 'Play of '98'. This scenario was written in 1904 at the request of Frank Fay, who suggested that 'Yeats in *Cathleen* has pointed out the right road for plays of that time' (*CW* III, 215).[57] Here, two peasant women, Bride and Kathleen, one a Catholic and the other a Protestant, take shelter to avoid the 'bloody villains is loose on the land' (*CW* III, 217). Both fear rape, and both agree that it is 'a bad day this day for the female women of Ireland' (*CW* III, 217). It is only after they begin to share stories about their experiences that sectarianism comes to the fore: when Kathleen uses the word 'heretic', Bride recognizes that her companion is a Protestant and, in turn, Kathleen identifies Bride as a Catholic. In Yeats's account of Synge's play, the two women then separate, preferring to risk attack than to hide together. Here, Synge offers a biting critique of sectarianism and the nationalist sanitization of history, focusing on an unresolved tension between the two women. As in his later *National Drama: A Farce* (*CW* III, 220–6), he uses the form of the dramatic dialogue dialectally. Even when not writing for the stage, he turns to drama rather than to prose as the medium for his satire because of the potential of the form for working through a binary argument to produce a more complex and ironic truth.

The reception of *The Well of the Saints* is a testament to the success of Synge's method. Joseph Holloway expressed his distaste for Synge's 'irreverent' drama; likewise, the reviewer for the *Freeman's Journal* termed the presentation of Martin Doul 'lacking in reverence' and 'a constant offence'.[58] The confusion of the *Freeman's Journal* reviewer, however, is tied to the ambiguity of Synge's artistic stance: 'Mr. Synge's plays are somewhat baffling. How are they to be interpreted? ... Is it an attempt to hold the mirror up to Irish nature? Are we to look at it for a treatment of the facts of Irish life ...? ... Whence is [Irish theatre] to derive its philosophy of life? From what source its psychology of character?'[59] For Yeats, writing after the production of *The Well of the Saints* in the Abbey's magazine, *Samhain*, this confusion was key to Synge's innovation:

---

[57] Mary C. King, 'Conjuring past or Future? Versions of Synge's "Play of '98"', *The Irish Review*, No. 26 (Autumn 2000), 71–9, p. 72.

[58] Hogan and O'Neill, eds., *Joseph Holloway's Abbey Theatre*, p. 53; Robert Hogan and James Kilroy, eds., *The Abbey Theatre: The Years of Synge, 1905–1909* (Dublin: The Dolmen Press, 1978), p. 19.

[59] Hogan and Kilroy, eds., *The Abbey Theatre: The Years of Synge*, p. 18.

Mr. Synge is the most obviously individual of our writers. He alone has discovered a new kind of sarcasm, and it is this sarcasm that keeps him, and may long keep him, from general popularity. Mr. Boyle satirises a miserly old woman and he has made a very vivid person of her, but as yet his satire is such as all men accept; it brings no new thing to judgement. We have never doubted that what he assails is evil, and we are never afraid that it is ourselves.[60]

It is this ambiguous satirical quality that Synge attributes to his reading of Rabelais. In *The Tinker's Wedding*, the play ends with the tinkers fleeing, '*leaving the PRIEST master of the situation*' (*CW* IV, 49). In *The Well of the Saints*, the comedy is directed in turns against the beggars, the villagers, and the Saint, and the play closes on a resigned discussion between the Saint and Timmy the Smith: Timmy warns that the blind people 'will be drowned together in a short while, surely', to which the Saint replies simply, 'They have chosen their lot', before proceeding into the church to marry Molly and Timmy in an ironically traditional comic conclusion (*CW* III, 151). One of Synge's early critics, the American scholar Stuart P. Sherman, also noted with Yeats Synge's divergence from classical comedy in terms of the clarity of the satirical attack, citing the example of the 'Play of '98':

In all the classical comedy of the world one is made aware of the seat whence the laughing spirit sallies forth to scourge the vices or sport with the follies and affectations of men. When the play is over, something has been accomplished toward the clarification of one's feelings and ideas; after the comic catharsis, illusions dissolve and give way to a fresh vision of what is true and permanent and reasonable. Synge's comedies end in a kind of ironical bewilderment. His, indeed, is outlaw comedy with gypsy laughter coming from somewhere in the shrubbery by the roadside, pealing out against church and state, and man and wife, and all the ordinances of civil life.[61]

Synge's 'outlaw comedy', characterized by its ironic ambiguity, is the result of his preoccupation with dialectical structures, as illustrated by *A Rabelaisian Rhapsody*. The argument between opposing theological, artistic,

---

[60] W. B. Yeats, ed., *Samhain: An occasional review* (Dublin: Maunsel & Co., 1905), pp. 4–5.
[61] Stuart P. Sherman, *On Contemporary Literature* (New York: Henry Holt, 1917), pp. 206–7.

and moral systems of thought is used to complicate binary positions, and it is in this form that Synge's satire functions most effectively. Rather than being detached from national life, however, as the *Freeman's Journal* reviewer suggests, Synge's drama is deeply rooted in his perception of contemporary political and cultural movements.

The Well of the Saints, in which a religious figure attempts, with what Hyde referred to as 'exaggerated episcopal severity', to convert two contrary and unassimilable blind beggars, can and should be read as the cumulation of Synge's developing spiritual, aesthetic, and social philosophy. In embodying the orthodoxy of St Patrick, the Saint of Synge's play becomes a figure about which the colonial, the spiritual, the aesthetic, and ultimately the modern can be discussed and defined. In Lady Gregory's plays, the reforming colonial figure was taking his place in both a historical and contemporary context. In 1904's *Spreading the News*, written for the opening night of the Abbey, an English Magistrate who is visiting a rural Irish community is figured in explicitly colonial terms. The Magistrate, who hopes to impose a 'system' on the 'disorder' of the place, often refers back to his position in a British colonial territory: 'This district has been shamefully neglected. I will change all that. When I was in the Andaman Islands, my system never failed. Yes, yes, I will change all that.'[62] Set in a context in which the colonial administrator expects 'Agrarian crime... Boycotting, maiming of cattle, firing into houses', Gregory's play is situated as a binary of the will to impose 'order' and the anarchic and comic tendencies of the 'disordered' community: in other words, the dynamic of the modernizer and the yet-to-be-modernized is invoked, with the modernizer promoting a form of stereotypically English rationalism.[63] As Anthony Roche writes, 'this pompous character is doomed to failure in the face of the verbal anarchy' of the community.[64]

Even the opening setting for Synge's play invokes an image of opposition: the roadside on the right, and the 'ruined doorway of a church' on the left. The two blind beggars, Martin and Mary Doul (Doul being a play on the Irish *dall* for 'blind'), are quickly established as savage in both humour and appetite. When they discover that a saint is coming who believes that 'young girls... are the cleanest holy people you'd see walking in the world', Mary laughs to herself: 'Well, the saint's a simple fellow, and it's no lie'

---

[62] Lady Gregory, *Seven Short Plays* (New York: Putnam, 1909), pp. 3–4.

[63] Lady Gregory, *Seven Short Plays*, p. 3.

[64] Anthony Roche, *The Irish Dramatic Revival, 1899–1939* (London: Bloomsbury, 2015), p. 103.

(*CW* III, 83). The piety of the Saint is immediately set up for ridicule. Against this irreverence, the Saint is depicted as severe, moralistic, and rule-bound: the opposition, in fact, is strikingly reminiscent of that between Thomas à Kempis and François Rabelais in Synge's earliest dialogue. When the Saint unwittingly insults Martin by calling the pair 'wrinkled and poor' and suggesting that they would not elicit the pity of 'the rich men of this world', Martin attempts a defence. One of Synge's drafts for this interaction is particularly revealing:

SAINT   It's a hard thing to be shut out from seeing the glory of the world ~~of God~~, and the shape of the cross, and the image of God himself ~~as it is~~ thrown upon men. . . . It isn't up among ^rich I do be^ going with the water from the blessed well but to the like of yourselves who are wrinkled and poor, a thing the rich men of this world would throw a coin to maybe, or a crust of bread.

MARTIN (*uneasily*)   When they look at herself, who is a fine woman, they do often throw two coins or a trifle of meat.

SAINT (*severely*)   What do we know of women who are fine or foul? What is any man at all but a thing of weakness and sin?

MARTIN (*under his breath*)   Oh, fasting is a great thing, fasting and praying is a great thing surely.[65]

We see here that Martin levels the same mode of complaint against the Saint's life and teachings as Rabelais does against Thomas à Kempis. The criticism of women is in line with the Patrick of 'St Patrick's Breastplate', in which the Saint calls the power of God to protect him from 'the spells of women, and smiths, and druids'.[66] Patrick's hymn, which asks for defence against 'the desires of nature', posits him in the ascetic tradition, and Synge's integration of Patrick's lines into the speeches of his Saint likewise aligns him with this image of the national figure. Martin's sarcastic muttering undercuts this image of piety, and suggests the ultimate recalcitrance of the beggars to Christian orthodoxy and reform. These are people, like the tinkers in Yeats's *Where There is Nothing* (1903), who 'never gave in to the preaching of S. Patrick'.[67]

[65] TCD MS 4338, ff. 7–8.
[66] 'The Breastplate of St Patrick', *All Ireland Review*, Vol. 3, No. 2, p. 1.
[67] Yeats, *Where There is Nothing*, p. 85.

The inevitable failure of the Saint's curing of the blind people is symptomatic of his inability to 'cure' their unorthodox views: their refusal to conform to capitalist strictures of work, their unwillingness to accept his complete authority, and, underlining these, their unshakeable bond with, and privileged access to, the natural world. In his long speech at the end of the first act, after the Douls have been cured for the first time and realized each other's outward ugliness, the Saint tries to coach them in a reformed understanding of their Christian duties on earth. In the published version, he emphasizes the asceticism that should follow from a mystical understanding of the world, and tries to impose on the beggars a sort of nature worship that is inimical to their own creed. In an earlier version, rather than emphasizing this new form of mysticism, the Saint instead underlines the importance of their participation in the workforce of the community: 'You'll be strange maybe, a short while, and queer in your thoughts, and you looking on the world, and then you'll get used to seeing, and begin doing your work' (*CW* III, 100). This draft reveals the Saint not only to be a figure of emergent capitalism and colonial 'conversion' but also as associated with the spiritual morbidity and sterility previously linked with the ascetic saints, nuns, and pious figures of Synge's earlier works. Colonial and capitalist concerns are thus brought into Synge's vision of opposition between the 'primitive', Rabelaisian peasantry and the emerging bourgeois sensibilities of the settled community.

In Yeats's preface to the first edition of the play, he frames Synge's dramatic dialect in direct opposition to capitalism. Firstly, Yeats criticizes 'the writers of our modern dramatic movement, our scientific dramatists, our naturalists of the stage' for their use of an 'impersonal language that has come, not out of individual life, nor out of life at all, but out of the necessities of commerce, of Parliament, of Board Schools, of hurried journeys by rail' (*CW* III, 65). He then goes one step further, suggesting that this impersonal language has become free-floating to the extent that it can be harnessed by capitalist power structures: 'One must not forget that the death of language, the substitution of phrases as nearly impersonal algebra for words and rhythms varying from man to man, is but a part of the tyranny of impersonal things' (*CW* III, 65). Synge's dramatic language is figured as a vital antidote to this 'tyranny', which is surely embodied in the Saint's hackneyed orthodoxy and recycling of familiar religious codes. In fact, Synge himself, in a draft preface for his earlier play *The Tinker's Wedding* (1904) (in which two tinkers attempt to trick and eventually attack a priest onstage) envisioned drama as anti-capitalist, invoking Marx (as does Yeats in his preface for *The Well*) when he writes that 'in literature...there is no division of labour'.[68] Synge also takes the opportunity in this draft to distinguish the moral world of the theatre from the wider world in which the theatre is situated. The first draft of the preface begins by defining his drama in opposition to the Decadent movement ('in these days the play-house is too often stocked with the drugs of many seedy problems, or with the Absinthe and vermouth of the last musical comedy') and defines the seriousness of literature not in its treatment of 'problems that are serious in themselves' but 'by the degree in which it gives the material, the nourishment, not very easy to define, on which our imaginations live'.[69] In the second draft, Synge continues this train of thought, and concludes, 'That is to say literature is necessary—all arts are necessary—yet they have nothing to do with rules of behaviour and the problems that are connected with the details of life.'[70] What is most important in Synge's vision of drama, therefore, is its imaginative qualities, its ability to promote humour and sustain a high level of mental activity.[71] These prefaces argue for the inherent irreverence of the theatre with regard to social and moral codes (in fact, Synge goes as far as to suggest that the theatre is amoral), and both promote personal, vibrant activity and language as an antidote to the 'seedy' problems of modern life and capitalist 'tyranny' and impersonality. However, *The Well of the Saints* does not simply reject capitalist modernity in its formal and linguistic structures; in fact, the action of the play, and the dynamics established between its principal characters, are designed to emphasize a general resistance in Revivalist theatre to the social, religious, and economic norms associated with anglicization and capitalist modernity.

When the scene opens on the play's second act, after the first cure has been performed, the audience are met with the hellish sound of beating hammers in Timmy's forge, and the despondent Martin Doul who has been forced to work there. This dehumanized man, abused as a 'lazy, basking fool' (*CW* II, 103) by a tyrannical employer renowned for his cruelty, is hardly what we might have expected after the Saint's talk of glorious miracles and blessings in Act I. Martin's unsuccessful integration into the world of work serves a plot function in that it makes him reconsider his sight, and his relationship with Mary; however, it is also indicative of other failed

---

[68] TCD MS 4336, f. 1. Yeats quotes Marx's *Capital* in his preface (*CW* III, 66).

[69] TCD MS 4336, f. ii.   [70] TCD MS 4336, f. iv.

[71] See TCD MS 4336, f. iv: 'wherever a country loses its humour as Ireland is doing, there will be morbidity of mind, as Baudelaire's mind was morbid, and many people going into the Asylums.'

conversions in the play. In an early draft, Synge has Martin complain to Timmy that 'I'm destroyed with the queer job they're after giving and I all the morning inside sweating and sneezing in the forge' (*CW* II, 108). Although the origin of the job is never explained, it is clear that it has been 'given' to Martin against his will, and that the requirement that he works 'all the morning inside' is contrary to the rapturous vision of nature in the Douls' earlier and later speeches. As in Synge's depiction of the relief workers in his articles 'From the Congested Districts' (discussed in the following chapter), degradation is seen to ensue from the imposition of an unnatural life on the 'natural' peasantry. The world of the forge establishes the degradation of forced labour and attempts at integrating nonconforming populations into capitalist modernity and social orthodoxy, and this is pitted at each point against the nature worship of the blind people and their psychic connection to the earth and its moods. Martin and Mary Doul oppose the Saint and the results of his 'cure' in the same way that Ossian opposes St Patrick, and their humour opposes the Saint in the same way that Rabelais's opposes Thomas à Kempis.

In the final act, after the Douls are reunited in their blindness, they return to a rapturous state of nature worship. The staging for the original production of *The Well of the Saints* was described as being made of 'flat cloths and faint tints [that] suggested surprising semblances of rugged lands and sombre skies'.[72] It was thus in line with Yeats's vision of a dramatic scenery which was not harnessed to reality but 'needed some imagination, some gift for day-dreams' in the audience.[73] Designed by Pamela Colman Smith, editor and illustrator of the esoteric literary magazine *The Green Sheaf* (where Synge's 'Dream of Inishmaan' was first published), and later designer of the famous Rider-Waite tarot deck, the set would undoubtedly have carried the implications of a spiritually inclined peasantry, in keeping with the Douls' harmony with the natural world.[74] In the final act, however, the blind people's rapture is soon undercut by a noise in the distance:

[72] L. J. M'Quilland, from *The Belfast Evening Standard*. Quoted in Hogan and Kilroy, eds., *The Abbey Theatre: The Years of Synge*, p. 21.

[73] W. B. Yeats, 'The Theatre' (1899–1900), in *Essays and Introductions*, 165–72, p. 169.

[74] Colman Smith provided illustrations for a number of occult publications, was a member of the Golden Dawn since 1901, and had designed the sets for an unrealized New York production of *The Countess Cathleen* and for the unproduced *Where there is Nothing*. See Joan Coldwell, 'Pamela Colman Smith and the Yeats Family', *The Canadian Journal of Irish Studies*, Vol. 3, No. 2 (November 1977), 27–34, pp. 28–9.

MARTIN DOUL   What's that is sounding in the west?

[A faint sound of a bell is heard.]

MARY DOUL   It's not the churches, for the wind's blowing from the sea.

MARTIN DOUL [*with dismay*].   It's the old saint, I'm thinking, ringing his bell.

MARY DOUL   The Lord protect us from the saints of God! [*They listen.*] He's coming this road, surely. (*CW* III, 131–3)

The crux of Synge's satire is reached in that final inversion, in which what he might term the 'inorganic morality' of the Saint is pitted against the 'organic morality' of the Lord.[75] Religion, in this way, is split into two forms: the organized and the organic. The sound of the Saint's bell jarringly cuts across the Douls' rhapsodic appreciation of the natural world. Nature and the Saint, in this way, are opposing entities. When the two begin to panic about the Saint's arrival, Mary suggests that Martin would 'have a right to speak a big terrible word' to interrupt the 'miracle' of the cure, but Martin asks, 'What way would I find a big terrible word, and I shook with the fear, and if I did itself, who'd know rightly if it's good words or bad would save us this day from himself?' (*CW* III, 135). By this point, the Douls can no longer trust whether the Saint is benevolent or otherwise, and so cannot decide whether a curse or a prayer would protect them against him. The ironic thrust of Synge's work has led to a position from which the distinction between the 'good works' of the Church and the evildoing of the devil has become impossible to determine.

The drive towards the assertion of individual imaginative integrity and freedom in Act III stems from this recognition on behalf of the Douls of their difference from the community not solely in terms of their blindness and occupation but also in terms of their right to remain unintegrated. In the final act, the blind people stand before the Saint, Synge stipulates, with 'piteous hang-dog dejection' (*CW* III, 137). The same phrase is later used to describe the despondency of a band of relief workers which Synge and Jack Yeats encounter in Connemara. The relief workers, forced into labour and watched by a 'swaggering' ganger, present yet another image of cultural interface in Synge's oeuvre in which the peasantry is denatured by the

---

[75] See TCD MS 4384, f. 66v.

imposition of capitalist modernity: 'every man and woman was working with a sort of hang-dog dejection that would be enough to make any casual passer mistake them for a band of convicts' (*CW* II, 296). As in 'Among the Relief Works', in which this image of the degraded peasant is contrasted with the happiness of those engaged in the more 'natural' work of kelp gathering, so in *The Well of the Saints* the intervention of the Saint is contrasted with the joy of the Douls in their own imaginative world. The dramatic development of Synge's vision of the peasantry in *The Well of the Saints* prepared him for his encounter with the effects of modernization and distress on the real-life peasantry in the Congested Districts just a few months later, and his subsequent portrayal of life on the western seaboard is inflected with his own literary artifices. By the time he wrote *The Playboy of the Western World* (1907), the scaffold of the dialectic had begun to be dismantled in favour of a more unharnessed Rabelaisianism. The figure of Father Reilly never appears on stage, and his authority is only felt through the priest-fearing and wimpish Shaun Keogh.

Over many years, Synge established a spiritual basis for his aesthetic, countering asceticism with pantheism, restriction with Rabelaisian excess. The various iterations of this conflict can be traced over numerous dialogues, scenarios, and plays in his oeuvre, and this dialectical structure became subsumed into a larger literary vision of nonconformity and multidirectional irony. In turn, Synge's spiritual and aesthetic opposition to ascetic or conforming figures began to influence his understanding of political and social change in contemporary Ireland. By mid-1905, when he arrived in the Congested Districts on commission with Jack B. Yeats for *The Manchester Guardian*, his vision of a modernizing society was already primed by years of aesthetic theorization and practice.

5

'From the Congested Districts'

The Crow and the Golf Ball

While travelling in the Congested Districts of Mayo and Connemara with Jack Yeats in early summer 1905, on commission for *The Manchester Guardian*, Synge wrote a short vignette which he later added to the fourth part of his as-yet-unpublished prose narrative, *The Aran Islands*. Synge's book underwent continuous revision until its publication in 1907 and was eventually picked up by George Roberts, managing director of the newly established Maunsel & Co., who had originally contacted Synge to seek permission to collect the *Manchester Guardian* articles into a book.[1] The vignette in question takes the form of an inserted 'set piece', situated directly between two translations of Irish poetry, and relates two incidents connected on a theme, revealing the effects of the *Manchester Guardian* commission in confirming Synge's oppositions to modernization in the west of Ireland and in prompting an increasing irony towards his earlier Romanticism. He writes:

> This morning, when I had been lying for a long time on a rock near the sea watching some hooded crows that were dropping shellfish on the rocks to break them, I saw one bird that had a large white object which it was dropping continually without any result. I got some stones and tried to drive it off when the thing had fallen, but several times the bird was too quick for me and made off with it before I could get down to him. At last, however, I dropped a stone almost on top of him and he flew away. I clambered down hastily, and found to my amazement a worn golf-ball! No doubt it had been brought out some way or other from the links in County Clare, which are not far off, and the bird had been trying half the morning to break it.

---

[1] Ann Saddlemyer, 'More Letters by John Millington Synge', *Irish University Review*, Vol. 45, No. 1 (Spring/Summer 2015), 25–30, p. 27.

J. M. Synge: Nature, Politics, Modernism. Seán Hewitt, Oxford University Press (2021). © Seán Hewitt.
DOI: 10.1093/oso/9780198862093.003.0006

Further on I had a long talk with a young man who is inquisitive about modern life, and I explained to him an elaborate trick or corner on the Stock Exchange that I heard of lately. When I got him to understand it fully, he shouted with delight and amusement.

'Well,' he said, when he was quiet again, 'isn't it a great wonder to think that those rich men are as big rogues as ourselves.'[2]

Ann Saddlemyer has identified just two 'set pieces' within Synge's prose works, in which the narrator draws heightened attention to his ability to process and experience an exceptional moment. Saddlemyer identifies the 'Dream of Inishmaan' from *The Aran Islands* and the experience recounted in Synge's 'Autobiography' of having a vision of two huge eyes in a Wicklow hillside as 'set pieces', but does not note the passage quoted above.[3] Saddlemyer's 'set pieces' were discussed in Chapter 1 as revealing and self-conscious moments in Synge's works that appear to act as a commentary on the narrator's own position within the text; however, the above passage is the most clearly self-aware of the three, and serves to add an ironic gloss to the rest of the narrative.

The above anecdote relates, broadly speaking, two 'tricks': one played on the author and crow, and the other played at one of the key symbols of international capitalism—the stock exchange. It is unlikely that either of the two incidents are true to life, since both were first written down by Synge years after his final trip to the Aran Islands and seem to have been prompted by his researches in the Congested Districts. Instead, the passage is a construct designed to give a pause for reflection, situated at the end of *The Aran Islands* as a sort of ironic authorial commentary on the book. Karen Vandevelde notes this passage as evidence that Synge 'acknowledges the confrontation between traditional Ireland on the one hand, and progress and prosperity on the other'; however, the inferences of such a suggestion are never extended: 'such references to progress and modernity occur in Synge's letters, prose, and manuscript drafts of plays, but not in the final versions of his dramas.'[4] Of course, as this book has already demonstrated,

[2] *CW* II, p. 175. Original found in TCD MS 4397, ff. 7r–v.
[3] Ann Saddlemyer, 'Synge and the Doors of Perception', p. 100.
[4] Karen Vandevelde, '"What's All the Stir about?": Gerald MacNamara, Synge, and the Early Abbey Theatre', *New Hibernia Review/Iris Éireannach Nua*, Vol. 10, No. 3 (Autumn 2006), 108–21, pp. 118–19.

Synge's exploration of 'progress and modernity' was more deeply interwoven into his works than this observation might suggest.

The shellfish that the crow has been trying to crack, and which turns out to be a golf ball, is an apt metaphor for the frustrating process of trying to access a 'primitive' culture that is being modernized, an idealized west of Ireland that is not quite as it appears. It relates, through Synge's association of the natural and spiritual, to the increasing difficulty of accessing the sublime (detailed in Chapters 1 and 2). Modernity creates a literal blockage in the natural processes of Inishmaan: the golf ball is the symbol of the disruption that occurs where the intractable, standardized modern object intrudes on the 'natural' or 'primitive' world. It is thus an explicit example of the 'tyranny of impersonal things' represented in *Riders to the Sea* by the mass-produced material of Michael's stocking or the 'foreign' development in the Congested Districts. The 'links in County Clare' is most probably Lahinch Golf Club, established in 1892 by a group of British army officers. Just as with the proposed golf links in Shaw's *John Bull's Other Island* (1904), Synge's reference to this development represents a new phase of modernity in Ireland as a mixture of touristic, capitalist, and imperialist pressures.[5] This phase, in Synge's context, is contentious in that it requires the standardized to be subsumed into the non-standardized, the unnatural into the natural. If, as discussed in Chapter 1, the flora and fauna of Aran represent for Synge an artisanal, unique landscape which opposes encroaching capitalism, then the golf ball, as a 'common' object, becomes the symbol of a modernity which is invasive and which jars the traditional, 'primitive', and natural processes of the island community.

The second 'trick' related in this passage, however, depicts not a blockage but a potential continuity. In both, the ability of people to intercept and manipulate natural processes is implicit, as though the 'tricks' were magical as well as ironical. The ironic, mischievous humour of the 'young man who is inquisitive about modern life' finds a correlative in the activity of the brokers at the stock exchange. Whereas the golf ball disrupts the natural world, which Synge has strongly associated with spiritualism, the 'primitive', and the Rabelaisian humour of the peasantry, the financial trickery of the brokers suggests a modernity into which the valuable qualities of the islanders might be accommodated. In fact, this trick raises two distinct levels of

---

[5] George Bernard Shaw, *John Bull's Other Island* (Harmondsworth: Penguin, 1984), pp. 152, 161.

irony: one which is metatextual, and the other which serves to reinforce Synge's ideal of the ironic humour of the peasantry.

What Synge shows us, in the inclusion of these two 'tricks', is the possibility for the communities in the Congested Districts to adapt to the strictures of capitalist modernity. In the scene with the golf ball, modernity causes a definite blockage in the natural process: it is represented by the uncrackable shellfish, the source of life and nourishment closed off by modern capitalist tourism, something monied, leisurely, commodified, and standardized taking the place of the original and natural object. In the second trick, the roguery of the islander is mirrored in the roguery of the broker, giving the potential of continuity, a sense of the potential of 'survival' through the modernization process, a potential for manipulating capital and commodity with humour and wit. Here, Synge's two related incidents plot the temporal, historical, and social implications of modernization; the confusion of organic and enforced progress; the confusion of the organic and the manufactured; and the ideal of a linear, evolutionary progression into modernity against a less reductive conception of multiple possible futures and pasts. In turn, this process of manuscript revision of earlier works leads to a growing ironization of any attempt to read the prose works as Romantic or atavistic depictions of a pre-modern Ireland. The social commentary of 'From the Congested Districts' is both the later expression of Synge's views on modernization and a platform from which these implicit views take on a more solid state. The social and economic upheavals taking place in the Congested Districts, where systematic modernization is most clearly evident, show just how deeply Synge's literary output is rooted in a reaction to contemporary Irish life, and how intertwined his social commentary is with the increasingly modernist temperament of his drama. These readings reflect the underlying tensions arising in Synge's *Manchester Guardian* articles, in which the author heavily critiques forms of modernization which he sees as unnatural, and attempts to suggest ways in which more organic progress might be achieved. During these travels, Synge's aesthetic concerns began to solidify into a more certain and explicit political viewpoint. This led to both a forward- and backward-looking progression in his oeuvre: he began to revise earlier works to 'update' them in line with a new, more modernist edge, and he started to theorize more openly that ironic humour could act as a form of political protest against what he perceived as the demoralizing effects of capitalist modernity as encouraged by the measures of the Congested Districts Board for Ireland (CDB).

The CDB was established in 1891 as part of the British government's 'constructive unionist' policy. Through 'a combination of coercive and conciliatory measures', the Board attempted to provide infrastructural improvements to the rural Irish economy to make the population more self-sufficient.[6] Active on the Aran Islands during the time of Synge's visits, the Board had been on his radar since early in his writing career as an agent of often undesirable change. *The Aran Islands* even opens with a thinly veiled attack on CDB improvements to Kilronan, which had been left with 'very little to distinguish it from any fishing village on the west coast of Ireland' (*CW* II, 47).[7] Though the Board was part of a more general trend in the late nineteenth century from the relief of local crises to a more structured emphasis on development, its efficacy has been questioned by historians.[8] Joseph Lee, for example, has argued that the CDB 'made little contribution to the modernization of Irish society', in part because it focused on supporting 'uneconomic work'.[9] However, as Janice Helland has shown, the Board's support for 'traditional' crafts such as needlework, lacemaking, and other industries predominantly engaging women workers was lucrative, and the profits were returned to the makers through a notable absence of middlemen, forming a network of 'fair trade' between western communities and international fashion markets.[10] However, as contemporary sources make clear, changes in fashion towards Irish homespuns were presented as a form of constructive unionism: the improvement of the 'cottage industries' being 'of infinitely more practical benefit to Irish peasants than HOME RULE'.[11]

---

[6] Ciara Breathnach, *The Congested Districts Board of Ireland, 1891–1923: Poverty and Development in the West of Ireland* (Dublin and Portland, OR: Four Courts Press, 2005), p. 11.

[7] The homogenizing effects of CDB improvement schemes are also emphasized in Robin Flower's travel narrative *The Western Island*, in which the process of removing the traditional 'rundale' system of farming on the islands, and replacing it with 'convenient blocks of arable and pasture', is seen as particularly traumatic, disrupting the people's knowledge of the land. See *The Western Island, or The Great Blasket*, with illustrations by Ida M. Flower (Oxford: Oxford University Press, 1978), pp. 37–8.

[8] For an analysis for this transition towards a developmental approach in the west of Ireland, see Carla King, '"Our Destitute Countrymen on the Western Coast": Relief and Development Strategies in the Congested Districts in the 1880s and 90s', in Carla King and Conor McNamara, eds., *The West of Ireland: New Perspectives on the Nineteenth Century* (Dublin: History Press, 2011), 161–84.

[9] Joseph Lee, *The Modernisation of Irish Society, 1848–1918* (Dublin: Gill & Macmillan, 1973), pp. 129, 124.

[10] See Janice Helland, '"Caprices of Fashion": Handmade Lace in Ireland, 1883–1907', *Textile History*, Vol. 39, No. 2 (2008), 193–222, p. 195.

[11] From an advertisement in the magazine *Gentlewoman*, 30 January 1897, quoted in Janice Helland, '"A Delightful Change of Fashion": Fair Trade, Cottage Craft, and Tweed in Late

Frederick Aalen has suggested that the reforming nature of constructive unionism made it a political Janus, both progressive and conservative: 'Reforms in Ireland were intended to make a relatively underdeveloped country more capable of laissez-faire; to present an attractive capitalist alternative to socialistic solutions and ultimately to strengthen individual enterprise and responsibility and the interests of property and the empire.'[12] Or, as Shaw's Englishman, Broadbent, puts it in *John Bull's Other Island*, the general aim was to 'take Ireland in hand, and by straightforward business habits, teach it efficiency and self-help on sound Liberal principles'.[13]

Because conditions in the west of Ireland were deeply politicized, nationalists faced repeated claims of exaggeration, and Unionists were met with accusations that they were downplaying the severity of distress.[14] However, due to the Revival's cult of the peasant, a matrix of artistic concerns were also entangled in the modernization projects in the districts. A contested literature arose out of the ongoing controversies regarding the distress in the Congested Districts, with reporters, political figures, and philanthropists all adding to the increasing mass of conflicting voices.[15] In 1905, C. P. Scott, editor of the liberal *Manchester Guardian*, wrote to Synge to request that he add his voice to the growing literature of the Congested Districts. At Scott's suggestion, Synge met with the nationalist politician John Muldoon, who offered to introduce him to a number of individuals who might help him in his reportage.[16] Writing to Scott after the meeting, Synge asked that he be allowed to 'work on the problem independently, rather than from the point

---

Nineteenth-Century Ireland', *The Canadian Journal of Irish Studies*, Vol. 36, No. 2 (Fall 2010), 34–55, p. 40.

[12] Frederick H. A. Aalen, 'Constructive Unionism and the Shaping of Rural Ireland, c. 1880–1921', *Rural History*, Vol. 4, No. 2 (October 1993), 137–64, pp. 138–9.

[13] Shaw, *John Bull's Other Island*, p. 158.

[14] Breathnach, *The Congested Districts Board*, p. 27.

[15] See, for example, James Hack Tuke, *The Condition of Donegal: Letters, with further suggestions for the improvement and development of the Congested Districts of Ireland and promotion of light railways, fisheries, etc.* (London: W.R. Ridgeway, 1889); Robert John Buckley, *Ireland as it is and as it would be under Home Rule: Sixty-Two Letters Written by the Special Commissioner of the Birmingham Daily Gazette Between March and August, 1893* (Birmingham, Birmingham Daily Gazette Company, 1893); Special Commissioner of the *Daily Express, Mr Balfour's Tours in Connemara and Donegal* (Dublin: *Dublin Daily Express*, 1890).

[16] Synge's articles show a significant knowledge of contemporary political writings on the Congested Districts. It is possible that these were suggested to him, or even supplied to him, by Muldoon. The works with which Synge was familiar were, at any rate, not all popular publications.

of view of the strictly orthodox nationalist.'[17] Scott agreed to this and suggested that Synge 'give the reader a sympathetic understanding of the people and the way their life is lived and let the political lesson emerge out of that'.[18] Either way, Synge still felt the confines of the commission, and his articles for *The Manchester Guardian* differ significantly in style, tone, and interest from his Wicklow and West Kerry essays. As he wrote to Stephen MacKenna, 'Unluckily my commission was to write on the "Distress" so I couldn't do any thing like what I would have wished to do as an interpretation of the whole life.'[19]

As Synge noted in a letter to his mother, the commission was demanding: 'it is ... not very easy here to rake up fresh matters for an article every second day.'[20] The difficulty of adding something new to a subject about which 'so much that is contradictory has been spoken and written' (*CW* II, 283) means that, for the most part, Synge does not suggest much that is original regarding practical schemes of improvement. Synge's experience in the Congested Districts is inflected by his socialism, and thus the aesthetic lessons he draws from his visits are rooted in a socialistic vision of a modernizing Ireland and are an extension of those elaborated in *The Well of the Saints*. In his *Manchester Guardian* essays, which have been somewhat overlooked in criticism, and which were dismissed by W. B. Yeats as 'something to be wished away' (perhaps because they disproved Yeats's vision of Synge as a man 'unfit to think a political thought'), the author is revealed as a man deeply engaged in contemporary political currents, and as an artist for whom the aesthetic is inextricable from the social.[21] Although these articles have been acknowledged as evidence of Synge's 'capacity for incisive social comment', showing him to be 'an acute commentator on social change', their importance for Synge's artistic philosophy has

---

[17] J. M. Synge to C. P. Scott, 23 May 1905. John Rylands Library, Manchester, MS GDN126/65.

[18] C. P. Scott to J. M. Synge, 26 May 1905. John Rylands Library, Manchester, MS GDN126/66. This degree of independence given to Synge by Scott was typical of the latter's dealing with his special correspondents. For example, when Scott commissioned J. B. Atkins to act as special correspondent for the Boer War, 'Atkins told him that his views on the War were not in complete agreement with those of the paper, but Scott replied that he trusted him to act as a truthful observer and that this was the quality he looked for in a correspondent.' J. L. Hammond, *C.P. Scott of the Manchester Guardian* (London: G. Bell & Sons, 1934), p. 53.

[19] J. M. Synge to Stephen MacKenna, 13 July 1905. *CL* I, p. 116.

[20] J. M. Synge to Kathleen Synge, 24 June 1905. *CL* I, p. 114.

[21] Nicholas Grene, 'Introduction', J. M. Synge, *Travelling Ireland: Essays 1898–1908* (Dublin: Lilliput Press, 2009), p. xiii; Yeats, *Essays and Introductions*, p. 319.

remained unexamined.[22] His earlier development of an aesthetic based on a strong association between the Irish peasantry and nature means that certain schemes of modernization are perceived as both a social and an aesthetic threat to an ideal Ireland. Throughout his articles 'From the Congested Districts', Synge draws on, and is susceptible to, wider political currents; however, his originality remains at this stage aesthetic, not political.

The socialism of William Morris, in which both Synge and Yeats held faith, emphasized the power of nature to oppose industrialism and commercialism. Taking inspiration from Thomas Carlyle's *Past and Present* (1843) (which Synge himself read in 1895, experiencing 'a sort of mystical ecstasy' (*CW* II, 12), alongside the Romantic poets and Ruskin's *Stones of Venice* (1851–3)), Morris advocated an aesthetic socialism in which all art must be based in nature.[23] As Alun Howkins notes, central to the myth of the ideal rural life was the idea of a 'natural' or 'organic' social order and society.[24] Importantly, Morris's sense of aesthetic value rests on the proximity of a piece of art to nature and natural forms. For him, each piece of art 'must be either beautiful or ugly; beautiful if it is in accord with Nature, and helps her; ugly if it is discordant with Nature, and thwarts her'.[25] This assessment of value is replicated by Synge throughout his oeuvre, and is particularly challenged by his experience in the Congested Districts. In *Socialism: Its Growth and Outcome* (1893), which Synge read and made notes on in 1895, Morris and E. Belfort Bax extend this measure of aesthetic value to problems of social degeneration: at periods when there is a 'rottenness of society', art suffers a 'degradation'. As capitalism spreads, the work of art becomes increasingly commodified, so that eventually 'the fine arts' are 'mere[ly] expensive and pretentious though carefully-finished upholstery'.[26] In turn, humanity itself is degraded, reflecting the compromised position of the arts. This theory is suggested by Morris and Belfort Bax in order to establish a defence of utopian communism (in chapter 17 of *Socialism*) and

---

[22] Elaine Sisson, '*The Aran Islands* and the travel essays', in Mathews, ed., *The Cambridge Companion to J. M. Synge*, 52–63, p. 57; McCormack, *Fool of the Family*, p. 23.

[23] Synge notes his reading for 1895 in TCD MS 4416. He also read a selection of Carlyle's essays and *The French Revolution* (1837), reading at least one of Carlyle's works each year between 1892 and 1895. See TCD MSS 4413–6.

[24] Alun Howkins, *Reshaping rural England: a social history, 1850–1925* (London: Routledge, 1991), p. 231.

[25] William Morris, 'The Lesser Arts', in *The Political Writings of William Morris*, 31–56, p. 33.

[26] William Morris and E. Belfort Bax, *Socialism: Its Growth and Outcome* (London: Swan Sonnenschein, 1893), pp. 131–2.

an affirmation of the ideal place of the arts within society.[27] Deploying ideas from social Darwinism, emphasis is placed on the theory that 'man is the creature of his surroundings, and that by diligent attention to the development of his nature he can be brought to perfection'.[28] As in his Wicklow essays, Synge pays particular attention to these discourses, noting in his journal that 'Human nature is itself a growth of the ages, and is ever and indefinitely moulded by the conditions under which it finds itself.'[29] A similar explanation is given by Morris and Belfort Bax for the possibility of human improvement as exemplified in the communes of Robert Owen, Saint-Simon, and Charles Fourier, and thus it carries the weight of a discourse which suggests that humanity can be consciously moulded towards 'perfection'.[30] This is key to Synge's notion that the disruption of a perceivably natural or organic society by governmental modernization constituted an aesthetic as well as a political threat.

The mystical attractiveness of such theories to Synge demonstrates the close interlinking of his three principal concerns: socialism, nature, and spiritual experience. He was by no means alone, however, in his linking of proximity to nature and the potential for mystical experience: both Yeats and AE saw in the Irish peasantry a recoverable link to the natural which would enable a connection with a visionary world in keeping with the writers' theosophical pursuits.[31] The association of socialism with nature became integral to many contemporary British and Irish political writings so that, theoretically at least, a reinstatement or preservation of nature could be used to counteract the forces of industrialism and capitalism. For many of Synge's contemporaries, the disappearance of 'nature' from social and political structures was seen as the key contributing factor to a confused and disorientating modern world.[32] Following on from this, nature, variously conceived, could function as a logical anchor in a social climate in which the direction of progress had become increasingly difficult to discern.

Modernity is seen by Synge, as by his fellow Revivalists, as having brought with it a spiritual disruption which must be repaired. As Roy Foster notes,

---

[27] Morris and Belfort Bax, *Socialism*, pp. 307–11.
[28] Morris and Belfort Bax, *Socialism*, p. 208.   [29] TCD MS 4379, f. 65r.
[30] Morris and Belfort Bax, *Socialism*, pp. 206–17, especially p. 208.
[31] See Leeann Lane, '"There are compensations in the congested districts for their poverty": AE and the idealized peasant of the agricultural co-operative movement', in Betsey Taylor FitzSimon and James H. Murphy, eds., *The Irish Revival Reappraised* (Dublin: Four Courts Press, 2004), 33–48, pp. 45–6.
[32] See particularly John Eglinton's *Some Essays and Passages*, selected by W. B. Yeats (Dundrum: Dun Emer Press, 1905), pp. 23–30.

Morris's emphasis on bringing art into everyday life was an attempt to do just this. As with Synge himself, Yeats and others turned to 'love of the Unseen life, love of country' in order to reinstate the spirituality supposedly inherent to the Irish.[33] Yeats would use this Morrisian rejection of the modern debasement of the arts in order to argue implicitly for an elite culture, 'a return to the essential aristocracy of folk tradition', though, for a short time, he adopted Morrisian communism.[34] Like Synge, Yeats encountered at the turn of the century not only Morris's works on utopianism and communes but also writings concerning other communist experiments, many of which were explicitly or implicitly concerned with ideas of spiritual and scientific 'race improvement'. The influence of these experiments, which caught Yeats's eye for their potential to demonstrate a potential pathway towards the repair of modern spiritual dislocation, are also evident in Synge's reactions to the schemes of livestock improvement in the Congested Districts and his understanding of the effects of the political, social, and natural environment on racial degeneration. During his reading in the 1890s, Synge encountered, through Morris, the histories of various utopian communes, and made notes on Marx and Engels's *Communist Manifesto* (1848).[35] Of particular interest, no doubt, were Robert Owen's 1823 plans for communistic villages as a remedy for Irish distress, which Morris and Belfort Bax refer to in their *Socialism*.[36] However, the notion of moral development in communes as a way of improving mankind, seen as paramount to the future of the Congested Districts by AE, and referred to often by Morris, Owen, and Yeats, was a less attractive concept for Synge. As we have seen, Synge did not subscribe to a pious moral vision of the peasantry, nor did he favour the conversion of an economically underprivileged people into 'a happy, industrious, and orderly community'.[37] Synge's paternalistic protection of the peasantry focused on their right to remain 'natural', by which he meant that they subscribed to an 'organic morality', and that their modes of industry were communal and often contentious in the environment of a standardizing capitalism. This background of socialist schemes for the improvement of the working classes and peasantry in the nineteenth century was taken up by Yeats and Synge through Morris. For Yeats, as Donald Childs has shown, Allan Estlake's *The Oneida Community* (1900), in which the author detailed the establishment and practices of John

---

[33] Foster, *W. B. Yeats: A Life*, I, p. 254.   [34] Foster, *W. B. Yeats: A Life*, I, pp. 64, 307.
[35] See TCD MS 4379.   [36] Morris and Belfort Bax, *Socialism*, p. 209.
[37] Morris and Belfort Bax, *Socialism*, p. 209.

Humphrey Noyes's Oneida Community in New York, acted as a catalyst for 'an early interest in eugenics that is in some ways as coherent and comprehensive as the well-documented later interest'.[38] Though, as Childs suggests, this interest took its tenets from experiments in racial improvement, it was also subsumed into the larger Yeatsian quest for a 'church' of art, and finds its way into his plays of the early 1900s through a focus on the ability of art to promote spiritual and biological regeneration. It is in this form that we also find these concerns replicated in Synge's articles 'From the Congested Districts' and later, in elaborate ways, in *The Playboy of the Western World*. Rather than being merely an Anglo-Irish aesthete traveller in the districts— what Nicholas Grene refers to as a 'dilettante in search of the picturesque', or what Christy Mahon in a draft of *Playboy* calls a 'tweedy suited poet'—Synge offered a keen critique of the practices of the CDB which condenses many contemporary concerns and has significant implications for our understanding of his own philosophy.[39]

As evolutionary theory was applied to sociology by contemporary thinkers such as Herbert Spencer, T. H. Huxley, Edward Caird, and Isaac Taylor, natural metaphors for social development became increasingly common.[40] The question of how a society should evolve while remaining true to natural law became fundamental to contemporary social commentators and political theorists, though the application of evolutionary biology to sociology entailed varying degrees of logical separation. In the works of Herbert Spencer, which Synge read extensively, and in sociologist Edward Caird's *Individualism and Socialism* (1897), read by Synge in its year of publication, the theory of evolution is applied to changes in socio-economic structures in order to plot the potential of 'reconciliation' between opposing world views.[41] For Caird, the application of evolutionary theory suggests that a society will become more 'natural' through the division of labour and increasing individualism within a cooperative social framework.[42]

---

[38] Donald J. Childs, *Modernism and Eugenics: Woolf, Eliot, Yeats, and the Culture of Degeneration* (Cambridge: Cambridge University Press, 2001), p. 186.

[39] Grene, *Synge: A Critical Study of the Plays*, p. 18; TCD MS 4331–3, f. 823.

[40] Synge read each of these prominent writers. See TCD MSS 4379 (Spencer), 4393 (Huxley), 4414 (Taylor), 4418 (Caird).

[41] See TCD MS 4418.

[42] See Edward Caird, *Individualism and Socialism*, especially p. 20, where Caird uses Spencer's theory of evolution to suggest that the division of labour and subsequent cooperation is a natural progression. Synge himself drew particular attention to Spencer's 'formula of evolution', noting it down in his notebook: 'Formula of evolution = Evol is an interpretation of matter and concomitant dissipation of motion, during which the matter ~~become~~ passes from

Caird emphasized that he was dealing with a 'modern Socialism' which allowed for individuality within a socialist framework (a particularly Syngean ideal), and saw the individual and society as being essentially reconcilable. Morris and Belfort Bax's ideal of a new moral consciousness, which would be 'in a sense a return on a higher level to the ethics of the older world', was one in which socialism would enact a complete unity between the individual and society, so that 'the identification of individual with social interests will be so complete that any divorce between the two will be inconceivable to the average man'.[43] Benjamin Kidd's *Social Evolution* (1894), on the other hand, which Synge read in 1895, launched a critique of such ideas, arguing that the social organism and the individual are innately antagonistic.[44] For Kidd, if evolution results in the ever-increasing capacity of the individual, and the demands of the social organism are ever increasing, the two can never be reconciled. Kidd's solution was that the state should use its power to lift individuals out of Darwinian competition, thus liberating them. If progress can only be achieved by man going against his social instinct, then the conditions of progress must be altered in order to retain 'nature' in human society.[45] During the first years of the twentieth century, a prevalence of similar concerns was repeated in the Irish context, most notably in the works of John Eglinton (pseudonym of W. K. Magee) and in the Revivalist magazine *Dana* (1904–5), which he edited alongside the playwright Fred Ryan.[46] Eglinton's writings employ a language and theory much in keeping with that of Spencer, Caird, and Kidd, emphasizing explicitly the importance of preserving 'nature' in the social fabric, for when 'nature is no longer in it ... endless disintegration is its portion'.[47]

an indefinite, incoherent homogeneity to a definite choherent heterogeneity; and during which the retained motion undergoes a parallel transformation.' TCD MS 4379 f. 92.

[43] Morris and Belfort Bax, *Socialism*, p. 298. [44] See TCD MS 4416.

[45] See Kidd, *Social Evolution*, pp. 79–82.

[46] Although scholars remain undecided about Synge's reaction to *Dana*, he did make notes on the journal and seems to have engaged positively with many of the debates therein. See TCD MS 4393, ff. 33r–v. In fact, as W. J. McCormack has noted, Synge's own politics seem to be gauged between those of the magazine's editors: 'Synge held very decided political views, sharpened by his tours of the west with Jack Yeats in June 1905; they meet [Fred] Ryan's in a detestation of middle-class greed, ... Magee's in a complicated anxiety about modernity.' *Fool of the Family*, p. 266. See also J. M. Synge to Stephen MacKenna, 19 June 1904, *CL* I, p. 88; Terry Eagleton, *Crazy John and the Bishop and Other Essays on Irish Culture* (Cork: Cork University Press, 1998), pp. 249–72; C. H. Houghton, 'John Synge as I Knew Him', in Mikhail, ed., *J. M. Synge: Interviews and Recollections*, 3–7, p. 6.

[47] Eglinton, *Some Essays and Passages*, pp. 28–9.

The articulation of a denatured modernity, and of a persistent tension between individual freedom and centralized economic and political structures, is prominent throughout the sociological works which Synge read. Synge's own views on modernization reveal an anxiety regarding the place of nature in a changing world, though he supplements contemporary socialism with his own theory of a 'primitive', spiritualized connection to nature. Not only is the place of nature important in the aesthetics of Revivalism, but it is also key to an analysis of social change which opposes capitalist standardization. In Synge's *Manchester Guardian* articles, these interlinked concerns are equally at play, and eventually culminate in the theorization of a more certain aesthetic and political stance. The aesthetic and spiritual importance of the natural world is asserted as fundamental to the 'primitive' health and tradition of the peasantry, and the relationship between individuality and state-imposed modernization is used to emphasize both the importance of ironic humour (which is a sign of implicit protest and inveteracy) and traditional life (which is non-standard and close to nature) in opposing systematic schemes of 'improvement'. Furthermore, turn-of-the-century concerns with degeneration are evident in Synge's own anxieties about the evolutionary process and the introduction of the 'foreign' into the Congested Districts. The Revival's focus on racial rejuvenation is replicated in Synge's essays through a complicated dilemma between the urges to preserve and to improve. Not comfortable with asserting a Yeatsian 'dream of the noble and the beggar-man', Synge makes political and aesthetic compromises to accept improvements in living standards which would ordinarily run counter to his fetishization of the natural.[48]

Again, Synge's early writings and notebooks provide important insights into the philosophy of nature and morality which his later works elucidate more fully. In his 'Autobiography', Synge establishes something close to what Robert Goodin has termed a 'green theory of value', whereby the degree to which a natural entity has been altered by humanity determines its depreciation of 'value'.[49] As Kate Soper notes, 'Ecological writing . . . very frequently works implicitly with an idea of nature as a kind of pristine otherness to human culture, whose value is depreciated proportionately to

---

[48] Writing of himself, Lady Gregory, and Synge in his poem 'The Municipal Gallery Revisited', Yeats wrote that 'We three alone in modern times had brought / Everything down to that sole test again, / Dream of the noble and the beggar-man.' *VP*, 603.

[49] See Robert Goodin, *Green Political Theory* (Oxford: Polity Press, 1992), p. 41.

its human admixture.'[50] From a young age, Synge tells us, he had an exacting sense of the value of natural things:

> I remember that I would not allow my nurses to sit down on the seats by the [River] Dodder because they were [man-]made. If they wished to sit down they had to find a low branch of a tree or a bit of rock or bank.... My brother also had this idea about 'made' things, perhaps he gave it to me. I had a very strong feeling for the colour of locality which I expressed in syllables of no meaning, but my elders checked me for talking gibberish when I was heard practising them. (*CW* II, 5)

Thus, the 'Autobiography' posits the younger Synge both as a commanding advocate of untouched nature and also, through his practising of unintelligible 'syllables', in the early stages of articulacy regarding the 'colour of locality', that most important aspect of his later works. Further on in the text, Synge elaborates on this idea:

> In my childhood the presence of furze bushes and rocks and flooded streams and strange mountain fogs and sunshine gave me a strange sense of enchantment and delight but I think when I [rested] on a mountain I sat quite as gladly looking on the face of a boulder as at the finest view of glen or river. My wish was that nature should be untouched by man, whether the view was beautiful or not did not interest me. A wood near Rathfarnham represented my idea of bliss until someone told me it was a piece of artificially arranged planting on an artificial hillock. I hated the neighbourhood from that day. This feeling has never entirely left me, and I remember fifteen years later after a long afternoon in a French forest that I enquired in the evening with real anxiety whether or not this forest was a mere plantation. (*CW* II, 12)

> I think the consciousness of beauty is awakened in persons as in peoples by a profound unsatisfied desire... Perhaps the modern feeling for the beauty of nature as a particular quality—an expression of divine ecstasy rather than a mere decoration of the world—arose when men began to look on everything about them with the unsatisfied longing which has its proper analogue in puberty... The feeling of primitive people is still everywhere

---

[50] Kate Soper, *What is Nature?: Culture, Politics, and the Non-Human* (Oxford: Blackwell, 1995), p. 16.

the feeling of the child; an adoration that has never learned or wished to admire its divinity.   (*CW* II, 13)

Synge's disdain for any sort of 'artificial' nature, which extends not only to man-made objects but also to managed landscapes, establishes an exacting 'green theory of value' which, as he makes clear, was carried through into adulthood. The 'sense of enchantment' in nature is deemed misplaced or ill-founded if it is a response to anything tainted by human processes. Synge's sense of aesthetic value is bound tightly to the concept of a 'pristine' nature, hence the pervasive anxiety in his Congested Districts essays concerning the displacement of the natural. In the first passage above, conventional beauty is irrelevant in comparison to the promise of an 'untouched' landscape. Although Synge registers an adult irony regarding his perhaps untenable standards for a pristine natural environment, the second passage elaborates on the spiritual basis for his views. As in his poem 'The Creed' (*CW* I, 6), in which Synge 'With Earth's young majesty would yearning mate', there is a sexual element to his conception of mystical closeness to nature. The 'modern feeling' for nature, which is rooted for him in seeing the world as 'an expression of divine ecstasy', is the result of a separation from the 'primitive' and unexamined experience of the natural world, which is child-like and, in contrast to the 'pubescent' stage, 'satisfied'. Again, the Romantic emphasis on the child's world view becomes subsumed into a primitivist discourse of closeness to nature: the modernizing world, which is increasingly 'man-made' and 'artificial', separates man from an unexamined 'adoration' of the natural environment.

For Synge, then, modernity again turns back to the 'divine ecstasy' of nature, but this is necessarily a self-conscious position. The world of the 'primitive', untouched by modernity, is figured as prelapsarian; however, it is the imposition of the artificial that has led to a 'modern' (in this case, Romantic) feeling for nature that is focused on its mystical qualities. Hence, Synge's own 'consciousness of beauty' is at once linked to the 'profound unsatisfied desire' of a postlapsarian world and is an attempt to recover the 'primitive' 'adoration' of nature that he sees as predating the modern condition. At this stage, the 'noble savage' of Romanticism does not seem far away. The ideal, for Synge, is an intimate relationship to the natural world that is innocent and untainted by modernity, and this is represented for him in the figure of 'primitive' humanity. Synge's paternalistic desire, in his Congested Districts articles, to protect the peasantry from what is figured as unnatural modernization, protests against the artificial standardizing practices of the Congested Districts Board and also attempts to retain the privileged position of the 'primitive' in a rural Irish context.

Like AE, Synge was concerned that the CDB's attempts to improve the material situation of the peasantry would lead to the destruction of their 'rich humanity'; unlike AE, Synge did not counter this by advocating the improvement of the peasantry on Christian and cooperative terms.[51] For both men, self-help was the ultimate goal; however, where AE saw in the Congested Districts a place where 'the people are the most backward and most teachable', Synge preferred to see the peasantry as recalcitrant, and as an opposition to the standardizing improvement schemes enacted under constructive unionist policy.[52] His focus on what is most natural extends from an 'enchantment' in the natural world to a moral code, whereby what is most natural is also what is most distanced from modern political, economic, and religious structures. In a notebook that he began in 1895, which he used for notes on the lectures of Paul Passy and Louis Petit de Julleville, and also to record his impressions of the Aran Islands on his second visit in 1899, Synge gives his definition of 'organic morality', which he contrasts with 'inorganic morality'. 'Organic morality', he writes, is 'life held to level of most inspired moments', whereas an 'inorganic morality' is 'life held to level of another [such] as Ch[ristianity] etc.'[53] The definition of 'organic' morality is clearly linked to Synge's spirituality ('inspired moments') and, by extension, to his vision of the 'primitive' who has a unique ability to access these moments. The 'inorganic', which is linked to the imposed moral strictures of a Church or government, is artificial because it does not take its cues from a spiritual communion with nature. Like Morris and Belfort Bax, who argued that 'the so-called morality of the present age is simply commercial necessity, masquerading in the forms of the Christian ethics', Synge saw that a return to 'organic morality' would provide a mechanism for the unweaving of capitalist ethics from religion.[54] Not only do the modes of production of the peasantry oppose the growth of industrialism, but their very character and moral code is antagonistic to the modern, 'inorganic' world view. Hence, Synge's philosophy of nature encompasses not only a relationship to the environment, and a strict privileging of the purely natural over the artificial, but also a morality that is rooted in this 'primitive' or spiritual connection with a divine universe. His 'green theory of value' denigrates not

---

[51] AE, 'The best place for co-operation', *Irish Homestead*, 14 May 1910, p. 399.
[52] AE, 'Local Organisation', *Irish Homestead*, 7 April 1906, p. 262.
[53] TCD MS 4384, f. 66v.   [54] Morris and Belfort Bax, *Socialism*, p. 10.

only human admixture in natural processes but also definably 'inorganic' aspects of morality. By implication, it also venerates the 'organic' and unconventional, which is thus the most natural form of morality.

There is, of course, something troubling about Synge's aesthetic privileging of the 'natural' with regard to the peasantry. The 'organic' morality of the Syngean peasant, characterized by that which is most vital, or joyous, is an antidote to racial degeneration. The contemporary, Europe-wide concern that evolutionary law had been thwarted in humans by improvements in living standards is echoed in Synge's antagonism towards the artificial 'golf ball' of modernity. The introduction of 'foreign' horses, or models of architecture, or forms of labour is seen as having a direct degenerative effect on the peasantry. Natural forms, which Synge theorizes in certain types of dress or modes of production, are imbued with the ability to counter this modern decline. Art's role in spiritual and biological regeneration was a key concern for Yeats, as Donald Childs has shown, and this led to a more distinctly eugenical interest in breeding which aimed to prioritize natural morality. As Childs notes, regarding Yeats's play *Where There is Nothing* (1903), the characters of the magistrates are criticized for their breeding practices: 'they have turned from the natural authority of the heart and mother wit to the abstract authority of genealogy, social position, and financial considerations.'[55] As in Synge's theory of morality and its application to the Congested Districts in his articles, Yeats shows a concern for the displacement of nature in favour of social strictures which he theorizes as leading to degeneration. The privileging of the 'natural', and the importance of a 'natural' art in regeneration, underlie both Yeats's early plays and Synge's responses to the modernization schemes of the CDB, in which art and nature are seen as simultaneously under threat and capable of enacting an alternative modernity.

The first article in the series, entitled 'From Galway to Gorumna', introduces the principal dilemma of Synge's response to modernization, to which he comes back repeatedly over the following weeks. He begins with an emphasis on the remoteness and wildness of the districts, which 'can only be visited thoroughly by driving or riding over some thirty or forty miles of desolate roadway' (*CW* II, 284). Driving towards Spiddal from Galway, Synge introduces us to an idealized peasantry under threat, while also drawing out his own privilege in the act of idealization:

---

[55] Childs, *Modernism and Eugenics*, p. 185.

These men are all dressed in homespuns of the grey natural wool, and the women in deep madder-dyed bodices, with brown shawls over their heads. One's first feeling as one comes back among these people and takes a place, so to speak, in this noisy procession of fishermen, farmers, and women, where nearly everyone is interesting and attractive, is a dread of any reform that would tend to lessen their individuality rather than any very real hope of improving their well-being. One feels then, perhaps a little later, that it is part of the misfortune of Ireland that nearly all the characteristics which give colour and attractiveness to Irish life are bound up with a social condition that is near to penury, while in countries like Brittany, the best external features of the local life—the rich embroidered dresses, for instance, or the carved furniture—are connected with a decent and comfortable social condition.   (*CW* II, 286)

From the very beginning, Synge establishes an uncomfortable moral tension. The qualities which he sees in the people, who are dressed in 'natural wool' and are all 'interesting and attractive', are threatened by the standardization of any reform which 'would tend to lessen their individuality'. As with AE, there is a strong urge to preserve hidden within the urge to improve. However, Synge recognizes, to a degree, his own privilege in valuing the 'colour and attractiveness' of the peasantry over their material well-being, and the following articles are an often-tortuous attempt to find a compromise between a 'comfortable social condition' and the 'natural', traditional life of the people. In the opening article, CDB reform is established as a process that threatens to drain the 'colour' from the countryside, and as a process through which 'individuality' is worn away until the 'characteristics which give...attractiveness to Irish life' are gone. The 'natural' clothing, and the vibrancy of the 'noisy procession' of people, is threatened by material improvement because the two are seen as essentially opposed. The modern improvements, which are feared to displace nature, will result in a peasantry of diminished vitality. Whereas in Brittany the 'best external features of the local life' are consonant with material well-being (thus meaning that an improvement in the latter need not degrade the former), in Synge's view of Ireland 'individuality' and 'a decent and comfortable social condition' seem mutually exclusive under the present government policy.

For Paul Murphy, Synge's vision of an 'economic double-bind' in the position of the peasantry is indicative of a latent desire 'to restore the feudal landowner/peasant relationship and remove the irksome *bourgeoisie*', in which Synge constructs a 'fantasy' peasant as a key component in 'an ideological assault on *bourgeois* economics and a defence of aristocratic values'.[56] It is undeniable that, throughout the essays, Synge's observations and suggestions are underpinned by this double bind, and any reform which does not allow the continuance of 'individuality' and traditional, natural processes is lamented. However, his articles 'From the Congested Districts' seek to unpick the 'double-bind' by identifying alternatives to 'foreign', state-imposed modernization. McCormack argues that it is 'impossible to assign [his] unambiguous detestation of William O'Brien's political initiatives to Synge's socialism'; however, Synge's socialism was influenced by a Morrisian emphasis on the importance of aesthetics in social change and took from contemporary theorists an emphasis on the place of nature in social reform.[57] As Donna Gerstenberger argues, 'Synge is not...in this series a blindly nostalgic lover of the past at the cost of the present. Instead, he is much concerned to correct the "traditional misconception of the country people" and, having done so, to offer concrete suggestions for the alleviation of their lot.'[58] In the context of Synge's reading, his aesthetic, and turn-of-the-century sociological works, his opposition to the CDB is undoubtedly 'socialist', though some might now be reluctant to recognize it as such.

His socialism, as his articles 'From the Congested Districts' clearly show, both shaped and was shaped by his aesthetic and spiritual values; hence, though Synge's disdain for standardizing material improvement comes from a privileged vantage point, it is just one essential aspect of the broader constellation of his beliefs and values, the whole of which is constructed so that the removal of 'nature' will lead to its collapse. In these essays, therefore, Synge is not only protesting against the treatment of the peasantry, whom he sees as largely demoralized, but also against a threat to his own carefully constructed aesthetic. That he conflates the interests of the peasantry with his own personal interests is regrettable; however, in his brand of socialism, life and art were often equally at stake. In an earlier draft of the first article in the series, rather than stating the 'economic double-bind' in the terms given above, Synge instead opts for phrasing which reveals the close links between his politics and his aesthetics:

by the misfortune of the Irish past the atmosphere and colour of the life that these people have made for themselves, all that is characteristic, that is

---

[56] Murphy, *Hegemony and Fantasy in Irish Drama*, pp. 29–31.
[57] McCormack, *Fool of the Family*, p. 228.
[58] Gerstenberger, *John Millington Synge*, p. 16.

to say that which appeals to the imagination is bound up with their simpleness and penury.[59]

Synge later substitutes 'all that appeals to the imagination' with 'all the characteristics which give colour and attractiveness to Irish life'; however, it is clear that the threat of standardization implicit in 'improvement' schemes is seen by him as a threat to both aesthetics and artistic potential. The removal of individuality, of the 'atmosphere and colour' of the peasantry, is seen as a threat not only to their well-being but also to a world in which imagination is encouraged. The 'atmosphere and colour' so strongly associated with access to the sublime in his earlier prose works are threatened by certain forms of material improvement, and so modernization becomes an implicit threat to spiritual transcendence.

The tendency of CDB modernization schemes to remove 'all that is characteristic', to replace the local with the standard, is a key focus of Synge's critique. One of the most controversial practices of the CDB was their attempt to affect the improvement of livestock in the districts via the introduction of foreign breeds.[60] In 'The Small Town', Synge notes the 'long-legged, gawky type' of horse which is prominent, and uses the example to comment not only on the ill-suited nature of the breed but also on how local opinion is regarded by the Board (*CW* II, 337). The introduction of a 'foreign' breed of horse, which is 'ill suited' to its new environment, is conceived as both unnatural (it ignores the purpose of evolutionary development) and as symptomatic of a wider disregard for local opinion. Rather than improving the current 'local' breed, the CDB's decision to import horses into the districts is seen both as a colonial interference and as a way to cheat 'natural' improvement through breeding. Synge makes a logical progression from the 'foreign' horse, which represents a disregard for nature, and the 'foreign' methods of the CDB, which disregard local knowledge and tradition. In both, the methods of improvement are seen in terms contrary to local, natural processes. The disruption of nature is coterminous with the injustice against the peasantry, and thus Synge's concern for the place of nature in society works alongside his socialism. Not only this, but

---

[59] TCD MS 4399, f. 3r.
[60] See Carla King, 'Our Destitute Countrymen on the Western Coast', p. 173. W. L. Micks, who was a member of the CDB, wrote of the Board's horse improvement scheme that 'none of the Board's schemes were so fiercely attacked'. *An Account of the Constitution, Administration and Dissolution of the Congested Districts Board for Ireland from 1891 to 1923* (Dublin: Eason & Son, 1925), p. 28.

the concern for the intrusion of the 'foreign' takes on a nationalist tone in the drafts of this article, in which Synge observes that:

> the light-hearted way in which foreign types are introduced in every direction by...men instead of trying to improve local breeds on their own lines is a good instance of the sort of work that results from the persuasion that nothing good can come out of Ireland.[61]

Here, of course, 'foreign' takes on a much broader and more accusatory meaning than in the published version, though the sense of intrusion and disruption is maintained. Although such a logical progression, from the disruption of nature to disruption of the 'natural' peasantry, is implicit throughout his earlier writings, in these essays it is brought to the forefront of both Synge's and his reader's consciousness.

In fact, each essay in 'From the Congested Districts' is designed specifically to alternate between the natural and unnatural in this way, with Synge moving phrases and scenes between articles in order to create contrasts which reinforce his concerns. The third article in the series, 'Among the Relief Works', is the most striking in its account of the degradation of the peasantry. Synge opens with a description of the highway infrastructure in Connemara, drawing attention to the road Jack Yeats and himself are travelling, which 'has been built up in different years of famine by the people of the neighbourhood working on Government relief works, which are now once more in full swing' (*CW* II, 296). Synge's opinion of the relief works is clearly evident in his description of the people as he approaches. This passage (as I showed in the previous chapter) extends the imagery of *The Well of the Saints* to social commentary:

> Then, at a turn of the road, we came in sight of a dozen or more men and women working hurriedly and doggedly improving a further portion of this road, with a ganger swaggering among them and directing their work. Some of the people were cutting out sods from grassy patches near the road, others were carrying down bags of earth in a slow, inert procession, a few were breaking stones, and three or four women were scraping out a sort of sandpit at a little distance. As we drove quickly by we could see that

---

[61] TCD MS 4397, ff. 53v–54r.

every man and woman was working with a sort of hang-dog dejection that would be enough to make any casual passer mistake them for a band of convicts. (*CW* II, 296)

The 'swaggering' government official, or 'ganger', juxtaposed with the panicked hurrying of the peasantry, establishes an undertone of threat and the abuse of power. Furthermore, the 'slow, inert procession' of workers reinforces a sense of 'dejection', exhaustion, and resignation. As Synge's journal testifies, this scene is also imbued with nationalist (or at least anti-unionist) sentiment: it is designed to illustrate the 'distance between the unionist official and the people'.[62] Jack Yeats's illustration for the article only goes to emphasize Synge's description: the peasants are downcast, their heads lowered; meanwhile, in the foreground, the 'ganger' stands upright in a bowler hat and suit, holding his lapels and watching the workers with little trace of sympathy (see Figure 5.1, below). The force of unionism and joyless work leads the people to physical and mental degeneration.

This 'procession' of men was originally described by Synge in a draft for 'The Kelp Makers', where there is a 'melancholy procession of men carrying bags of earth'. The reason for Synge's restructuring of his articles becomes clear if we compare the key arguments of the two published pieces. The 'dejection' of the relief workers stems implicitly from the unnaturalness of their labour; on the other hand, Synge's principal aim in 'The Kelp Makers' is to emphasize the importance of subsidizing local, traditional (read 'natural') industry. In moving the description of the procession of men to 'Among the Relief Works' as opposed to leaving it in 'The Kelp Makers', Synge establishes a distinct contrast in the articles between the 'natural'/ 'traditional' form of industry and the unnatural, degrading form of the CDB's 'novel' schemes.[63]

However, this is not solely an aesthetic point, and Synge was clearly well read in political reportage from the districts, which he uses to assess the economic and political arguments for certain schemes of aid. At the beginning of 'The Kelp Makers', he criticizes a 'large volume issued a couple of years ago by the Department of Agriculture and Technical Instruction for

---

[62] TCD MS 4399, f. 20v.

[63] TCD MS 4399, f. 32r. In this way, Synge meets Horace Plunkett's contemporaneous views on the criticism of 'novel schemes' and the importance of self-reliance, though Synge is decidedly less severe in his belief in the economic independence of the peasantry, advocating schemes of development which promote the ability of the peasantry to develop independently. See Horace Plunkett, *Ireland in the New Century* (London: John Murray, 1904), pp. 175, 245.

IN THE "CONGESTED DISTRICTS."

AMONG THE RELIEF WORKS.

BY J. M. SYNGE.   ILLUSTRATIONS BY JACK B. YEATS.

Beyond Carraroe, the last promontory on the north coast of Galway Bay, one reaches a group of islands which form the lower angle of Connemara. These islands are little more than a long peninsula broken through by a number of small straits, over which, some twelve years ago, causeways and swing bridges were constructed, so that one can now drive straight on through Annaghvaan, Lettermore, Gorumna, Lettermullen, and one or two smaller islands. When one approaches this district from the east a long detour is made to get round the inner point of Great-man's Bay, and then the road turns to the south-west till one reaches Annaghvaan, the first of the islands. This road is a remarkable one. Nearly every foot of it, as it now stands, has been built up in different years of famine by the people of the neighbourhood working on Government relief works, which are now once more in full swing, making improvements in some places, turning primitive tracts into roadways in others, and here and there building a new route to some desolate village.

We drove many miles, with Costello and Carraroe behind us, along a bog road of curious formation built up on a turf embankment, with broad grassy sods at either side—perhaps to make a possible way for the bare-footed people,—then two spaces of rough broken stones where the wheel-ruts are usually worn, and in the centre a track of gritty earth for the horses. Then at a turn of the road we came in sight of a dozen or more men and women working hurriedly and doggedly improving a further portion of this road, with a ganger swaggering among them and directing their work. Some of the people were cutting out sods from grassy patches near the road, others were carrying down bags of earth in a slow, inert procession, a few were breaking stones, and three or four women were scraping out a sort of sandpit at a little distance. As we drove quickly by we could see that every man and woman was working with a sort of hang-dog dejection that would be enough to make any casual passer mistake them for a band of convicts. The wages given on these works are usually a shilling a day, and as a rule one person only, generally the head of the family, is taken from each house. Some-times the best worker in a family is thus forced away from his ordinary work of farming or fishing or kelp-making for this wretched remuneration at a time when his private industry is most needed. If this system of relief has some things in its favour, it is far from satisfactory in other ways and is not always economical. I have been told of a district not very far from here where there is a ganger, an overseer, an inspector, a paymaster, and an engineer superintending the work of two paupers only. This is possibly an exaggerated account of what is really taking place, yet it probably shows, not too inexactly, a state of things that is not rare in Ireland.

A mile or two further on we passed a

similar band of workers, and then the road rose for a few feet and turned sharply on to a long causeway with a swing bridge in the centre that led to the island of Annaghvaan. Just as we reached the bridge our driver jumped down and took his mare by the head. A moment later she began to take fright at the hollow noise of her own hoofs on the boards of the bridge and the blue rush of the tide which she could see through them, but the man coaxed her forward, and got her over without much difficulty. For the next mile or two there was a continual series of small islands and causeways and bridges that the mare grew accustomed to, and trotted gaily over, till we reached Lettermore, and drove for some distance through the small hills of stone. Then we came to the largest causeway of all, between Lettermore and Gorumna, where the proportion of the opening of the bridge to the length of the embankment is so small that the tide runs through with extraordinary force. On the outer side the water was banked up nearly a yard high against the buttress of the bridge, and on the other side there was a rushing, eddying torrent that recalled some mountain salmon stream in flood, except that here, instead of the brown river water, one saw the white and blue foam of the sea.

The remainder of our road to the lower western end of Gorumna led through hilly districts that became more and more white with stone, though one saw here and there a few brown masses of bog or an oblong lake with many islands and rocks. In most places if one looked round the hills a little distance from the road one could see the yellow roofs and white gables of cottages scattered every-where through this waste of rock, and on the ridge of every hill one could see the red dresses of women who were gathering turf or looking for their sheep or calves. Near the village where we stopped things are somewhat better, and a few fields of grass and potatoes were to be seen, and a certain number of small cattle grazing among the rocks. Here also one is close to the sea, and fishing and kelp-making are again possible. In the village there is a small private quay in connection with a shop where everything is sold, and not long after we arrived a hooker sailed in with a cargo of supplies from Galway. A number of women were standing about expecting her arrival, and soon afterwards several of them set off for different parts of the island with

a bag of flour slung over an ass. One of these, a young girl of seventeen or eighteen, drove on with her load far into Letter-mullen, the next island, on a road that we were walking also, and then sent the ass back to Gorumna in charge of a small boy and took up the sack of flour, which weighed at least 16 stone, on her back, and carried it more than a mile, through a narrow track, to her own home. This practice of allowing young girls to carry great weights frequently injures them severely, and is the cause of much danger and suffering in their after lives. They do not seem, however, to know anything of the risks they run, and their loads are borne gaily.

A little further on we came on another stretch of the relief works, where there were many elderly men and young girls working with the same curious aspect of shame and dejection. The work was just closing for the evening, and as we walked back to Gorumna an old man who had been working walked with us, and complained of his great poverty and the small wages he was given. "A shilling a day," he said, "would hardly keep a man in tea and sugar and tobacco and a bit of bread to eat, and what good is it at all when there is a family of five or six maybe, and often more?" Just as we reached the swing-bridge that led back to Gorumna another hooker sailed carefully in through the narrow rocky channel with a crowd of men and women sitting along the gunwale. They edged in close to a flat rock near the bridge and made her fast for a moment while the women jumped out on shore, some of them carrying bottles, others with little children, and all dressed out in new red petticoats and shawls. They looked as they crowded up on the road as fine a body of peasant women as one could see anywhere, and were all talking and laughing eagerly among themselves. The old man told me in Irish that they had been at a pattern—a sort of semi-religious festival like the well-known festivals of Brittany—that had just been held some distance to the east on the Galway coast. It was reassuring to see that some, at least, of these island people are, in their own way, prosperous and happy. When the women were all landed the swing-bridge was pushed open, and the hooker was poled through to the bay on the north side of the islands. Then the men moored her and came up to a little public-house, where they spent the rest of the evening talking and drinking and telling stories in Irish.

Figure 5.1 Jack B. Yeats, illustration for J. M. Synge, 'In the "Congested Districts": Among the Relief Works', *The Manchester Guardian*, 17 June 1905, p. 7. © Estate of Jack B. Yeats, DACS London/IVARO Dublin, 2020.

Ireland' for the absence of attention to the kelp industry, 'which is a matter of the greatest importance to the inhabitants of a very large district' (*CW* II, 307).[64]

The kelp industry, as Synge sees it, is socially important to the peasantry of the district, and he advocates the introduction of regulations 'to ensure the people a fair market for their produce'.[65] The purpose of protecting this industry is revealed in his drafts as a way of ring-fencing the 'gaiety' of the people against a modernity which is seen in opposition to mental and physical health:

> There is a curious contrast to be noticed in all the districts where there is acute distress between the gaiety of even the poorest people when they are engaged in their [?] tradition ~~natural work~~, and the dejection of those employed on the relief works.[66]

The 'gaiety' associated with the 'natural'/'tradition[al]' work of kelp-making is contrasted sharply with the 'dejection' of the relief works. Synge originally contrasts the relief workers and the kelp makers within the space of a single article, but he separates the 'unnatural' from the 'natural' in his published articles to provide a more binary contrast. The aesthetic appeal of the kelp-making process seems to be of importance in Synge's categorization of the trade as 'natural work'. While carrying the weed to be burnt, 'several bare-legged girls' are heard 'crooning merry songs in Gaelic', and the scene is altogether more hopeful:

> The whole scene, with the fresh smell of the sea and the blueness of the shallow waves, made a curious contrast with the dismal spectacle of the relief workers we had just passed, for here the people seemed as light-hearted as a party of schoolboys. (*CW* II, 308)

---

[64] The book to which Synge is referring is most probably William P. Coyne, ed., *Ireland: Industrial and Agricultural* (Dublin: Browne & Nolan, 1902), which ran to 525 pages. The Department of Agriculture and Technical Instruction was established in 1900 and headed by Horace Plunkett and T. P. Gill, whom Synge knew as the editor of the *Dublin Daily Express*, to which Synge contributed reviews. For more on the foundation of the D.A.T.I. and its political implications, see Nicholas Whyte, *Science, Colonialism and Ireland* (Cork: Cork University Press, 1999) and Andrew Gailey, *Ireland and the Death of Kindness: The Experience of Constructive Unionism, 1890–1905* (Cork: Cork University Press, 1987), p. 51. Horace Plunkett's controversial book *Ireland in the New Century*, which was hotly debated in the pages of *Dana*, dealt with the establishment of the new department. See especially chapters X–XI.

[65] TCD MS 4399, f. 32r. [66] TCD MS 4399, f. 31r.

The aesthetic appeal of the scene is associated directly with its 'light-heartedness'; and, conversely, the 'naturalness' of the work becomes linked to its aesthetic appeal. In this way, again, the defence of traditional or 'natural' ways of life is both artistic and political. The 'slow, inert procession' (*CW* II, 296) of the relief workers contrasts directly with the imaginative peasantry described in the opening of the first article, who are a 'noisy procession of fishermen, farmers, and women, where nearly everyone is interesting and attractive' (*CW* II, 286). 'Foreign', imposed labour results, both in Synge's and Jack Yeats's depictions, in a dejection which is 'inert', both slow-moving and, in the chemical sense, unreactive. The interest and attraction of the peasantry, both in visual and vital terms, is drained away. Elsewhere, a group of boatbuilders, working by the shore, 'reminded one curiously of some old picture of Noah building the Ark' (*CW* II, 312): their lifestyle is almost prelapsarian, and their aesthetic pre-modernity hints at their potential to offer a remedy for modernity's dislocation of the spiritual from the product of labour.

These articles make an implicit link between the collapse of this traditional trade and the standardization of building methods in the district. Though the rearrangement of holdings by the CDB is 'appreciated by the people', the new building materials and designs 'are perhaps a less certain gain' and, for Synge, 'give the neighbourhoods where they have been made an uncomfortable look that is...felt by the people' (*CW* II, 314). The substitution of iron roofs for the traditional thatch and the implications of more 'sweeping improvements' result, Synge suggests, in a loss of traditional knowledge, and also have an adverse consequence on the aesthetics of the community which in turn affects the psychological health of the peasantry. Additionally, the improvements (according to one notebook) 'tend to force the people away from a certain traditional life that is full of charm and interest'.[67] Rather than a government board 'improving' the housing on a 'foreign' model, the article concludes that

> it is far better, wherever possible, to improve the ordinary prosperity of the people till they begin to improve their houses themselves on their own lines, than to do too much in the way of building houses that have no interest for the people and disfigure the country.... the people should be left as free as possible to arrange their houses and way of life as it pleases them.   (*CW* II, 314–5)

[67] TCD MS 4400, f. 27r.

An earlier draft of this conclusion reinforces the architectural basis for Synge's emphasis on local tradition:

> If, however, the proportion of well-to-do people could be raised, it is at least possible that the people would begin to improve their houses and their standard of life on their own lines and they would escape the fearful workhouse-like look of the new.[68]

The concern that the newly built houses look like 'workhouses' again suggests Synge's association with degradation and demoralization and aesthetics which are not in tune with the landscape and 'natural work' of the people. For Synge, any modernization carried out should be done so as 'to disorganise as little as possible the life and methods of the people' (CW II, 315). His aesthetic eye is always at work, and the sense that modern housing might 'disfigure' the country relies on Synge's own prioritization of a harmony with nature and his disdain for anything 'artificial'. Synge's sense of aesthetic consonance with the landscape is an example of a sort of geomancy in these articles, in which certain practices and traditions are 'in touch' with nature while others are categorized as unnatural or anti-nature.[69] These geomantic aspects retain the spirit, 'atmosphere', and 'colour' of the locality and promote imaginative health.

The bind, therefore, is to find a scheme of improvement which is both 'organic' and progressive, one which ensures the place of nature in the modern world while also improving the economic and social position of those living in the Congested Districts. However, Synge's plan for the 'organic' improvement of housing was precariously placed within contemporary tenancy and land-purchase systems. After discussing the various shortcomings of different rent systems at the end of 'The Smaller Peasant Proprietors', he notes the principal difficulty in the relationship between rent and improvement: namely, that a tenant who improved their property was often subjected to an increase in rent, while 'the careless tenant had his rent lowered' (CW II, 323). As Timothy Guinnane and Ronald Miller note, 'Without leases landlords could always raise rents or eject a sitting tenant, giving tenants no incentive to invest in their holdings, as the landlord

---

[68] TCD MS 4400, f. 31r.
[69] For more on geomancy, architecture, and the 'spirit of place', see Sheldrake, *The Rebirth of Nature*, pp. 146–51.

could appropriate the value of any investment the tenant might make.'[70] Additionally, the tenant had no incentive to care for the landlord's improvements to the property, and so neither was encouraged to make long-term investments. Synge introduces the reader to the schemes of the CDB which allow this sort of stagnation to be sidestepped:

> These matters are well-known; but at the present time the state of suspended land purchase is tending to reproduce the same fear in a new form, and any tenants who have not bought out are naturally afraid to increase the price they may have to pay by improving their land. In this district, however, there is no fear of this kind, and a good many small grants have been given by the Board for rebuilding cottages and other improvements. A new cottage can be built by the occupier himself for a sum of about £30, of which the Board pays only a small part, while the cottages built by the Board, on their own plan, with slated roofs on them, cost double, or more than double, as much. We went into one of the reslated cottages with concrete floor, and it was curious to see that, however awkward the building looked from the outside, in the kitchen itself the stain of the turf smoke and the old pot-ovens and stools made the place seem natural and local. That at least was reassuring.   (*CW* II, 323–4)

The 'old fear of improvements, caused by the landlord system' (*CW* II, 323) is no longer an issue thanks to peasant proprietorship and grants from the CDB. This proprietorship, which allows the rebuilding or improvement of holdings 'by the occupier himself', is clearly favoured by Synge as a method which allows for the continuation of tradition and the 'atmosphere and colour' of the districts. Although the outside of the improved cottage looks 'awkward', the interior scene is tellingly described as 'natural and local'. In a later article on 'The Small Town', Synge depicts the cottage of a returned emigrant in similarly approving terms: 'Her cottage was perfectly clean and yet had lost none of the peculiar local character of these cottages' (*CW* II, 338). The continuance of tradition and the ability of the 'local' and 'natural' to exist within a superficially 'foreign' and 'awkward' construction is 'reassuring' for Synge because it enshrines the place of the natural within the modern and shows the possibility for a positive, local modernization.

---

[70] Timothy W. Guinnane and Ronald I. Miller, 'The Limits to Land Reform: The Land Acts in Ireland, 1870–1909', *Economic Development and Cultural Change*, Vol. 45, No. 3 (April 1997), 591–612, p. 593.

Hence, Synge's opposition is to a demoralizing, standardizing, and 'inorganic' modernity rather than to modernization as a rule. After the *Playboy* riots, he wrote an additional concluding paragraph for his essay 'The People of the Glens' (originally published in *The Shanachie* in March 1907) which was removed from the text used in *In Wicklow, West Kerry and Connemara*. As with the 'set piece' added to *The Aran Islands*, this paragraph shows again how his works were redrafted in accordance with contemporary events and his evolving artistic and political consciousness. After noting that there is some physical degradation amongst the peasantry ('it is possible to find many individuals who are far from admirable either in body or mind' (*CW* II, 224)), Synge takes the opportunity to attack the 'theology' of the urban Irish elite:

> One would hardly stop to assert a fact so obvious if it had not become the fashion in Dublin, quite recently, to reject a fundamental doctrine of theology, and to exalt the Irish peasant into a type of almost absolute virtue, frugal, self-sacrificing, valiant, and I know not what. There is some truth in this estimate, yet it is safer to hold with the theologians that, even west of the Shannon, the heart of man is not spotless, for though the Irish peasant has many beautiful virtues, it is idle to assert that he is totally unacquainted with the deadly sins, and many minor rogueries. He has, however, it should never be forgotten, a fine sense of humour and the greatest courtesy. When a benevolent visitor comes to his cottage, seeking a sort of holy family, the man of the house, his wife, and all their infants, too courteous to disappoint him, play their parts with delight. When the amiable visitor, however, is once more in the boreen, a storm of good-tempered irony breaks out behind him that would surprise him if he could hear it. This irony I have heard many times in places where I have been intimate with the people, and I have always been overjoyed to hear it. It shows that, in spite of relief-works, commissions, and patronizing philanthropy—that sickly thing—the Irish peasant, in his own mind, is neither abject nor servile.[71]

Ironic humour, which stands in opposition to systematic modernization, finds explicit expression in this addition to 'The People of the Glens', where it serves not only to bolster Synge's views on modernization and the peasantry but also to rebuke those who protested against his depiction of

[71] J. M. Synge, 'The People of the Glens', in *The Shanachie: An Illustrated Irish Miscellany*, Vol. II (Dublin: Maunsel & Co., 1907), 39–47, p. 47.

the peasantry in *The Playboy*. In this way, Synge's work in 'From the Congested Districts' was the beginning of a more direct theorization of ironic humour as a form of 'protest' against the 'dejection' of 'relief-works, commissions, and patronizing philanthropy'. The precarious place of 'nature' within a modernizing society becomes the cue for Synge's assertion of his trademark Rabelaisian humour as a way of reinvigorating a denatured world. In this way, it could function as a second form of re-enchantment, or as an act of regeneration.

Synge's unconventional, and certainly controversial, use of ironic humour as a method of protest formed an integral part of the fabric of the 'Congested Districts' articles before they were sent to Scott at *The Manchester Guardian*. There are numerous instances in which Synge uses a sort of violent comedic episode to counteract the 'dejection' of the social and political situation in the districts. A few pages after the 'crow and golf ball' passage in his 'Congested Districts' notebook, Synge writes a short description of the Aran Islanders which, from the evidence of various manuscript deletions, could easily be a concealed description of the people in the Congested Districts. Certainly, the passage about the Aran Islanders was written during or shortly after Synge's travels for *The Manchester Guardian*, and is again indicative of his focus on the grotesque or Rabelaisian characteristics of the peasantry as a method of opposing 'foreign', standardizing modernization:

> Many of these people have an extraordinarily frank viciousness, many of them are drunkards, and all are filthy, yet with them one is possibly in better company than when one is with the rather well bred . . . people in the cities of Ireland who hunger and thirst for all that is vulgar in the world.[72]

The growing sense of the importance of ironic, 'vulgar', or 'vicious' humour in the peasantry as a protest against urbanity and middle-class, religious, and nationalist morality is contemporaneous with Synge's commission for *The Manchester Guardian*, and is in part retrospectively applied to *The Aran Islands*. Though he had noted earlier the censoring tendencies of the Revival, which (as he suggested in a review of Lady Gregory's *Cuchulain*) 'omitted certain barbarous features' of the Irish language tradition, thus cleansing them of some of their 'wildness and vigour' (*CW* II, 368–70), it was only later that such an opinion became fully politicized. Just as the place of nature

---

[72] TCD MS 4397, f. 9v.

in modernizing societies leads to Synge's reassessment of his own earlier works, adding a layer of authorial irony, so the 'answers' to this denaturing process, namely ironic humour and a sort of Rabelaisian grotesque, start to be written into Synge's view of the peasantry. This is a reaction both to the response of critics to *The Shadow of the Glen* and *The Well of the Saints*, and to the demoralizing effects of systematic modernization in the west of Ireland. The Syngean peasant is, as always, a confluence of both artistic and political imperatives.

The idealization of the peasantry in the Revival has been well documented, as has Synge's divergence from the pastoral, spiritualized, 'twilight' figure of the peasant.[73] Jack Yeats and Synge held similar political views; both were dismayed by the relief works, and both sought to counter the 'dejection' of the peasantry with images of vitality.[74] However, there is a common misconception that Synge was countering an idealization of the peasantry which rested on their perceived closeness to nature, their benignity, and their spirituality. Rather, Synge's vision of 'the wildness, violence, cruelty, and verbal extravagance at the heart of peasant life' reinforces this closeness but also realigns it.[75] The 'wildness' is tied to his theory of 'organic morality', which is in turn tied to a closeness to nature. For Synge, closeness to nature and spirituality does not result in an ideally nationalist or Catholic view of the peasant; on the contrary, it poses a challenge to both these views and to the dominant political regime of constructive unionism. In fact, it is the anarchic contrariness of the peasantry which Synge values above all else, and this is a sign of their pre-modernity, their organicism, and their spiritual vitality. In this way, Synge's vision of the peasant is, by this stage, avowedly modernist.[76]

There are numerous passages in the drafts of the 'Congested Districts' articles which do not appear in the published texts, and it is clear to see that the commonality between them is their attention to a sort of violent and

[73] See, for example, Deborah Fleming, 'A man who does not exist': The Irish Peasant in the Work of W. B. Yeats and J. M. Synge (Ann Arbor: University of Michigan Press, 1995); Hirsch, 'The Imaginary Irish Peasant'; Maurice Harmon, 'Cobwebs before the Wind: Aspects of the Peasantry in Irish Literature from 1800–1916', in Daniel J. Casey and Robert E. Rhodes, eds., Views of the Irish Peasantry 1800–1916 (Hamden, CT: Archon, 1977), 129–59.

[74] See Bruce Arnold, Jack Yeats (New Haven and London: Yale University Press, 1998), pp. 136–40.

[75] Hirsch, 'The Imaginary Irish Peasant', p. 1126.

[76] For a discussion of the distinction between Romantic and modernist primitivism, see Garrigan Mattar, Primitivism, Science, and the Irish Revival, p. 4.

unconventional humour. These were evidently removed because the commission was designed to raise awareness and funds for the districts.[77] Synge's social conscience and political awareness, in this instance, lead to a tactful act of self-censorship. In a deleted passage from his article on 'The Village Shop', set in the 'inner lands of Mayo' where, although the destitution is less intense, there are still villages 'built on the old system ... and filled with primitive people' (*CW* II, 329), Synge recalls a relatively harmless scene of roguery, in which the publican and other customers tease an old man for flirting with a married woman.[78] This whole passage is enclosed in a circle of blue pencil, the line of which extends down into a long question mark at the bottom of the page. Clearly, Synge was uncomfortable with the story in the context of his commission: its comedy, which is based on a tale of a runaway wife and extramarital flirtation, does not fit into the sort of narrative which might return charity from the Manchester people. However, its example of the peasantry's humour and sense of irony is attractive to Synge, who uses such instances to counter the scenes of degradation depicted elsewhere.

Another excised passage, from his article on 'The Small Town', deals again with an incident which touches perhaps too closely on an ironic or 'vicious' humour. The published article draws our attention to several local characters, including a set of 'strolling singers and acrobats' who give a performance and some brokers who have 'fantastic talk'; however, the image of the town is decidedly closer to Morris's utopian London than to the humour of two of Synge's literary heroes, Ben Jonson and François Rabelais. In his notebook, Synge describes an altercation on the street which is 'rowdy' and 'wonderful':

> The town crier is still a prominent person in these smaller towns and [in] the market ... one appeared to make some announcement about a lost purse or something of this kind. He had hardly said a score of words when a rowdy character rushed up one of the side allies [*sic*] and began hooting and booing at him till he drove him off the field. This it appeared

---

[77] Synge clearly bears in mind the potential of charity from the *Manchester Guardian* readership, mentioning the good work done as a result of funds raised in the past. In 'Erris', another article set in the 'inner lands of Mayo', he writes: 'Typhus is less frequent than it used to be, probably because the houses and holdings are improving gradually, and we have heard it said that the work done in Aghoos by the fund raised by the "Manchester Guardian" some years ago was the beginning of this better state of things.' (*CW* II, 327)

[78] TCD MS 4398, f. 30r–31r.

was a former crier who had been dismissed and ever since he pursues the new one with a wonderful epithet. 'Go along', he said, 'you old jackdaw. Go along, you jack in the box, you thieving villain.'[79]

The 'peculiar character' (*CW* II, 334) of the town is given as a mix of its old-fashioned charm and its tendency for something more akin to *Bartholomew Fair*. Again, it is not hard to see Synge's reasoning behind his decision not to include this passage. The image of two competing town criers, one 'hooting and booing' and hurling insults at the other, is full of the ironic resonances of Synge's comedies, and shows Synge's attraction to this aspect of the peasantry. The jovial, comedic, and often dark humour of *The Well of the Saints* and *The Playboy of the Western World* is given in the articles 'From the Congested Districts' as a protest against degrading schemes of modernization (as Synge makes explicit in his revised ending to 'The People of the Glens'), but the published articles have a tendency to prioritize the political imperative of the commission over the more anarchic incidents related in the notebooks.

These acts of self-censorship show Synge's capability to shift between his prioritization of the aesthetic and the political in his writings in order to aid the people. However, although Synge discerns the effects of, and remedies for, modernization, the aesthetic lesson he draws from contemporary political currents and actions in the west of Ireland are more important, and more original, than his contributions to journalism and social commentary. The 'possible remedies' which Synge arrives at in the final article of the series are not particularly unique or radical in themselves. His remarks on emigration match Horace Plunkett's (whose *Ireland in the New Century* was hotly debated in the pages of *Dana*) to the degree that they recognize that improving conditions will likely 'increase the outflow' of population, and both agree on the relative 'paternalism' of the CDB.[80] Likewise, *The Irish Times* was advocating the need for the CDB to provide improved transport links in Connemara.[81] Importantly, however, Synge advocates self-government as the measure preliminary to all others. The relative conventionalism of his conclusions tends to obscure the particularly personal route by which he arrives at them. There is a confluence of contemporary

---

[79] TCD MS 4397, f. 50v.

[80] Plunkett, *Ireland in the New Century*, pp. 39, 244. Plunkett made a tour with H. Moran, Chief Land Inspector of the CDB, in order to inspect the Congested Districts, just over a month before Synge and Yeats began their travels. See *Irish Independent*, 29 April 1905, p. 6.

[81] 'Connemara and the Congested Districts Board for Ireland', *Irish Times*, 10 Nov 1904, p. 6.

socialistic concern regarding the 'place' of nature in modern society and Synge's own (by this point) quite elaborate oppositions to systematic modernization. Though the practical implications of his articles might not have been radical, the effects of the *Manchester Guardian* commission became, for Synge, intensely literary. The CDB's schemes of modernization threatened 'nature', 'individuality', and the spiritual, and Synge's literary reaction would lead him to the specific form of vicious and ecstatic ironic humour which would both make and challenge his reputation.

Throughout these articles, Synge displays a deep engagement with, and susceptibility to, wider political currents; hence, though he does not dictate the political terms, his process of drawing aesthetic lessons from them again reinforces a reading of his work as a developing reaction to modern life. The place of nature is a permanent fixture; however, the increased threat to the natural results in a development of Synge's artistic philosophy, which begins to encompass a more ironic and 'brutal' aesthetic. These essays, therefore, mark a decisive shift in Synge's theory and work: the connection between the aesthetic, the moral, and the political is made explicit; the displacement of nature becomes the key objection to a certain form of 'artificial' modernization; and ironic humour begins increasingly to function as an act of protest.

6

Degeneration, Eugenics, and *The Playboy of the Western World*

During the 1880s and 1890s, anthropological, ethnographical, and literary attempts were made to distinguish the characteristics of the 'Celt'. Earlier characterizations, particularly from Ernest Renan and Matthew Arnold, of the Irish as spiritual, effeminate, irrational, and naturally submissive were variously adopted and revised in order to suit political and aesthetic opinion.[1] Building on earlier nineteenth-century works, new scientific and anthropological theories were deployed in order to 'unravel the tangled skein of the so-called "Irish race"'.[2] Perhaps inevitably, the 'racial' qualities of the more 'primitive' Irish, notably the western peasantry, were conceived by many Revivalist writers in degenerationist terms, seeing the modern (urban, middle-class) population as having 'fallen' from a more heroic past. In some cases, this degeneration was perceived in a social sense, and thus attributed to cultural and economic factors; in others, it was more explicitly understood as a form of genetic, racial degeneration, thus requiring the sort of regenerative eugenic measures which proliferated in scientific and political discourse in the closing decades of the nineteenth century. The political implications of social Darwinism were central to attempts to 'regenerate' the Irish in cultural and racial terms, and were thus central to attempts to 'revive' Irish culture.

Genetic views of degeneration permeated contemporary ethnographic studies, such as those of Haddon and Browne on the Aran Islands, in which the natives were measured, analysed, and found to be generally better-looking, and less susceptible to disease, than their mainland cousins.[3]

---

[1] For a discussion of the historical basis of these debates, see Joep Leerssen, *Mere Irish and Fíor-Ghael: Studies in the Idea of Irish Nationality, its Development and Literary Expression prior to the Nineteenth Century* (Cork: Cork University Press, 1996), especially pp. 377–9.

[2] D. J. Cunningham and A. C. Haddon, 'The Anthropometric Laboratory of Ireland', *Journal of the Anthropological Institute*, Vol. 21 (1891), 35–9, p. 36.

[3] A. C. Haddon and C. R. Browne, 'The Ethnography of the Aran Islands, County Galway', *Proceedings of the Royal Irish Academy*, Vol. 2 (1891–3), 768–830, pp. 779, 798.

J. M. Synge: Nature, Politics, Modernism. Seán Hewitt, Oxford University Press (2021). © Seán Hewitt. DOI: 10.1093/oso/9780198862093.003.0007

The image of the islands as 'free from syphilis and sexual vice' (a point which informs Synge's *The Aran Islands*) caused them to be perceived as a health retreat. Scott Ashley even suggests that Synge's visits might have been partly motivated by his ill health.[4] By positing the Aran Islanders as the remnant of a pure race, descended from the Firbolgs, they could be held up as an example of Irishness free from British domination.[5] As a health retreat, the islands could be figured as a source of individual revitalization; but as the site of a pre-modern and supposedly pre-colonial culture, their potential for rejuvenation was extended to a national scale. For Synge, these ideas intersected with his ongoing campaign against aesthetic Decadence, as his preface to *The Playboy of the Western World* makes clear. Wildness, joy, 'natural form', writing that is 'rich and copious' and rooted in the vitalizing source of peasant and Irish-language culture: all are set against an etiolated Ibsenite literature of 'joyless and pallid words' (*CW* IV, 53). This is politicized not only in the 'fully flavoured' speech of *The Playboy*, but also in the play's emphasis on regenerative violence, its co-option of 'wildness' as a concerted and conscious attack on the audience.

For Synge, as we have seen, the view of a 'timeless' and depoliticized Irishness was anathema, though more Romantic Celticist discourses do infiltrate his vision. For him, the Irish peasantry, demoralized and degenerated through homogenizing imperial schemes, might be reinvigorated through a reconnection both with more socialistic, communal work practices and with their 'natural' life. An outbreak of ironic, Rabelaisian humour had the power to counter the demoralization effected by foreign, bourgeois expectation. The citation of economic and social causes for degeneration had a precedent in late Victorian anthropology, particularly the works of E. B. Tylor, who notes injustices against the poor as forcing physical conditions which could lead to degeneration.[6] Synge followed suit, positing economic and cultural remedies to social degeneration. However, by this stage he was also rebelling against the artistic restraints of the dominant nationalist discourses of the Revival.

In *The Playboy*, a force of Romantic revolutionism is unleashed, with Synge deploying a satiric and multifaceted ironic attack on both the aesthetic

---

[4] Scott Ashley, 'Primitivism, Celticism and Morbidity in the Atlantic fin de siècle', in Patrick McGuinness, ed., *Symbolism, Decadence and the Fin de Siècle: French and European Perspectives* (Exeter: Exeter University Press, 2000), 175–93, p. 189.

[5] See Scott Ashley, 'The poetics of race in 1890s Ireland: an ethnography of the Aran Islands', *Patterns of Prejudice*, Vol. 35, No. 2 (2001), 5–18, p. 9.

[6] See Beer, *Open Fields*, p. 86.

and the political fronts. Gregory Castle has read the play as a dramatic enactment of this protest, seeing it, both as text and performance, as 'a kind of performative justice that seeks to redress the discursive violence perpetrated by Revivalist, nationalist and anthropological representations'.[7] As Sinéad Garrigan Mattar has shown, Synge's study of Celtology and primitive society led him to adopt a vision of original Irishness at odds with many of his contemporaries, and his modernist vision of the peasantry set his works against those who preferred to imagine Irishness in terms more commensurable with late Victorian morality.[8] Synge's writings between 1905 and 1907 strike against conservative nationalist movements and work to subvert their deployment of a rhetoric of racial piety by depicting an enervated peasantry revitalized by protest against those attempting to mould the 'soft wax' of contemporary Ireland along increasingly restrictive lines.[9] Revivalist attempts to circumscribe Irish identity within a wholesome, puritanical version of Gaelic Ireland—what John Hutchinson has succinctly described as a place 'free from all the evils of modernity—a secular literature, alcoholism, sexual immorality, socialist agitations and materialist ideals'—were mocked in *Playboy*'s elaborate deployment of racial and degenerationist discourses.[10]

As John Brannigan has noted, Yeats's attempts to understand the Revival in the light of the new political developments in Ireland after the War of Independence (1919–21) led him to characterize his work and the work of his contemporaries as involved '"in a deepened perception of all those things that strengthen race", by which he means the race-consciousness and racial memory of the Irish'.[11] Implicated in this vision of racial 'strengthening' were key Revivalist works, including Lady Gregory's *Cuchulain of Muirthemne* (1902) and Synge's *The Playboy of the Western World*. The initial Anglo-Irish formulation of the Celt, which attempted to root itself in a twilit past and hence avoid sectarian and class politics, gained prominence in the 1880s and 1890s; but, as Geraldine Higgins notes, this 'cultural, race-based identity . . . soon had to vie with a politicized, Catholic

---

[7] Castle, *Modernism and the Celtic Revival*, p. 145.

[8] See Mattar, *Primitivism, Science, and the Irish Revival*, pp. 130–84.

[9] Yeats describes the project of Irish identity formation during the Revival as a question of 'how one might seal with the right image the soft wax before it began to harden'. *Autobiographies*, p. 101.

[10] John Hutchinson, *The Dynamics of Cultural Nationalism: The Gaelic Revival and the Creation of the Irish Nation State* (London: Allen & Unwin, 1987), p. 140.

[11] John Brannigan, *Race in Modern Irish Literature and Culture* (Edinburgh: Edinburgh University Press, 2009), p. 23.

version of the Gael'.[12] The awakening of what AE referred to as the 'memory of race', prompted by Standish O'Grady's seminal three-volume series *History of Ireland* (1878–81), led to a 'search for the qualities that might be described as the essence of the race'.[13] The formation of a unique racial and cultural basis for the Irish is reflected in early Revivalist theatrical attempts to consolidate an apolitical audience around an aesthetic project based in a unified view of the national character. Over time, however, 'Irishness increasingly revealed itself unable to efface fully the differences among the diverse individuals who composed these audiences'.[14] As the audience at the Abbey altered (as it did when ticket prices were reduced prior to the first production of *The Playboy of the Western World*), the illusion of a cohesive Irish audience was dispersed, and this was recognized by Yeats, who gradually amended the ideal of a theatre for 'all Irish people' to one for 'vigorous and simple men' fractured along lines of gender, class, and education.[15] Synge's increasingly combative turn against a homogeneous and idealized Irish peasant (and Irish audience) is reflected, in this way, in the changing tenor of Yeats's thought.

Theories of race, here, intersect with social and cultural theories of degeneration: the categories, as Synge's work demonstrates, are often blurred, so that where cultural regeneration might be posited as a remedy in some instances, in others eugenic regeneration is implied. In *Playboy*, Synge comes close to a eugenic discourse; however, his 'solution' (so far as a play as ambiguous as *Playboy* can ever be said to deal in 'solutions') is concerned with social and economic causes. Removing social and economic restrictions on marriages; untying concerns of property from matters of sexuality; reforming demoralizing schemes of modernization; and an overall revolution against social convention in favour of 'organic' morality: all are figured as potential forms of regeneration. His socialism, but also his sense

---

[12] Geraldine Higgins, *Heroic Revivals from Carlyle to Yeats* (Basingstoke: Palgrave Macmillan, 2012), p. 16.

[13] Higgins, *Heroic Revivals*, p. 40. See also AE [George William Russell], 'Standish O'Grady', in *Imaginations and Reveries* (Dublin and London: Maunsel & Roberts, 1921), 2nd edn., 12–21, p. 13.

[14] Paige Reynolds, *Modernism, Drama, and the Audience for Irish Spectacle* (Cambridge: Cambridge University Press, 2007), p. 12.

[15] See Reynolds, *Modernism, Drama, and the Audience for Irish Spectacle*, p. 12. Quotations from Gregory, *Our Irish Theatre*, p. 20, and W. B. Yeats, 'Discoveries' (1906), in *Essays and Introductions*, 261–97, p. 265. Morash suggests that Synge was 'more clear-sighted' regarding the factious nature of the Abbey audience than other playwrights. See *A History of the Irish Theatre, 1601–2000*, p. 117. For more on the controversy over ticket prices at the Abbey previous to the production of *Playboy*, see Adrian Frazier, *Behind the Scenes*, p. 173.

of Romantic (even anarchic) revolutionism, are thus fundamental to the sophisticated protest of *The Playboy*.

That Synge's play might draw on eugenicist discourses has been suggested in passing by a number of critics, though Susan Cannon Harris was the first to undertake a proper study of the confluence of the contemporary concern for 'public health' in relation to the adverse reaction to Synge's play.[16] Harris, who notes that the premiere of *Playboy* coincided with the foundation of the Eugenics Education Society in England in 1907, uncovers the nexus of national health concerns in nationalist newspapers (particularly Arthur Griffith's *Sinn Féin*), and sees contemporary eugenicist readings of Synge's play as symptomatic of broader concerns about social hygiene and racial purity. Harris shows that nationalist concerns for the condition of the Irish race, combined with a distrust of British government schemes, led to various public health initiatives being seen as 'assault[s] on the Irish race'.[17] As the pages of *Sinn Féin* in the weeks leading up to the first production of *Playboy* attest, 'Griffith and his contributors identified imperial science, when practiced in Ireland, as a vector of disease and degeneration rather than as a prophylactic.'[18] Synge maintains a parallel association of imperialism with degeneration, though this is understood in very different terms, as we will see. Griffith's acceptance of the principles of eugenics led him to view *Playboy* as an attack on Irish racial health akin to those made by imperial agents. Harris's work shows, therefore, that the reaction to *Playboy* was in part influenced by a contemporary concern with racial degeneration, linked to concerns about depopulation and critiques of economic policy but also to narratives of imperialism. However, Harris's argument is less concerned with the text itself than with what was read into it by its first audiences. Harris's critique has since been built upon by Nicholas Crawford, who has argued that the modernism of Synge's play can be interpreted as a rebellion against literary influence, allegorized both in Synge's presentation of Christy's growth as an 'evolutionary fantasy of

---

[16] See, for example, George Cusack, '"In the gripe of a ditch": nationalism, famine and The Playboy of the Western World', in George Cusack and Sarah Goss, eds., *Hungry Words: Images of Famine in the Irish Canon* (Dublin and Portland, OR: Irish Academic Press, 2006), 133–58. Cusack identifies the 'eugenic tone' of the proposed marriages in *Playboy*, and sees this as a demonstration of 'the Darwinian mentality which underlies the villagers' understanding of their own situation' (p. 144).

[17] Susan Cannon Harris, 'More than a Morbid, Unhealthy Mind: Public Health and the Playboy riots', in Stephen Watt, Eileen Morgan, and Shakir Mustafa, eds., *A Century of Irish Drama: Widening the Stage* (Indianapolis: Indiana University Press, 2000), 72–94, p. 73.

[18] Harris, 'Public Health and the *Playboy* riots', p. 73.

language', a 'linguistic eugenics', and in terms of the overarching narrative of the play, wherein Christy aims to 'kill his father and reinvigorate his heritage' by marrying Pegeen Mike.[19]

As we have seen in 'From the Congested Districts' and his Wicklow essays, however, Synge was drawing on degenerationist discourses both before and during the time he was composing *Playboy*. The text itself, and not just the reaction to the performed play, draws on these debates. Though Crawford recognizes the debt to eugenics in the narrative of *Playboy*, he does not foreground, as this chapter does, Synge's engagement with contemporary politics as couched in eugenicist terms, nor does he explore Synge's own well-documented concern with heredity and evolutionism. In *Playboy*, Synge moves closer to the development of a eugenic discourse more commonly associated with later modernisms, such as Yeats's authoritarianism, or Pound's fascism. Whereas Yeats would later criticize Russian communism for wielding 'the necessary authority' but incorrectly thinking 'the social problem economic and not eugenic and ethnic', however, Synge's deployment of eugenic discourses veers away from ideas of ethnic purity and towards a critique of bourgeois morality, capitalist economics, and imperialism.[20] As a form of discursive retribution against certain restrictive politics, *Playboy* deploys a drama of sexual selection in a degenerated landscape in order to posit ironic humour, imaginative freedom, and 'savage' violence as a revitalizing impulse.[21] In a number of logical reversals of the doctrines of Irish racial purity, the characters in both *Playboy* and a number of other unperformed scenarios propound a violent vitality as preferable to a degenerate modern Ireland, and posit the restrictive nationalism of the likes of Sinn Féin and the Gaelic League as conversely degenerationist.

Critics have often been tempted by the ambiguity of Synge's text to 'solve' the problem of the play through allegorical and mythological readings, and eugenicist or Darwinian readings risk simply adding to this trend. To see Christy as a Christ figure, or a modern-day Cuchulain, or a mock Oedipus, or even a mock Christ, are not invalid readings per se, but they do incline towards taking unconscious or semi-conscious parody to the level of

[19] Nicholas Crawford, 'Synge's *Playboy* and the Eugenics of Language', *Modern Drama*, Vol. 51, No. 4 (Winter 2008), 482–500, p. 483.

[20] W. B. Yeats, 'On the Boiler' (1939), *Explorations* (New York: Macmillan, 1962), 407–44, p. 424.

[21] For an exploration of regenerative violence in Irish modernism texts, see Sarah Cole, *At the Violet Hour: Modernism and Violence in England and Ireland* (Oxford and New York: Oxford University Press, 2012), pp. 131–96.

authorial intention.[22] As Nicholas Grene argues, 'the action of the play is rooted in substantial and immediate reality, without mythical or literary *arrière-pensées*.'[23] Synge's relationship to Darwinism, however, is well documented, though his concern with heredity (and especially with notions of racial improvement and degeneration) is less so. Ronan McDonald has skilfully shown how ancestral guilt and a preoccupation with heredity feeds into Synge's drama, most notably with regard to the Oedipal plot of *Playboy*, though this reading is primarily focused on Synge's own personal–political Anglo-Irish relationship to the peasantry.[24] Childs, too, has identified Synge's *Playboy* as exhibiting a knowledge of eugenicist discourses, and lists Synge as one of a number of modernists whom new studies in eugenics and literature must address, though Childs's own work focuses on W. B. Yeats, who exhibits (particularly in *On the Boiler* (1939), and through his membership of the Eugenics Society) a more direct and authoritarian relationship to notions of selective breeding.[25] Unlike with Yeats, however, Childs suggests that Synge's 'pervasive irony' means that determining the author's own opinion on eugenics is 'impossible'.[26]

Eugenics in Ireland only fully took hold in Protestant Belfast, with the Catholic Church (though it was sympathetic to the general idea) remaining cautious about the interventions in family life proposed by negative eugenics.[27] The fact that Ireland was less industrialized than Britain, and that eugenics was generally symptomatic of a fear of the urban poor, meant that the rural populations of the western seaboard who were idealized by various nationalisms were not seen as threatening to racial purity. Rather, they were the essence of it, though what characterized this essence was contested territory. In 1906, M. J. Nolan, medical superintendent of the

---

[22] For Christy as Christ, see Stanley Sultan, 'A Joycean Look at The Playboy of the Western World', in Harmon, ed., *The Celtic Master*, 45–55; for Cuchulain, see Declan Kiberd, *Synge and the Irish Language* (London and Basingstoke: Macmillan, 1979), pp. 115–21; for mock Oedipus, see Warren Atkin IV, '"I Just Riz the Loy": The Oedipal Dimension of "The Playboy of the Western World"', *South Atlantic Bulletin*, Vol. 45, No. 4 (Nov. 1980), 55–65; for mock Christ, see Howard D. Pearce, 'Synge's Playboy as Mock-Christ', in Thomas R. Whitaker, ed., *Twentieth Century Interpretations of The Playboy of the Western World: A Collection of Critical Essays* (Englewood Cliffs, NJ: Prentice-Hall, 1969), 88–97.
[23] Grene, *Synge: A Critical Study of the Plays*, p. 133.
[24] Ronan McDonald, *Tragedy and Irish Literature: Synge, O'Casey, Beckett* (Basingstoke: Macmillan, 2002), pp. 54, 71.
[25] For more on Yeats's promotion of selective breeding, see W. J. McCormack, *Blood Kindred: W. B. Yeats: The Life, The Death, The Politics* (London: Pimlico, 2005), pp. 257–69.
[26] Childs, *Modernism and Eugenics*, p. 10.
[27] Greta Jones, 'Eugenics in Ireland: The Belfast Eugenics Society, 1911–15', *Irish Historical Studies*, Vol. 28, No. 109 (May 1992), 81–95, pp. 91–5.

Down District Asylum, proposed a number of eugenic measures which he intended to ensure racial regeneration across the whole of Ireland. These were particularly concerned with marital arrangements (especially consanguineous marriages), reproduction, and the sectioning of the mentally ill.[28] Unfortunately, this does not appear to be the M. J. Nolan with whom Synge corresponded after the *Playboy* riots, who identifies himself in his letters as a Dublin-based fruit-seller.[29] The Belfast Eugenics Society, which launched in 1911, survived only until 1915, and the Dublin society, which was proposed in 1911, seems never to have established itself. Discussions of marital regulation and the control of reproduction and the mentally ill, however, were widespread in Ireland in the years 1906 and 1907, and these discourses are clearly influential on Synge's work.[30] However, Synge's concern is less with eugenics as a principle than with eugenics as analogous to the restriction of Irish identity to something less vigorous or vital, and to the imposition of 'unnatural' regulation and competition into the lives of the peasantry, thus removing them more completely from their 'authentic' connection to the landscape. *The Playboy of the Western World* mobilizes eugenic language in both these senses, using a Darwinian process of sexual selection in order to critique the debilitating effects of homogenizing capitalist modernity.

Synge's deployment of these discourses in *Playboy* did not go unnoticed, and contemporary reactions illustrate how closely his play interacted with the cultural and political zeitgeist of the Revival. Writing in *The Irish Times* during the week of riots sparked by the first production, the popular social and cultural commentator P. D. Kenny rallied to the defence of that 'highly moral play'.[31] For Kenny (who was also a keen advocate of national self-criticism), Synge's play depicted with 'merciless accuracy' the social, cultural, and economic degradation of the western peasantry, and the audience's adverse reaction was the symptom of its unwillingness to face facts: 'It is as if we looked in a mirror for the first time, and found ourselves hideous. We fear to face the thing.... We scream.'[32] Kenny's contention that Synge's play was 'highly moral' (his was almost a lone voice in an otherwise

---

[28] See Jones, 'Eugenics in Ireland', p. 87.

[29] For Synge's correspondence with M. J. Nolan, see TCD MS 4424–6, Items 301, 305, 496, 498, 532, 535, 544, which range between 6 February 1907 and 7 March 1909.

[30] Jones, 'Eugenics in Ireland', p. 91.

[31] P. D. Kenny, 'That Dreadful Play', *The Irish Times*, 30 January 1907, p. 9.

[32] Kenny, 'That Dreadful Play', p. 9. See D. P. Moran, *The Philosophy of Irish Ireland*, ed. Patrick Maume (Dublin: University College Dublin Press, 2006), especially p. 79.

general attack on *The Playboy*'s 'unmitigated, protracted libel') stems from his reading of the play as a commentary on both nationalist squeamishness and the thwarting of the doctrine of the 'survival of the fittest' amongst the peasantry.[33] A number of contemporaneous interpretations of Synge's *Playboy* saw the courting competition in the play (between Shawn, Christy, Pegeen, and the Widow Quin) in specifically Darwinian terms: alongside Kenny's analysis, for example, a Mr Sheehan spoke during the Abbey's 'Freedom of the Theatre' debate (chaired by Kenny himself) to say that 'he had never seen the doctrine of survival of the fittest treated with such living force as by Mr. Synge in his play'.[34] Even Lady Gregory, to whom we should grant more authority as an explicator of *The Playboy*'s significance for Synge, suggested that the play presented the original Dublin audience with the 'foreshadowing of what will happen if emigration goes on carrying off, year by year, the strongest, the most healthy, the most energetic'.[35] Gregory's theory is backed up in the manuscript drafts of *Playboy*, where Michael is frustrated at his inability to get a good pot-boy: 'where would I get one unless I sent the Town-Crier shouting through the streets of New York?'[36] Kenny's analysis went further, focusing on the character of Shawn Keogh ('Shaneen'), and identifying *The Playboy* as a critique of the social malaise of the Mayo Congested Districts in more strictly Darwinian terms:

> Character wants freedom, and so escapes, but the 'Shaneens' remain to reproduce themselves in the social scheme. We see in him how the Irish race die out in Ireland, filling the lunatic asylums more full from a declining population, and selecting for continuance in the future the human specimens most calculated to bring the race lower and lower.

---

[33] The reviewer for *Freeman's Journal*, writing on the Monday of the opening week of *The Playboy*, expressed his indignation against 'this squalid, offensive production', which was an 'unmitigated, protracted libel upon Irish peasant men and, worse still, upon Irish peasant girlhood'. See 'The Abbey Theatre, "The Playboy of the Western World"', *Freeman's Journal*, 28 January 1907, p. 10. For a full documentary account of the media reaction to Synge's play, see James Kilroy, *The 'Playboy' Riots* (Dublin: Dolmen, 1971).

[34] *Freeman's Journal*, 5 February 1907, pp. 6–7. Reprinted in Kilroy, *The 'Playboy' Riots*, p. 86.

[35] Lady Gregory, 'An Explanation', *The Arrow*, 4 (1 June 1907), p. 3. Quoted in Paige Reynolds, 'Reading Publics, Theater Audiences, and the Little Magazines of the Abbey Theatre', *New Hibernia Review/Iris Éireannach Nua*, Vol. 7, No. 4 (Winter 2003), 63–84, p. 80.

[36] TCD MS 4331–3, f. 82. 'New York' is given variously as Cork and Tralee, and Synge eventually settles on Castlebar in the published text, perhaps in order to emphasize the isolated location of the shebeen from even local urban areas. See TCD MS 4331–3, f. 105.

'Shaneen' shows us why Ireland dies while the races around us prosper faster and faster.[37]

This is a fine example of the slippage between discourses of social and genetic degeneration: adverse political and economic conditions, in Kenny's analysis, lead eventually to genetic racial degeneration through breeding of less desirable 'specimens'. We find the same slippage, and consequent regenerative reversal, employed by Synge. Rather than suggesting eugenic solutions (such as restrictions on, or promotion of, desired sexual relations), Synge suggests altering sociocultural conditions in order to promote cultural (and even perhaps biological) regeneration.

As Lionel Pilkington has observed, Kenny and Synge shared a 'network of similar political views', particularly with regard to certain forms of nationalist orthodoxy.[38] Kenny's *Economics for Irishmen* (1906), which ran to several editions, began with a strongly worded attack on Irish nationalist thought, which 'confines itself largely to praising itself, which, in man or nation, is a sign of weakness, and a loss of strength'.[39] *Economics* was originally published in the Dominican monthly *Irish Rosary*, though a chapter criticizing the clergy was only added to the book later, to the irritation of Kenny's former sponsors.[40] Kenny was a vocal critic of Irish social mores, and particularly resentful of the education system, the clergy, and the United Irish League, whom he saw as 'hostile to new ideas and enforcing conformity'.[41] His book attempts to diagnose the economic troubles of Ireland in terms of this perceived ineptitude for self-criticism, and the 'misdirection' of the 'national mind', which has led to a 'decadent scene of social friction' and a degradation in the life of the peasantry.[42] Here, Kenny's anti-decadent language is reminiscent of Synge's own, though Synge employs the language of disease and degeneration perhaps more openly. Writing to Stephen MacKenna, Synge pitted himself against a 'purely fantastic, unmodern, ideal, spring-dayish, Cuchulanoid National Theatre', adding that 'I think squeamishness is a disease and that Ireland will gain if Irish writers deal manfully, directly, and decently with the entire

---

[37] Kenny, 'That Dreadful Play', p. 9.

[38] Lionel Pilkington, '"The Most Unpopular Man in Ireland": P. D. Kenny, J. M. Synge and Irish Cultural History', *The Irish Review*, No. 29 (Autumn 2002), 51–7, p. 52.

[39] P. D. Kenny, *Economics for Irishmen* (Dublin: Maunsel, 1906), p. 1.

[40] Patrick Maume, *The Long Gestation: Irish Nationalist Life, 1891–1918* (New York: St. Martin's Press, 1999), p. 84.

[41] Maume, *The Long Gestation*, p. 83.   [42] Kenny, *Economics*, pp. 8–9, 131.

reality of life.'[43] Synge's critique of an ideal national drama draws on the same terms as Kenny's critique of national self-image in his *Economics*.

Of course, Kenny's analysis of Synge's play could be attributed to the prejudices of his own social commentary, and we might put aside its assertions as bearing no more consequence to Synge's own vision of the play than any other contemporary review. It would seem, in fact, that Kenny's appraisal of Synge's play was an extension of his own thought with regard to land management, employment, and 'human progress' in rural Ireland. The similarity between Kenny's *Economics* and Synge's *Playboy* was even the subject of crossed wires in the correspondence between Synge and the Scottish artist James Paterson, who was commissioned to paint Synge's portrait. Writing to Synge after having read *Playboy*, Paterson commented that 'Some things in the play I understood better from "Economics for Irishmen".'[44] Assuming that Synge had sent both texts together, Paterson had little trouble in viewing them as complementary.[45] Even though this was not the case, Paterson's sense that Kenny's book and Synge's play were in some way kindred is not unfounded. In *Economics*, Kenny laments that:

Even the institution of marriage among us is vitiated by our agrarian peculiarities, husbands and wives being selected, not on the standard of their character, and not on any other natural basis that could encourage social and moral elevation, but rather on the standard of the farms with which they are associated. As I have shown before, the better the farm, the more useless the man, in many cases if not generally; but it is the farm that is married, so that the farmer reproduces his imbecility for his country's benefit, while the man of ability emigrates. Agitation and the Acts of Parliament accommodating it have made the incapable farmer the stand-ard for the rest, suspending the competitive process, which alone could bring out character in the people, and now we pay for it in lunatic asylums filling up, from a population that goes down. In Great Britain, with the tenure of the land open to the fittest man, he, and not the imbecile privileged by statute, is the man most likely to reproduce himself, thereby

---

[43] J. M. Synge to Stephen MacKenna, 28 January 1904. *CL* I, pp. 74–5.

[44] TCD MS 4424–6, Item 308. Letter from James Paterson to J. M. Synge, dated 26 February 1907.

[45] TCD MS 4424–6, Item 308. Letter from James Paterson to J. M. Synge, dated 26 February 1907.

preserving a capable race on the soil, which is always the primary source of sound human stock in any country.[46]

The economic situation of land ownership has primacy, for Kenny, in the degeneration of the 'human stock' of the country. As Synge picks up in his notes on Darwin's *The Descent of Man* (see below), the modern form of sexual selection rests on status and wealth, rather than on physical attributes or aesthetics. The 'suspension of the competitive process', for Kenny, is framed as unnatural both in economic and biological terms. Furthermore, the unwillingness to admit such 'facts' has led to a 'weakness' in the national life of Ireland, resulting in 'decadence'. That Kenny should focus on marital law and custom in this instance gives us an insight into why the courtship plot of Synge's *Playboy* should have caught his eye.

Even from an early age, Synge's own illness led him to take a serious decision regarding his future life. Before encountering Darwinism, he tells us in his 'Autobiography', he became concerned with notions of heredity through his naturalist pursuits, particularly his breeding of rabbits:

> This ill health led to a curious resolution which has explained in some measure all my subsequent evolution. Without knowing, or, so far as I can remember, hearing anything about doctrines of heredity I surmised that unhealthy parents should have unhealthy children – my rabbit breeding may have put the idea into my head. Therefore, I said, I am unhealthy, and if I marry I will have unhealthy children. But I will never create beings to suffer as I am suffering, so I will never marry.   (*CW* II, 9)

Synge's contention that this resolution might act as a key to 'all [his] subsequent evolution' is intriguing, not least because of his propensity to judge both real-life social, economic, and cultural conditions as well as literary styles by their degree of healthiness. After the *Playboy* riots, the literary implications of this concern seem to have dogged him even more thoroughly, and one of his last surviving notebooks (written in 1907) contains a series of thoughts on the definition of 'healthy' and 'unhealthy' literature.[47] On reading Darwin, however, this nexus of concerns with evolution and heredity was extended. Famously, on reading a passage 'where [Darwin] asks how can we explain the similarity between a man's

---

[46] Kenny, *Economics*, pp. 131–2.   [47] See TCD MS 4405.

hand and a bird's or bat's wing except by evolution', Synge 'writhed in an agony of doubt' (*CW* II, 10). He continues,

> I had of course heard of atheists but as vague monsters that I was unable to realize. It seemed that I was become in a moment the playfellow of Judas. Incest and parricide were but a consequence of the idea that possessed me.
>
> (*CW* II, 11)

The depiction of the processes of evolution and natural selection in Darwin led in the young Synge's mind to both immorality and various aberrations of the system of heredity itself. 'Incest and parricide', after all, are both acts which are deemed contrary to reproduction, in the case of the former, and heredity, in the case of the latter. This observation is striking when considered alongside *Playboy*, itself a play which flirts with incest (in the suspicion that the Widow Casey was Christy's wet nurse) and which relates two (failed) acts of parricide. Synge, revising his 'Autobiography' sometime around 1907, must certainly have been struck by this coincidence, if indeed it was not intentional.[48]

Synge's preoccupation with heredity was particularly focused on the act of courtship, and on sexual selection and its effects on the characteristics of a species. In his notes on Darwin's *The Descent of Man, and Selection in Relation to Sex* (1871), Synge paid particular attention to Darwin's descriptions of the 'love of savages for ornament', and to the idea that 'Birds are the most aesthetic of all animals (except man)'.[49] Darwin puts forward a number of unsettling ideas in his *Descent*, bolstering his arguments with those of his cousin Francis Galton and W. R. Greg, pioneers of the British eugenics movement, though he is careful to distinguish his own conclusions from theirs. Darwin, for example, notes the 'problem' of the high birth rate among 'the very poor and reckless', in contrast to the low birth rate in the 'superior class', and makes a specific example, quoting Greg, of the 'careless, squalid, unaspiring Irishman' who 'multiplies like rabbits'.[50] This would certainly have caught Synge's attention, as would the preceding passages referring

---

[48] Alan Price suggests that Synge's typewritten sheets of revisions for the 'Autobiography' were 'made probably in 1907'. See *CW* II, p. 3, n. 1.

[49] TCD MS 4379, ff. 76r, 79r. For Darwin's description of 'ornament' in 'savage' peoples, and the 'influence of beauty in determining the marriages of mankind', see Darwin, *The Descent of Man*, pp. 640–44. For Darwin's work on the 'taste for the beautiful' in birds, see *Descent*, pp. 455–98.

[50] Darwin, *Descent*, pp. 163–4.

to Galton's work, *Hereditary Genius: An Inquiry into Its Laws and Consequences* (1869), published only two years prior to Darwin's book.[51] However, Darwin suggests that there are 'some checks in this downward tendency', particularly in that 'the intemperate suffer from a high rate of mortality, and the extremely profligate leave few offspring'.[52] Although Synge's notes are relatively selective, he does pick up on the idea that 'sexual selection today ... hinges on wealth and social [status]', a potential cause of 'degeneration' in the physical characteristics of a species, unless one also suggests that the wealthier and higher-status individuals are also the most developed.[53] The same idea arises in Kenny's *Economics*, as seen above. Either way, Synge is sure to note Darwin's caveat that sympathy is found in 'the noblest part of our nature', and that (in Synge's paraphrase) 'if we were intentionally to neglect the weak and helpless (for the good of the race) it could only be for a contingent benefit with an overwhelming present evil'.[54] This note is clearly a quotation from Darwin and not a personal 'admission of [Synge's] socialist politics', as Christopher Collins has asserted, though Synge's political bias is obviously instrumental in his note-taking.[55]

That sexual selection and ornament, both in musical and visual terms, were of importance to Synge is shown also in a now lost letter to his friend Robert Peers, a linguistics enthusiast whom he met while staying in Germany. In his reply, Peers answers a series of questions posed by Synge regarding sexual selection in birds, and also on the development of the eye. It should be noted, before quoting from this letter, that Peers was at this time serious about spelling reform, and his correspondence is carried out phonetically. Synge even wrote some verses for him on the 'Reformer and Conservative in Spelling', and seems to have picked up on Peers's interest by reading *The Phonetic Journal*, a copy of which is found in Synge's miscellanea at Trinity College Dublin.[56] Peers, who was clearly engaged in contemporary debates on evolution, pointed Synge to *The Descent of Man*, but summarized Darwin's argument thus:

---

[51] See Darwin, *Descent*, pp. 159–62.   [52] Darwin, *Descent*, p. 164.

[53] TCD MS 4379, f. 76r.   [54] TCD MS 4379, f. 80r. See Darwin, *Descent*, p. 159.

[55] Collins, *Theatre and Residual Culture*, p. 14.

[56] For Synge's poem, see TCD MS 4361, f. 6. One of Synge's copies of the weekly magazine *The Phonetic Journal*, which was 'devoted to the propagation of Pitman's Shorthand (Phonography) and phonetic reading, writing and printing', is in TCD MS 4368. The date of the journal is 26 October 1895, nearly a year after Synge and Peers corresponded on sexual selection, suggesting a continued interest on Synge's part.

He thinks that it iz diu tu the selekshon ov the femailz, hwo in sum spesheez hav regular konserts ov mail voisez given befoar them, and hwen the onkoarz ar aul thru, the femail givz her timid 'Yes' tu the mail hwos tenor or bais iz the best in her estimaishon, and thai theirupon wauk of arm in arm. The rezult iz that the mail desendants ov the kupel hav gud voisez in aul probabiliti, and the uther mailz, hwo hav tu reteir bei the bak dor ov the theater with no Fraus, dei in negleckt, without progeni. Hens, the rais az a hoal, haz a beter voiz in the mail memberz that it had sum teim befoar. The reason hwei the karakteristiks ov the mail bird ar not inherited bei the femal tu in the progeny iz not az yet fuli eksplaind, ani moar than it iz hwei yur fais iz bearded hweil yur sisters iz not.[57]

Peers's tongue-in-cheek analogy of the concert and the theatre, with the female of the species sitting in judgement of the male, would perhaps have rung true for Synge, a young violinist dealing with his own lack of romantic success. As Synge himself noted, the 'Music[al] faculty [was] probably first used and perfected in relation to the propagation of the species'.[58] It is clear from Peers's reply, here, that Synge was consciously linking Darwinian notions of sexual selection in birds to what he perceived as a lack of ornament in vertebrates, particularly human beings. The image of the female choosing between potential mates might also set the precedent for Synge's own presentation of Pegeen's choice of the newly eloquent playboy in Christy Mahon. Peers continues,

hwen yu sai that seksual diferensez ar not meerli az komon in the Manmalia az in birds, ei du not se hwair yu get fakts tu substantiat yur viu. Taik our oan human rais. Ar thair not seksual diferensez enuf thair? Houever, on luking at yur leter again, ei se that yu sai 'ornamental diferensez' ar not so komon. Ei shud sai that that waz so. The moar meerli nesesari diferensez heer seem to predominait over thoaz that mai be eksplaind on the biuti standpoint. Posibili the kompetishon haz bin stonger [sic] on land than in the air, or in the habitat ov Mamalz than in that ov birdz, thus giving moar chans for the evolushon ov the les absoliutli necesari feetiurz.[59]

---

[57] TCD MS 4424–6, Item 29. Letter from Robert Peers to J. M. Synge, dated 7 August 1894.
[58] TCD MS 4379, f. 76r.   [59] TCD MS 4424–6, Item 29.

Synge's insistence on ornamental differences, both in his notes on Darwin (which may, in fact, have been made after Peers's suggestion to reread *Descent*) and in his letter to Peers, suggests his preoccupation with the predominance of cultural and social differences in mankind in lieu of natural bodily ornamentation. Evolution, Synge notes, occurs on both the sociocultural and biological planes. This correspondence, of which this letter is unfortunately the only extant example, would certainly have furnished critics with a greater insight into Synge's particular concerns with regard to heredity and selection: Peers mentions previous discussions of August Weisman's theory of heredity (published a year earlier, in 1893) as a retort to Herbert Spencer, and also suggests a knowledge of contemporary debates by referring to Ernst Haeckel's *The History of Creation* (1884) as being 'ofensiv az tu Weisman'z Theori'.[60]

Just a year later, around the same time he was reading Darwin's *Descent*, Synge was also engaged in a broad study of evolutionism, social Darwinism, and natural theology, drawing on the work of Henry Drummond (discussed in the second chapter of this book) and Benjamin Kidd's *Social Evolution*, both published in 1894.[61] From this reading, it would appear that Synge was actively seeking out spiritual and political refutations to the more sinister leanings of social Darwinism prevalent in the 1890s. As Gregory Claeys has shown, there was no single political corollary for social Darwinism, and not all forms of it were illiberal: authors used it, for example, to bolster arguments for collectivism, for socialism, and for anarchism.[62] Hawkins has suggested the term 'reform Darwinists' for those theorists, including A. R. Wallace and Ernst Haeckel, who utilized Darwinism to argue for greater equality, public welfare, and democracy.[63] In the case of Kidd's *Social Evolution*, the state was figured as a potentially benevolent institution that could alter social and economic conditions in order to assist social evolution and allow individual freedom to flourish. Kidd also, like Drummond and others, argued that increased religious sensitivity was the direction of the evolution of human society.[64] The return to nature, variously conceived in matters of property, sexual relationships, and morality,

---

[60] Peers is most likely referring to Weismann's *The Germ-Plasm: A Theory of Heredity* (1893).

[61] See Synge's diary for 1895, TCD MS 4416.

[62] Gregory Claeys, 'The "Survival of the Fittest" and the Origins of Social Darwinism', *Journal of the History of Ideas*, Vol. 61, No. 2 (April 2000), 223–40, p. 228.

[63] Mike Hawkins, *Social Darwinism in European and American Thought, 1860–1945* (Cambridge: Cambridge University Press, 1997), p. 151.

[64] Kidd, *Social Evolution*, p. 245.

was thus not necessarily a conservative move. Synge's engagement with social Darwinism likewise seeks in the matrix of contemporary theories those which sanction a liberal rather than restrictive or authoritarian politics.

One of Synge's principal critics during the pre-*Playboy* years was Arthur Griffith, editor of the *United Irishman* and later founder, in 1905, of Sinn Féin. Griffith's conservative agenda during this period included, as Geraldine Higgins suggests, the policing of gender and nationalist–cultural politics: 'His creed of "home and hearth nationalism" combined protective chauvinism and protectionist economics.'[65] One of Griffith's main attacks on Synge came during the production of *The Well of the Saints* (1905), during which the row over Synge's earlier play, *The Shadow of the Glen* (1903), was revived in the pages of the *United Irishman*.[66] During this time, Synge began to pen a series of satirical scenarios in which he mocked what he viewed as pious and conservative strains of nationalism. In these plays, ideas of selective breeding and racial degeneration are paramount, and are the subject of Synge's most vicious attacks. Griffith's concern for a conservative 'Irish-Ireland' identity was translated by Synge in these scenarios into one which would result, through a series of comic logical turns, in racial degeneration. Synge satirizes rather than endorses Griffith's attempts to preserve a pious racial purity, reversing the eugenic principle of racial improvement. In two different scenarios, he draws out the darkly comedic and farcical logic of ideas of Irish racial and cultural purity. In the first, set after 'the Gaels have conquered' Ireland again, a pan-Celtic congress is held in Dublin and a contest is underway. In an eerily prophetic note, this pan-Celtic congress to determine the essence of the 'Irish race' was imagined by Synge as occurring in 1920; in fact, in 1922, the first 'Irish Race Congress' was held at the Hotel Continental in Paris. Ironically, alongside Lady Gregory's *The Rising of the Moon*, Synge's own *Riders to the Sea* was chosen to represent the best qualities of the Irish race.[67] In Synge's imagined congress, a competition is being held in which 'a large prize is offered for any Irishman who can be proved to know no English':

> They bring in each man in turn, throw a light on him and say 'God save Ireland' and 'To Hell with the Pope'. Men are detected again and again.

---

[65] Higgins, *Heroic Revivals*, pp. 78–9.

[66] For a documentary history of this controversy, see Hogan and Kilroy, eds., *The Abbey Theatre: The Years of Synge*, pp. 9–18.

[67] For more on this congress and its literary influences, see Brannigan, *Race in Modern Irish Literature and Culture*, pp. 16–77.

One is found at last who baffles all tests. In delight the congress is called in
in glorious robes; the victor is put up to make a speech in Irish, he begins
talking on his fingers – he is deaf mute and advocates a deaf mute society as
only safeguard against encroaching Anglo-Saxon vulgarity!

(CW III, 218)

That the members of the pan-Celtic congress expect the Irishmen to
react in prescribed ways to the phrases 'God save Ireland' and 'To Hell
with the Pope' suggests an alignment of Irishness with nationalism and
Catholicism, closely associating this imagined committee with the tenets
of national identity outlined by Arthur Griffith in the *United Irishman*.
Not only this, but Synge's scenario ridicules the naivety of a congress
which advocates national self-harm as the only way of denying anglicization. The 'Irish-Irelanders', typified in the figures of Arthur Griffith
and D. P. Moran (whom P. J. Mathews has termed a 'racial nationalist'),
are satirized as having the potential to bring about severe racial disfigure-
ment in their quest to circumscribe a moral Irishness protected from
'vulgarity'.[68]

In the second possible scenario for 'Deaf Mutes for Ireland', which
follows on from the first, Synge takes the concept of deaf-muteness as a
representation of a stubborn and futile resistance to natural evolution
to a more stark and violent level. In this scenario, it is the year 2000.
Synge's extension into the distant future allows him to imagine a time in
which biological degeneration from restrictive nationalism will have
taken a firm hold. Here, an American nerve doctor is investigating the
epidemic of deaf-muteness in Ireland, and reads out a tract he has found
on the subject:

About the year 1920 it was discovered that the efforts of the Gaelic League
to withstand the inroads of Anglo-Saxon vulgarity, American commercialism, French morals and German free-thought <had been unsuccessful,
therefore> the executive of the Gaelic League and the United Irish
League decided that drastic measures must be taken without delay if the
sacred entity of the Irish and Celtic soul was to be saved from corruption.

---

[68] P. J. Mathews, *Revival: The Abbey Theatre, Sinn Féin, the Gaelic League and the
Co-operative Movement* (Cork: Cork University Press, 2003), p. 98. Moran's insistence on the
Gaelic race, on being 'original Irish', is certainly an attempt to circumscribe nationalist politics
to racial identifiers. See Moran, *The Philosophy of Irish Ireland*, p. 26.

At a crowded meeting it was resolved that as Ireland could not speak Irish rather <than> us<ing> the filthy accents <of> England she would be speechless. Young and intelligent organizers were at once secured, and before long they had touched the saintly and patriotic hearts of the sweet-minded Irish mother<s>. From their cradles the future hopes of the Gaels—and indeed of Europe and the civilized world—heard no more dirty English stories, no more profane swearing, and their innocent <hearts were> delighted only by the inarticulation of those divine melodies which are the wonder and envy of all nations. A sympathetic conservative secretary was easily induced to force deaf-muteness on the Board of National Schools and in a few years the harsh voice of the National schoolmaster was heard no more. In a little while the degrading tourist traffic ceased entering. A gang of cattle maimers from Athenry broke into Trinity College on <St.> Patrick's Day and cut out the tongues of all the professors, fellows and scholars, the students had become so engrossed with football that they were not regarded as human enough to require this mark of Nationality.   (CW III, 218–19)

Synge is clearly critical of the attempts of the Gaelic League and United Irish League to withstand the influence of international change. As in his letter addressing the League, entitled 'Can We Go Back into Our Mother's Womb?', Synge depicts the proselytizing mission of these Irish-language enthusiasts (whom he relegates to the position of 'senile and slobbering' amateurs) as unmanly, and associated with the 'hysteria of old women's talk'. The 'old and magnificent language of our manuscripts' and the rich dialects of Irish spoken in the west are compared to the 'incoherent twaddle' of the Gaelic Leaguers (CW II, 400). In 'Deaf Mutes', Synge goes further, depicting the League's isolating nationalism and their bland and amateur use of Irish in terms of natural, enforced, and selectively bred disability. The 'mark of Nationality' becomes having no tongue, and the sign of a pure-bred and innocent Irish child is their deaf-muteness. Synge argues that the current Gaelic League is bound for failure, and again rails at the unnatural-ness of their project. As in 'Can we go back into our mother's womb?', the restrictive definitions of nationality proposed by certain newspapers and societies are shown to be working against an evolutionary imperative identified by Synge as tending towards internationalism and pluralism rather than towards isolationism. His understanding of such a process, in fact, may well have been influenced by his readings in Spencerian evolutionism, which defines the evolutionary process as one moving from homogeneity to heterogeneity.[69] Within the tenets of Spencer's theory, then, the homogenizing effects of both modernization and certain forms of cultural nationalism, and the perceived threat of a return to an undifferentiated state, can be read as working against the evolutionary imperative.[70] In 'Deaf Mutes for Ireland', Synge outlines the degeneration which he suggests will result from the imposition of nationalist orthodoxies on the creativity and potential internationalism of Ireland. Conservative nationalism, here, becomes a force for dividing nation from nature.

The more explicit move into social and political criticism that 'Deaf Mutes for Ireland', alongside Synge's other skit of nationalist demands for a 'national drama', *National Drama: A Farce* (c.1905), is reflected in his decision to anchor *The Playboy of the Western World* in an identifiably contemporary setting, both in terms of time and place. In *National Drama*, a committee meets to ascertain a definition of what might constitute an Irish national drama, and the character of Jameson is clearly a mouthpiece for Synge's own views on the subject. Fogarty, who is a 'country upper class Catholic' (*CW* III, 221), begins by going into the club room and reading a series of titles from the bookshelf. Examples include 'The Pedigree of the Widow of Ephesus' (confirming the dating of this farce to after the renewed controversy regarding *The Shadow of the Glen*), and 'The Whole History of Hungary for Beginners, by an Eminent Writer', mockingly referring to Arthur Griffith's 'Hungarian Policy' for nationalist parliamentary abstention, outlined in a series of twenty-seven articles in *United Irishman* between 21 January and 2 July 1904, and later published under the title *The Resurrection of Hungary* in December of the same year. Other books on the shelf include 'The Plays for an Irish Theatre, abridged and expurgated by a Catholic critic', and a book on 'The Re-afforestation of the Sea-Shore', which perhaps refers to (and reflects Synge's disparaging opinion of) Oliver J. Burke's *The South Isles of Aran, County Galway* (1887), which he was sent by the nationalist (and later MP) John Muldoon, after Synge wrote to him asking for introductions to help during his travels in the Congested

---

[69] 'Evolution is an integration of matter and concomitant dissipation of motion; during which the matter passes from an indefinite, incoherent homogeneity to a definite, coherent heterogeneity; and during which the retained motion undergoes a parallel transformation.' Spencer, *First Principles*, p. 358. This definition is transcribed by Synge into his notebook for 1894–5. TCD MS 4379, f. 91v.

[70] Daniel Pick explores the implications of this idea for French decadent writers in particular. See *Faces of Degeneration*, p. 88.

Districts.[71] The censorship of the 'Plays for an Irish Theatre' series, mockingly encapsulated in the imagined subtitle 'abridged and expurgated by a Catholic critic', quickly establishes Synge's antagonism towards these upper-class Catholics, who have 'strong patriotic principles, and a considerable thirst' (CW III, 221). On the same lines as his letter to MacKenna regarding a 'spring-dayish' theatre, Synge has Murphy (another protagonist) advocate a drama that 'shines throughout with the soft light of the ideal impulses of the Gaels' (CW III, 222). Molière, it is argued by Flaherty, cannot be considered a national dramatist because he spends too much time mocking the French; Murphy, on the other hand, suggests that, because France is a decadent country ruined by vice, Molière had no choice and so can be excused. Jameson interjects occasionally to remind the two others of Ireland's own vices ('There are 27 lunatics per thousand in Ireland, the highest figure on earth' (CW III, 223)), and rebukes the idea that an Irish drama 'should hold up the mirror to the Irish Nation and it going to Mass on a fine springdayish Sunday morning' (CW III, 224).[72]

As in a draft of When the Moon Has Set, where Synge's proxy character Colm attributes the 'melancholy degradation' of Ireland, which is 'worse than anything in Paris', to '[t]he old-fashioned Irish conservatism and morality', in his National Drama conservative morality and views of a pious national character are seen to tend towards mental illness.[73] For Synge, the 'national element in art is merely the colour, the intensity of the wildness or restraint of the humour' (CW III, 225), and is not connected to morality or to politics. In National Drama, we see that the controversies over his plays led Synge to a greater self-reflexivity (writing a play about the definition of drama reads as a particularly modernist act), and in both 'Deaf Mutes for Ireland' and National Drama we witness Synge pushing back strongly against the confines of contemporary political definitions, and seeing these (whether in terms of mental or physical health) as contributing factors towards enforced degeneration. Importantly for Playboy, in which

---

[71] Burke discusses the reafforestation of the seashore and the Aran Islands as a way of bringing back some of the spirituality of the Druids who once used such forests for worship. See Oliver J. Burke, The South Isles of Aran, County Galway (London: Kegan Paul, Trench & Co., 1887), especially pp. 15, 82. For John Muldoon's letter to Synge, see TCD MS 4424–6, Item 172. Letter from John Muldoon to J. M. Synge, dated 31 May 1905.

[72] The increase in asylum patients in the late nineteenth century in Ireland is attributed by Catherine Cox to both a growth in the size and number of lunatic asylums themselves and the fact that, because of limited provision of care, a larger number of the mentally ill were institutionalized. See Catherine Cox, Negotiating Insanity in the Southeast of Ireland, 1820–1900 (Manchester: Manchester University Press, 2012), pp. 5–6, 241.

[73] TCD MS 4351, f. 31.

bourgeois Catholicism is critiqued as a stifling form of social oppression, *National Drama* associates the views of the 'Catholic critic' with a bourgeois mentality; hence, his attack on the views of Catholic critics is also an attack on bourgeois values, and by extension an attack on the capitalist modernity he views as detrimental to the peasantry. In this way, his turn towards a more combative theory of drama is rooted in the antagonism towards the middle classes which manifested itself both as a reaction to the critics of his work and as a reaction to the social conditions in the Congested Districts. This turn, therefore, is as much a political as an aesthetic reaction to the new urgency of Synge's socialism.

A number of critics have mentioned *Playboy*'s contemporary setting in passing, though some have continued to level the criticism that Synge produced a drama that exhibited an 'almost total absence of historical references'.[74] Joseph Devlin, Brenda Murphy, and Herbert Howarth all note the links between Synge's travels in the Congested Districts and his decision to set his play in Mayo, with Devlin asserting that *Playboy* 'clearly takes place amid the economic distress' of Mayo which Synge bore witness to in his articles, and Murphy arguing that 'the crucial interaction between Christy and the people of Mayo is defined by the specific social, political, and economic situation in which they find themselves'.[75] The influence of Synge's travels in the Congested Districts, and his awareness of contemporary social and political debates, should not be understated when discussing *Playboy*, which more recent criticism has acknowledged as 'resolutely present-orientated'.[76] Unlike *The Well of the Saints*, which masqueraded as a play with a historical setting (though it was in fact an exploration of cultural modernization), *The Playboy of the Western World* makes no pretence at being temporally distant: there are references in the performed text to the second Boer War (1899–1902), to agrarian crime, and to land agents and bailiffs, and these go even further in the drafts, which name particular landlords, agents, bailiffs, and even Colonel Lynch and Sean

---

[74] Deane, *Celtic Revivals*, p. 55.

[75] Joseph Devlin, 'J. M. Synge's *The Playboy of the Western World* and the Culture of Western Ireland under Late Colonial Rule', *Modern Drama*, Vol. 41, No. 3 (Fall 1998), 371–835, p. 375; Brenda Murphy, '"The Treachery of Law": Reading the Political Synge', *Colby Quarterly*, Vol. 28, No. 1 (March 1992), 45–51, p. 47. See also Herbert Howarth, 'The Realist Basis of Surreality', in Whitaker, ed. *Twentieth Century Interpretations of The Playboy of the Western World*, 106–11.

[76] Shaun Richards, 'The Playboy of the Western World', in Mathews, ed., *The Cambridge Companion to J. M. Synge*, 28–40, p. 28. See also McCormack, *Fool of the Family*, p. 320, and Volpicelli, 'Bare Ontology', p. 121.

MacBride, who raised the Irish Transvaal Brigade in support of the Boers.[77] Synge's renewed interest in the effects of a stagnating economy and political system in the Congested Districts is also reflected in his reading matter during this period. In particular, he recommended to James Patterson two recent novels by George Birmingham (James Owen Hannay), *The Seething Pot* (1905) and *Hyacinth* (1906), which deal with contemporary Irish sectarian and political conflict and were both the cause of considerable controversy amongst Irish Catholics and nationalists.[78] Alongside his own satirical takes on cultural stagnation in Ireland, this interest in other contemporary accounts underlines Synge's renewed sense of political and literary purpose in attacking nationalist orthodoxies.

In a letter to MacKenna, Synge insisted on the importance of the Mayo setting of the play, writing that 'The story—in its *essence* [the word underscored four times]—is probable given the psychic state of the locality.'[79] In the same letter, Synge asserted that he had written to the press with source materials and 'evidence' for the probability of the plot of *Playboy* in order to 'controvert critics who said it was *impossible*'.[80] In other words, Synge saw the play not as an accurate representation of facts or actual events but as an impression of the probable symptoms of the social and economic life of the county. Both contemporary and subsequent debates about the justifiability of Synge's vision, therefore, are beside the point. Though *The Playboy* is not an allegory, it is a representation of the socio-economic life of Mayo which draws on literary, scientific, and economic sources to produce a dramatic 'mirror' of the 'essence' of contemporary malaise. In fact, though Synge made sure to assert in an interview that his play was not an act of 'holding the mirror up to nature', he privately conceded to M. J. Nolan that 'you speak very accurately and rightly about Shakespeare's "mirror"'.[81] We cannot know exactly what Nolan's remarks were regarding Shakespeare's

---

[77] See *CW* IV, pp. 69–71, and TCD MS 4331–3, ff. 36–7, 197.

[78] See James Patterson to J. M. Synge, 31 January 1907, TCD MS 4424–6, Item 298. For more on the reception to Birmingham's political fiction, see Masahiko Yahata, 'George A. Birmingham, "Hyacinth" (1906): What Turns a Patriot into an Exile', *The Harp*, Vol. 10 (1995), 8–13. W. J. McCormack notes that George Birmingham also lived in Greystones while the Synge family were holidaying there, suggesting that the two families were somewhat connected. See *Fool of the Family*, pp. 65–6.

[79] Ann Saddlemyer, 'Synge to MacKenna: The Mature Years', *The Massachusetts Review*, Vol. 5, No. 2 (Winter 1964), 279–96, p. 289.

[80] Saddlemyer, 'Synge to MacKenna', p. 289.

[81] Interview with the *Dublin Evening Mail*, 29 January 1907, p. 2, quoted in Kilroy, *The 'Playboy' Riots*, p. 23. See also J. M. Synge to M. J. Nolan, 19 February 1907, TCD MS 4424–6, Item 305.

wphrase; however, Synge's following remarks suggest that they were corresponding about the ignorance of the Dublin audience regarding the Irish peasantry: 'what it seems so impossible to get our Dublin people to see, obvious as it is—that the wildness and, if you will vices of the Irish peasantry are due, like their extraordinary good points of all kinds, to the <u>richness</u> of their nature—a thing that is priceless beyond words.'[82] Again, Synge is asserting that the suggestion of 'vice' is another method of emphasizing the 'richness', or unruliness, of the peasantry, and that his perception of their difference from urban audiences is at the root of their use as an antidote to capitalist modernity.

This is important to a discussion of the Darwinian influences on *Playboy* because the play's emphasis on unruliness, and on the 'law-breaker', is specifically related to discourses of degeneration. The echoes of a Romantic insistence on revolution are felt not only in Synge's political influences (William Morris, in particular) but also in the importance he attached to the necessity of a 'law-breaker' in cultural regeneration, which he made consonant with his developing aesthetic and spiritual stance. In a draft of a letter to Stephen MacKenna, Synge added a postscript that argued that 'the Law-Maker and the Law-Breaker are both needful in society', and that 'the Law-Maker is tending to reduce Ireland or parts of Ireland to a dismal morbid hypocracy [*sic*] that is not a blessed unripeness'.[83] The word 'morbid' had been co-opted at this time into the eugenicist movement's rhetoric of degeneration, and Synge's emphasis on the 'law-breaker' as an antidote to this 'morbidity' (in his view, the opposite of humour) is stated in his letter to MacKenna as the antithesis of a specifically Irish form of degeneration, which is the product of state control and the propagation of restrictive orthodoxies. The older Yeats, in later years, wondered if Maud Gonne's socialism was 'a characteristic of his [Pound's] generation that has survived the Romantic Movement, and of mine and hers that saw it die – I too a revolutionist – some drop of hysteria still at the bottom of the cup?'[84] What Yeats later characterized as 'hysteria', however, was felt at the time (as Elizabeth Cullingford has noted) as a 'romantic commitment to rebellion, national and social'.[85] Synge, too, we might say, had some drops left 'at the bottom of the cup'—remnants of a Romantic fervour for rebellion that

---

[82] TCD MS 4424–6, Item 305.

[83] J. M. Synge to Stephen MacKenna, 28 January 1904, *CL* I, pp. 74–6.

[84] W. B. Yeats, *A Vision: The Revised 1937 Edition*, ed. Margaret Mills Harper and Catherine E. Paul (New York: Scribner, 2015), pp. 5–6.

[85] Cullingford, *Yeats, Ireland, and Fascism*, p. 17.

expressed itself in the development of his theatre and in his political philosophy. In fact, Synge's understanding of the 'law-breaker' (as spelled out in his drafted letter to MacKenna) was inflected by William Blake (via Yeats and Ellis). In his notes on their *Works of William Blake* (1893), Synge wrote that 'the genius within us is law-breaking and only becomes peaceful and free when it grows one with the ~~universal~~ poetic genius. the universal mood.'[86] Society is not only saved from morbidity by the lawbreaker, but the human genius is itself lawbreaking, and only through this regenerative lawbreaking can it attain harmony with a pantheistic idea of the 'universal mood'. A return to a harmonious 'natural' state (both in terms of morality and social structure) requires a form of regenerative violence, a sort of anarchic 'breaking' of convention.

Both Synge's view of contemporary Mayo and his setting of *Playboy* emphasize a demoralized, degenerated, and occupied landscape, with 'a thousand militia—bad cess to them!—walking idle through the land' (*CW* IV, 63), and his characters make constant reference to previous biological health of mythic proportions as a form of protest against both imperialism and the oppression of the 'law-makers'. Pegeen, introducing the audience to the idea of Shawn Keogh as a contrast to the former heroism of the district, lists the injured, degenerated, and ill people who wander Mayo. As Paige Reynolds has noted, Shawn is associated closely with bourgeois Catholicism: he is 'the exemplar of the middle class. He regards marriage as neither a sacrament nor the culmination of a great romance, but instead as "a good bargain".'[87] Already, the play's construction of heroism is pitted against the stifling, materialistic influence associated with the growing middle classes. Shawn attempts to counter this vision of Mayo as a fallen landscape, but Pegeen snaps at him viciously:

PEGEEN [*looking at him teasingly, washing up at dresser*]: It's a wonder, Shaneen, the Holy Father'd be taking notice of the likes of you, for if I was him, I wouldn't bother with this place where you'll meet none but Red Linahan has a squint in his eye, and Patcheen is lame in his heel, or the mad Mulrannies were driven from California and they lost in their wits. We're a queer lot these times to go troubling the Holy Father on his sacred seat.

---

[86] TCD MS 4379, f. 51v.
[87] Reynolds, *Modernism, Drama, and the Audience for Irish Spectacle*, p. 65.

SHAWN [*scandalized*]:   If we are, we're as good this place as another, maybe, and as good these times as we were for ever.

PEGEEN [*with scorn*]:   As good, is it? Where now will you meet the like of Daneen Smith knocked the eye from a peeler, or Marcus Quin, God rest him, got six months for maiming ewes, and he a great warrant to tell stories of holy Ireland till he'd have the old women shedding down tears about their feet. Where will you find the like of them, I'm saying? (*CW* IV, 59)

Pegeen's lament for heroism in the district valorizes agrarian violence. In fact, the first act of *Playboy* suggests more orthodox nationalist undertones than the play delivers. Shawn's concept of people who are 'as good' now as they ever were is qualified later when he suggests that 'it's a good job' that Pegeen's recalled heroes are no longer around, 'for...Father Reilly has small conceit to have that kind walking around and talking to the girls' (*CW* IV, 59). Father Reilly's orthodoxy hangs over the play: in fact, in Brian Brady's 1995 production of *Playboy* at the Abbey, the director had a mute Father Reilly stand on stage to emphasize his importance.[88] The threat of the priest, which is given voice by Shawn's fear of clerical repercussion, is blamed implicitly for moral and physical degeneration. In addition to this, for Pegeen, the newly arrived Christy comes to signify a sort of protection from the colonial administration: Philly suggests that 'the peelers is fearing him', and Pegeen agrees that 'if I'd that lad in the house, I wouldn't be fearing the loosèd khaki cut-throats, or the walking dead' (*CW* IV, 75). Christy is imagined, in this way, as an emblem of defiance against authority, the archetypal 'law-breaker' who will rejuvenate the district and unshackle the people, mentally if not physically, from the oppression of the 'law-makers', from bourgeois values and imperialist economic structures and their resultant 'morbidity', returning it to a form of 'organic' harmony.

In *Playboy*, the imagined heroism of a previous time is representative of a race yet to be fully demoralized by colonial and economic modernity. James Connolly would later assert, in many ways in line with Synge, that 'the conquered, robbed, slave-driven, brutalized, demoralized Irishman [is] the product of generations of landlord and capitalist rule', linking national characteristics (or stereotypes) to economic and class conditions rather

---

[88] See Collins, *Theatre and Residual Culture*, p. 219.

than racial essences.[89] As with Synge, Connolly's insistence on a Celtic communism as a method of revitalization critiques capitalist modernity and argues that national characteristics seen as innate are in fact based in material and historical conditions. By suggesting a different brand of modernity, both Connolly and Synge imagine new directions for a self-governing Ireland. In *Playboy*, the newly arrived Christy Mahon, as an 'emptiness' ready to be filled with 'potential meanings', is made into an emblem of the shebeeners' own desire for a regenerative lawbreaker who might replicate the heroic figures of their collective (and collectively imagined) past.[90] The need for revitalization is fed by the shebeeners' construction of Christy into the image of a redeemer whose presence might rupture the economic and social demoralization of the district. As Pegeen asks Shawn Keogh in a draft, 'What would we do in this place without dead men ~~or dark deeds~~ ... to put life in us at all?'[91]

The ways in which a hero might be constructed eugenically are the subject of much debate amongst the peasant community in the play. The heroic history of Ireland is rehearsed by the shebeeners when Christy voices his concern about the body of his father being found by the authorities, giving one of the clearest examples of imagined physical degeneration. Even the apparent weakness of Old Mahon's skull is implicitly invoked as a contrast to those of previous generations of invading warriors or prelapsarian pagans:

JIMMY   Did you never hear tell of the skulls they have in the city of Dublin, ranged out like blue jugs in a cabin of Connaught?

PHILLY   And you believe that?

JIMMY [*pugnaciously*]   Didn't a lad see them and he after coming from harvesting in the Liverpool boat? 'They have them there,' says he, 'making a show of the great people there was one time walking the world. White skulls and black skulls and yellow skulls, and some with full teeth and some haven't only but one'.

---

[89] James Connolly, *Collected Works*, Vol. I (Dublin: New Books, 1987), p. 20. David Lloyd discusses Connolly's relationship to modernity in *Irish Times*, pp. 101–26.

[90] Una Chaudhuri, 'The Dramaturgy of the Other: Diegetic Patterns in Synge's *The Playboy of the Western World*', *Modern Drama*, Vol. 32, No. 3 (Fall 1989), 374–86, p. 376.

[91] TCD MS 4331–3, f. 187.

PHILLY   It's no lie, maybe, for when I was a young lad, there was a graveyard beyond the house with the remnants of a man who had thighs as long as your arm. (*CW* IV, 135)

It is possible, in the final image, that Synge is referring to Cornelius Magrath, the 'Irish giant', whose skeleton is still held at Trinity College Dublin, and who was the subject of a long article by Daniel Cunningham (the same Cunningham who worked with Haddon in his attempts to categorize the 'Irish race'), published by the Royal Irish Academy. In this article, Magrath's long thigh bones are illustrated and discussed, along with detailed tables of skull measurements and indices.[92] In a draft of this exchange, Old Mahon (who is, at this stage, 'Old Flaherty'), compares the exhibition of the skeletons of 'great people' to the use of 'horse shows and cattle shows to let all people see what is good'.[93] Here, Synge invokes the language of agricultural and livestock improvement to signify the shebeeners' belief that a similar process might be used to 'improve' human characteristics. As Old Mahon laments (quite ironically, given the condition of his own skull), 'there isn't any man in Ireland under fifty or three score with a decent stubborn scull [sic] on him.'[94] This obsession with physical strength provides a sharp contrast to the sickly figure of Shawn Keogh. Such ideas of racial improvement by example draw on a common Revivalist trope, which linked contemporary Ireland to a similar period in ancient Greece, 'before her first perfect statue had fixed an ideal of beauty which mothers dreamed of to mould their yet unborn children'.[95] This trope, repeated by Yeats in *The King's Threshold* and by contributors to the pages of *Sinn Féin*, suggests a historical moment in which racial characteristics might be 'fixed' and then improved by attention to aesthetics in all realms of public life.[96] The idea of biological regeneration by example is quietly undermined in another draft by an ironic reversal. Jimmy, on hearing about the skulls in Dublin, concludes, 'If that's the truth the Dublin people should be a low mad lot and it's no lie. (Contemptuously).—Looking on sculls [sic].'[97] Here, the eugenic

---

[92] D. J. Cunningham, 'The Skeleton of the Irish Giant, Cornelius Magrath', *The Transactions of the Royal Irish Academy*, Vol. 29 (1887–92), 553–612.

[93] TCD MS 4331–3, f. 530.   [94] TCD MS 4331–3, f. 530.

[95] George Russell (AE), 'Nationality and Cosmopolitanism in Literature', in John Eglinton, W. B. Yeats, AE, and W. Larminie, *Literary Ideals in Ireland* (London: T. Fisher Unwin, 1899), 79–88, p. 84.

[96] W. B. Yeats, *VPl*, pp. 264–5; W. E. Fay, 'A Note on National Games', *Sinn Féin*, 12 January 1907, p. 4.

[97] TCD MS 4331–3, f. 552.

interests of the urban classes are revealed as a form of degeneration. The interest shown by the shebeeners in the heroic past, however, establishes Synge's Mayo as a place seeking its own regeneration, either by turning towards a more vital past or by overthrowing a stifling present.

That the shebeeners' conceive of Christy as heroic both in deed and stature, and thus as a key to racial renewal, is evident in the courting competition between Pegeen and Widow Quin. For Christy, who has seen himself previously in 'the divil's own mirror' (*CW IV*, 95), his own personal history is couched in the terms of victimization and familial and racial degeneration, and this is rhetorically reversed so that he begins to believe in himself as 'master of all fights from now' (*CW IV*, 173). Old Mahon, in an early version of the play, describes his son not as 'a dirty, stuttering lout' (*CW IV*, 121) but as 'a misbred looking lout', and Christy explains that his family account for him in specifically degenerationist terms.[98] He gives the following version of a conversation between his mother and father:

> Then says she 'it's that lad has brought ill luck on you'—my father'd a decree for debt again him from the shop—'for your family's after living in this place says she, since the days of the days of the [*sic*] fire worshipper and pagans and the grand high times of Ireland and they never troubled till this day the way it's plain surely it's that lad—(meaning myself)—has brought ill luck upon your race.'[99]

In this excised passage, Christy's previous life is directly contrasted with the heroism of 'the grand high times of Ireland'; however, there is a subtle hint that it is the gombeen system, rather than biological degeneration, that is responsible for the family's 'ill luck'. A stifling economic system is blamed implicitly, though Christy's mother incorrectly assigns the blame to Christy himself. The use of eugenic language, therefore, can be representative of the wider 'demoralization' at the heart of Synge's critique of the socio-economic condition of the Congested Districts.

As Synge notes when reading Darwin, economic and social criteria are seen to have usurped sexual selection on 'natural' terms, with partners being chosen for the status rather than their aesthetic or biological qualities. As in *The Shadow of the Glen*, *Playboy* launches a sustained critique of this bourgeois intervention into biological evolution and sexual desire.

---

[98] TCD MS 4331–3, f. 558.   [99] TCD MS 4331–3, f. 76.

The motive of positive sexual selection in the play is at the heart of the shebeeners' acceptance of Christy's supposed patricide. When the Widow Quin asks Christy why he killed his father, Christy claims that he was being asked to marry the Widow Casey, 'when all know she did suckle me for six weeks when I came into the world' (*CW* IV, 103). This quasi-incestuous union is not just presented as a potential offence to propriety, but also to the natural law of selection: the Widow Casey, as Christy describes her, is 'A walking terror from beyond the hills, and she two score and five years, and two hundredweights and five pounds in the weighing scales, with a limping leg on her, and a blinded eye' (*CW* IV, 101). Hearing this, Sara gives her approval to Christy's actions: 'You were right surely' (*CW* IV, 103). It is not only Christy's 'heroic' deed, but that this deed is an assertion of the laws of sexual selection, that is applauded by the shebeeners. Again, as in *The Shadow of the Glen*, Synge attacks the institution of the 'loveless marriage', though here it is on more openly biological and evolutionary grounds. This idea is then replicated in Pegeen's decision to choose Christy over Shawn Keogh. Despite her father's concerns over her 'making him a son to me and he wet and crusted with his father's blood', she asks (rhetorically), 'Wouldn't it be a bitter thing for a girl to go marrying the like of Shaneen, and he a middling kind of scarecrow with no savagery or fine words at all?' (*CW* IV, 153). Here, Pegeen privileges sexual attraction over material concerns, 'savagery' over civilization, opposing Shawn's bourgeois version of marriage (he sees it as a 'bargain') and choosing a more vital mate. In selecting Christy, Pegeen rejects bourgeois social mores. This is at the heart of the play's promise of revitalization.

By the end of *Playboy*, Michael has accepted Christy as his future son-in-law on the basis of the eugenic principle of racial improvement, and his risk in allowing Christy to marry Pegeen is seen as a specifically patriotic act.

MICHAEL   It's many would be in dread to bring your like into their house for to end them maybe with a sudden end; but I'm a decent man of Ireland, and I'd liefer face the grave untimely and I seeing a score of grandsons growing up little gallant swearers by the name of God, than go peopling my bedside with puny weeds the like of what you'd breed, I'm thinking, out of Shaneen Keogh. (*CW* IV, 157)

Michael is prepared to be killed by his son-in-law if it means repopulating the country with 'little gallant swearers'. Following Synge's early principle, gleaned from his rabbit-breeding, Michael assumes that the children Pegeen would 'breed...out of Shaneen Keogh' would be 'puny weeds'. In Synge's vision, the lawbreakers and 'gallant swearers' are coveted in place of the pious peasantry cultivated in nationalist circles. The revitalization which will occur from the match between Pegeen and Christy will set the population against the bourgeois track of Shaun Keogh, promising a future race bred against the grain of a demoralizing modernity.

The process of configuring the first performances of *The Playboy of the Western World* in eugenic terms was started relatively soon afterwards by Yeats, though he tended to recognize Synge's literary rather than his political radicalism, positioning *The Playboy* (both as event and text) as a counter to bourgeois nationalism. Like Synge, Yeats reverses the eugenic idea, positing the audience, rioters, and critics variously as syphilitic and impotent. For Yeats, in his poem 'On Those Who Hated "The Playboy of the Western World"', 'Griffiths and his like' are figured as 'eunuchs' who 'rail and sweat' at the sight of Synge's intellectual and moral prowess, imaged in the 'sinewy thigh' of Don Juan.[100] Here, Synge himself becomes a sort of Christy Mahon, breaking through the sterility of national degradation, and his critics (and, by implication, their form of nationalism and their literary aesthetic) are figured as an evolutionary dead end. Earlier, in his essay 'J. M. Synge and the Ireland of his Time' (1910), Yeats was careful to include an anecdote in which he describes watching the theatre riots as a moment of national renewal shouted down by a diseased mob:

> As I stood there watching, knowing well that I saw the dissolution of a school of patriotism that held sway over my youth, Synge came and stood beside me, and said, 'A young doctor has just told me that he can hardly keep himself from jumping on to a seat, and pointing out in that howling mob those whom he is treating for venereal disease.'[101]

As in Synge's own vision, the stifling atmosphere of repressive nationalism (which is perpetrated by a syphilitic mob, representing national ill health) is purged by the lawbreaking hero or event. Even Synge's own 'Curse' on the rioters, directed at 'a sister of an enemy of the author's who disapproved of

---

[100] W. B. Yeats, 'On those that hated "The Playboy of the Western World", 1907', *VP*, 294. In a letter to Lady Gregory, Yeats confirms the subject of this poem as 'Griffith and his like'. W. B. Yeats to Lady Gregory, 8 March 1909, Allan Wade, ed., *The Letters of W. B. Yeats* (New York: Macmillan, 1955), p. 525. For a discussion of these connections, especially in relation to Yeats's later interest in eugenics, see Childs, *Modernism and Eugenics*, pp. 207–11.

[101] Yeats, *Essays and Introductions*, p. 312.

"The Playboy"' (*CW* I, 49), calls for a series of afflictions to befall his detractor. In a singularly vicious account, Yeats tells us that when Synge showed the poem to him, 'he said with mirthful eyes that since he had written it her husband had got drunk, gone with a harlot, got syphilis, and given it to his wife'.[102] One early critic, C. E. Montague (who had helped to edit *The Manchester Guardian* from 1895 to 1906, while C. P. Scott was an MP), described both the audience and the theatre itself in terms of a sickness which Synge could cure: 'In his harsh, sane, earthen humour, biting as carbolic acid to slight minds, they find a disinfectant well worth having, at the lowest, in an ailing theatre.'[103] These attempts, after the fact, to construe the rioters as unhealthy, both in physical and moral terms, position *Playboy*, Christy Mahon, and Synge himself as a revitalizing and oppositional presence, a 'rushing up of the buried fire, an explosion of all that had been denied and refused, a furious impartiality, an indifferent turbulent sorrow.'[104] Those who opposed Synge's work chose similar terms of attack, spreading rumours that the playwright had died 'as a consequence of his Parisian decadence'.[105]

Christy's 'savagery', his position as the lawbreaker who will free the shebeeners from the 'morbidity' of their oppressed life in the district, is combined with an imagined vision of racial and cultural regeneration through sexual selection, and thus the syphilitic audience functions as an extension of the dead hand of a restricting mainstream culture. In *Playboy*, custom and law are sidestepped by the power of the individual, and a gap is opened for a revitalization of the race. Though Yeats and others memorialized the play as radical in literary terms, its political radicalism was most effectively recognized by the later Abbey playwright, Teresa Deevy. In her one-act 1935 play *The King of Spain's Daughter*, which opened for (and interpreted) *The Playboy of the Western World* at the Abbey, Deevy reflected the stagnation of the Mayoites in the situation of her protagonist, Annie Kinsella, who must choose between two unsatisfactory men (one who is 'a big lounging figure' and the other who is 'too soft-hearted for any woman') or a life of factory work.[106] The stage directions place her between two road barriers, one reading 'No Traffic' and the other 'Road Closed'.[107] As Cathy

---

[102] Yeats, *Memoirs*, p. 202.
[103] C. E. Montague, *Dramatic Values* (London: Methuen, 1911), p. 15.
[104] Yeats, *Memoirs*, p. 223.   [105] See McCormack, *Fool of the Family*, p. 170.
[106] Teresa Deevy, *The King of Spain's Daughter*, in Angela Bourke et al., *The Field Day Anthology of Irish Writing, Volume V: Irish Women's Writing and Traditions* (Cork: Cork University Press, 2002), 1001–7, pp. 1002–3.
[107] Deevy, *The King of Spain's Daughter*, p. 1001.

Leeney has suggested, this setting figures the protectionist economics of de Valera's Ireland in personal terms, where the economic and cultural entrapment of the country is explored through the marriage plot of the play.[108] Annie is trapped not only in her poor choice of potential husbands but also in her economic dependency on the men in her life. Suggesting that she might run away instead of being forced into factory work or marriage, Jim warns her of her father's temper: 'He'd go after you: he'd have you crippled.'[109] Annie, who is chastised for the mutability of her imaginative world, eventually invents a violent mate for herself by reimagining Jimmy Harris (whom her mother refers to as 'a good, sensible boy') into the image of a lawbreaker who might liberate her from the repressive world she inhabits. The play closes strikingly:

MRS MARKS A good, sensible boy.

ANNIE Boy! (*She laughs exultantly*) I think he is a man might cut your throat!

MRS MARKS God save us all!

ANNIE He put by two shillin's every week for two hundred weeks. I think he is a man that - supposin' he was jealous - might cut your throat. (*Quiet, - exultant: she goes*)

MRS MARKS The Lord preserve us! that she'd find joy in such a thought![110]

Annie's joy at creating a violent image of Jimmy reflects the 'power of a lie' to break through (even if only imaginatively) the 'morbidity' of the lawmaker. In this way, Deevy shows an intimate understanding of Synge's political radicalism in her echoing of economic entrapment imaginatively ruptured by the potential of violence, drawing a line of literary heredity between her own work and Synge's before the latter's drama had been effectively canonized as both anti-modern and ahistorical. For both dramatists, the marriage plot allows for sexual selection to be figured as a moment of potential personal and national renewal, where the economic causes of demoralization are usurped by a violent energy.

Synge had already, even prior to his work in the Congested Districts, come to see the effects of imperialism and capitalist modernization in degenerationist terms; however, the restriction of the concept of Irishness, specifically with regards to literary representation, prompted a dramatic

---

[108] Cathy Leeney, *Irish Women Playwrights, 1900–1939: Gender & Violence On Stage* (New York: Peter Lang, 2010), pp. 162, 172.

[109] Deevy, *The King of Spain's Daughter*, p. 1005.

[110] Deevy, *The King of Spain's Daughter*, p. 1007.

theorization of protest. The discourse of racial improvement, and the question of in what form to set the 'soft wax' of Ireland and Irish identity, led Synge to satirize more conservative visions of national destiny in eugenic terms, reversing the rhetoric of improvement as 'morbid' and calling instead for a violent, revitalizing energy. This reading was compounded in later accounts and writings by Yeats, Deevy, and Synge himself, positing the lawbreaker (as someone who might destroy pallid and oppressive convention) as a racial rejuvenator. Synge's radicalism lies in his reading of degeneration in economic and political rather than ethnic terms, and in his construction of a drama which simultaneously challenges bourgeois morality and the real social effects of capitalist economics. Synge's reading in evolutionary theory, focusing as it did on sexual selection and 'ornament', was made consonant with his economic and social vision, whereby the substitution of class hierarchies and capital for 'natural' sexual attractors led to a society in which the population was degenerating. His critique of imperialism and modern conservative social convention led him to call for a reassertion of the laws of sexual selection, and to focus on the anarchic power of Rabelaisian humour and heroic energy, to combat the submissiveness and demoralization which he views as the implicit aims and effects of capitalist modernity.

Christy Mahon (and, in posterity, Synge himself) becomes the emblem of revitalization, a symbol of an alternative and postcolonial modernity which (in typically Syngean terms) can be imaginary as well as practical. The play, in this way, conveys the ability to reassert a powerful and vital modernity, and is the apotheosis of Synge's long-developed theories regarding comedy and nonconformity. It is the product of his travels in the Congested Districts, though its tail stretches back to some of Synge's earliest concerns in evolution and heredity. For Synge, 'all decadence is opposed to humour', and the 'extravaganza' of *Playboy* becomes a dramatic model of the lawbreaker, a model of Rabelaisian humour and vitality that will combat both the 'joyless and pallid' modern literature and the 'morbidity' of modern bourgeois Ireland.[111] Synge's modernism, as *The Playboy of the Western World* shows most clearly, is simultaneously a form of political and literary protest. Rooted in his socialism and informed by his long-standing engagement with modernization, it is the apotheosis of his tendency towards a literary experiment which works in tandem with an ever-developing political, social, and aesthetic consciousness.

---

[111] TCD MS 4405, f. 10r. See also *CW* IV, 53.

Conclusion

In a memorandum left alongside Synge's first completed play, *When the Moon Has Set*, W. B. Yeats wrote that, although Lady Gregory and himself decided to reject the work, it might have had 'a slight stage success with a certain kind of very modern audience' (*CW* III, 155, n.1). The modernity Yeats detected in *When the Moon Has Set*, however, is much different in both texture and intent than what this book has characterized as the modernity of Synge's later plays and prose works. Rather, Synge's first play, set in an Anglo-Irish 'Big House', is an awkward mixture of Ibsenism, Decadence, and the Revivalist peasant play, though Yeats's characterization most likely attends to the former two influences. However, despite its clunky construction and heavy-handed didacticism, *When the Moon Has Set* contains the kernels of many of the concerns traced throughout this book, and is instructive as a foil for Synge's later work because it demonstrates Synge's early aesthetic, social, and spiritual philosophy but does not display its dramatic praxis, which would only develop once subjected to the modernizing pressures of Ireland during the first decade of the twentieth century.

Vivian Mercier suggests that we find in Synge's first play 'the starkest expression of the basic Syngean conflict', between 'Puritan rejection and fear of life' (embodied in the character of Sister Eileen) and 'the forces of earth and acceptance of life' (embodied in Synge's proxy character, Colm).[1] Although this is true, in that these factors broadly form the basis of Synge's philosophy, this book has shown that, over the course of his career, this conflict was complicated and politicized, and Synge was forced to evolve or reaffirm his artistic and political values in new and often experimental ways. Early versions of Synge's play emphasize his concern with madness and degeneration, but also show that he was assigning these social issues to the stifling influence of religion on Irish society. Hearing about Colm's cellist friend in Paris, who drinks absinthe and vermouth, sleeps under a black quilt, and has two skulls on his mantlepiece, Sister Eileen tells him, 'You

---

[1] Mercier, *Modern Irish Literature: Sources and Founders*, p. 205.

J. M. Synge: Nature, Politics, Modernism. Seán Hewitt, Oxford University Press (2021). © Seán Hewitt. DOI: 10.1093/oso/9780198862093.003.0008

should make him live more wisely or he will go out of his mind'. Colm retorts that, 'in the life of the cloisters, and in this life of Ireland, men go mad every hour' (CW III, 160). Hence, Synge's antagonism to artistic Decadence is established, but even at this early stage he was much more concerned with the social causes of Decadence and with a life lived out of touch with nature. Colm suggests, characteristically, that a pantheistic world view is the antidote to this degenerative tendency, 'for God is in the earth and not above it' (CW III, 164), and 'the people who rebel from the law of God are not those who are essaying strange notes in the dark alleys of the world but the fools who linger in the aisles droning their withered chants with senile intonation' (CW III, 176).

Thus, what *When the Moon Has Set* illustrates is Synge's basic aesthetic and philosophic stance before it was politicized, before it had to contend with the realities of a modernizing Ireland, and before he had learnt his mastery of dramatic composition. His opposition to the supposed degeneration of Irish society due to the 'stagnation' of religion and social institutions (CW III, 176), as this book has demonstrated, would be extended to a more wide-ranging vision of degeneration at the hands of state modernization schemes and restrictive nationalist identity-building; his preoccupation with a pantheistic spirituality would become attached, through his political thought, to ideas of production, creativity, and individuality; and his vision of the revitalizing 'rebel' would find increasing urgency through his concept of both dramatic and political protest. It was through careful and persistent social observation, through reading and through a commitment to a vision of literature as subject to the evolutionary principle, that Synge experimented his way towards a more dynamic, ironic, and, indeed, modernist literature.

In his final, unfinished work, *Deirdre of the Sorrows* (1910), as a number of critics have suggested, Synge seems to have reverted to many of the concerns underpinning his first play, even choosing to conclude the first act with a set of pagan wedding vows strikingly similar to those with which Colm wed Sister Eileen at the end of *When the Moon Has Set*.[2] McCormack suggests that Synge's *Deirdre* 'marks a reversion, in style, in substance, and in its larger orientation'; however, it would be unfair to suggest that this means that 'the notion of progression, steady or otherwise, is not adequate to the facts of Synge's writing life as we know them'.[3] In fact, as this book has

---

[2] See CW III, p. 177, and CW IV, p. 215.   [3] McCormack, *Fool of the Family*, p. 366.

shown, taking Synge's works chronologically demonstrates a very distinct progression, and if *Deirdre* shows 'a reversion' of this progress, it must also be granted that the work is, like the 'half-finished piece of tapestry' (*CW* IV, 183) which hangs on the stage in its opening scene, incomplete. Sinéad Garrigan Mattar notes that 'paganism, violence, and sexuality are all returned to their "proper" places in *Deirdre*', suggesting that the world of the saga in the play remains 'too perfect' to accommodate a modernist primitivism.[4] Indeed, the play does seem to mark a departure from the trajectory traced in this book, though Synge did note that it 'required a grotesque element' which he had not managed to fully work into the manuscript as he left it (*CW* IV, 179). He worried that 'the "Saga" people might loosen [his] grip on reality', and was treating the play as 'an interesting experiment', something 'to change [his] hand'.[5] It is possible, therefore, that the engagement with sociopolitical issues which energized his other plays was more distant in his composition of *Deirdre*, allowing his Romanticism to take precedence. Either way, he was concerned that his act of protest in *Playboy* had brought 'so much unpopularity' to his fellow directors and the acting company that he was placed 'in a rather delicate position'.[6]

Recently, Nicholas Grene has argued that the lack of what might have been Synge's later work, due to his early death, makes it difficult to situate him as a modernist writer in a way that is not true for Yeats and others, who lived long enough to produce more recognizably modernist works.[7] However, many of Synge's incomplete plays demonstrate an identifiable trajectory. Along with his outlines for 'Deaf Mutes for Ireland', he also left an outline for a 'Comedy of Kings', probably written in the autumn of 1906, in which the stage is laid out with a series of beds. The kings lie in the beds, and at the front of the stage are seven archetypes: 'the hawker, horseman, houndman, boatman, Harper, storyteller, and gravedigger' (*CW* III, 230). Their movements throughout the scene are detailed, but their characters are not fleshed out, hinting towards the later drama of Yeats and other European modernists. Another scenario, for 'Lucifer and the Lost Soul', written in January 1908, draws on the early themes of *A Rabelaisian Rhapsody*. The lost soul, arriving in Hell, reveals that he spent his time on

---

[4] Mattar, *Primitivism, Science, and the Irish Revival*, pp. 179, 184.
[5] Letter from J. M. Synge to Frederick J. Gregg, 12 September 1907, *CL* II, p. 56; Letter from J. M. Synge to John Quinn, 4 January 1908, *CL* II, pp. 121–2.
[6] Letter from J. M. Synge to Frederick J. Gregg, 12 September 1907, *CL* II, p. 56.
[7] Nicholas Grene, 'J. M. Synge: Late Romantic or Protomodernist?', pp. 88–9.

earth in very bad company ('In Maynooth...with all nice little priests, talking ever and always'), his sin being writing 'mighty flat' pages for a paper called the 'Catholic Young Man' (*CW* III, 231). If *Deirdre of the Sorrows* is tragic, 'proper', and generally uncombative, this is hardly an indication that all of Synge's possible future plays would have followed such a pattern. In fact, the outlines of plays he wrote over his final years suggest an even more modernist output than that which he was able to produce in his lifetime.

In general, as this book has shown, Synge's Romantic inclinations did not preclude him from modernism; on the contrary, it was the tension between Romanticism and modernity that propelled the development of his drama. Katharine Worth has suggested that, after Beckett, Synge's modernity has become much more apparent to both audiences and critics.[8] Indeed, Synge's influence on twentieth-century modernism (and on postmodernism) is yet to be fully explored, and has the potential to reveal more clearly the interrelation between Revivalism and modernism both in Ireland and more broadly. Whereas a number of later Irish writers, such as Flann O'Brien, Patrick Kavanagh, and St. John Ervine, attacked Synge as a romanticizer of rural life, 'a faker of peasant speech', approaching him as the prime exemplar of the untrustworthiness of the Irish Revival in general, others recognized his radicalism and positioned him as a modernizing force, a precursor to their own modernist projects.[9] Flann O'Brien, taking cues from Daniel Corkery's *Synge and Anglo-Irish Literature* (1931), saw Synge's drama as a continuation of the 'stage Irishman', a problem that 'probably began with Lever and Lover'—who, as shown in the third chapter of this book, Synge rejected as out of touch—writing that 'in this Anglo-Irish literature of ours (which for the most part is neither Anglo, Irish, nor literature) (as the man said) nothing in the whole galaxy of fake is comparable with Synge'.[10] For O'Brien, in typical fashion, Synge's fakery was not long confined to the stage and was adopted as a national stereotype: 'And

---

[8]   Worth, *The Irish Drama of Europe*, p. 121.

[9]   St. John Ervine as quoted in Daniel Corkery, *Synge and Anglo-Irish Literature: A Study* (Dublin and Cork: Cork University Press, 1931), p. vi.

[10]   Myles na Gopaleen (Flann O'Brien), *The Best of Myles: A Selection from* 'Cruiskeen Lawn', ed. with a preface by Kevin O'Nolan (London: Picador, 1977), p. 234. Daniel Corkery was more positive in his assessment of Synge, arguing that he set himself apart from his ascendancy-class background because he lived with and tried to understand 'the people'. Corkery maintained, however, that Synge was unable to recognize the religious consciousness of the peasantry, and that 'his range of mind was limited, and was not quite free from inherited prejudices'. *Synge and Anglo-Irish Literature*, p. 79.

now the curse has come upon us, because I have personally met in the streets of Ireland persons who are clearly out of Synge's plays.'[11] Interestingly, the discourses of disease and infection which surrounded the first production of *Playboy* and which continued in portrayals of Synge as either a cure for, or vector of, ill health, are continued in O'Brien's criticism. If Lever and Lover were the beginning of the 'trouble' of Anglo-Irish fakery, 'in Synge we have the virus isolated and recognisable', and thus prepared for eradication.[12]

Other writers recognized Synge's radicalism and posited him as a vital influence on the development of modern literature. Djuna Barnes, for example, in an article for the *New York Morning Telegraph* in 1917, recognized Synge's 'method of work' as 'much more like the modern generation', emphasizing him as a writer for whom 'grim brutality and frankness and love are one, the upper lip is romance, but the under is irony'.[13] Adding an illustration of Mary Doul to her piece (see Figure C.1, below), Barnes brought Synge's female characters into line with her own aesthetic of subverted (or 'corrupted') femininity (exemplified a little earlier by her pamphlet of 'rhythms' and drawings, *The Book of Repulsive Women* (1915)), linking them visually with Decadent tropes but also subsuming them into a lineage of modernist images.[14] Whereas Barnes focused on the Syngean grotesque, others focused on a perception of his iconoclasm and soothsaying. In a very different mode to Barnes, some critics of Paul Henry's paintings, in the years following Synge's death, attributed Henry's increasingly modernist aesthetic to the influence of the dramatist, suggesting that Henry had 'flung away the accepted formulas' in painting as boldly as Synge had done on the stage: 'In place of the glamour of false romance you get the veracity of the thing seen.'[15]

In fact, it was Synge's emphasis on the brutal (espoused most explicitly in the preface to his *Poems*), and his ironic undercutting of Romanticism that appealed to modernists more generally. Ezra Pound, in his early study on

---

[11] O'Brien, *The Best of Myles*, p. 235.   [12] O'Brien, *The Best of Myles*, p. 234.

[13] Djuna Barnes, 'The Songs of Synge: The Man Who Shaped His Life as he Shaped His Plays', *New York Morning Telegraph*, 18 February 1917.

[14] See Djuna Barnes, *The Book of Repulsive Women: Eight Rhythms and Five Drawings* (Los Angeles: Sun & Moon Press, 1989). For more on fin de siècle images of women, see Bram Dijkstra, *Fantasies of Feminine Evil in Fin-de-Siècle Culture* (Oxford and New York: Oxford University Press, 1986).

[15] Quotations from a review of Henry's exhibition *Paintings of Irish Life*, held in Belfast, from *The Northern Whig*, 13 March 1911. S. B. Kennedy suggests that Henry's position as a founding member of the Allied Artists' Association in 1908 reveals Henry 'nail[ing] his colours firmly to the modernist mast'. See S. B. Kennedy, 'An Enduring View of Irish Identity: Paul Henry and the Realism of Fiction', *Irish Arts Review Yearbook*, Vol. 15 (1999), 98–107, pp. 99–100.

Figure C.1 Djuna Barnes, illustration of a scene from J. M. Synge's *The Well of the Saints*. 'Could we hide in the bit of briar that is growing at the west of the church?' (1917). From *Poe's Mother: Selected Drawings of Djuna Barnes*, ed. Douglas Messerli (Los Angeles: Sun & Moon Press, 1996), p. 111.

The Spirit of Romance (1910), found common cause with Synge's translations of Villon, in whom he saw the virtues of 'unvarnished, intimate speech', the 'voice of suffering, of mockery, of irrevocable fact'.[16] Furthermore, as James Longenbach has shown, rather than it being Pound who 'dragged the reluctant Yeats into the twentieth century', Pound himself assigned this role to Synge:

> There is little use discussing the early Yeats, everyone has heard all that can be said on the subject. The new Yeats is still under discussion. Adorers of the Celtic Twilight are disturbed by his gain of hardness. Some of the later work is not so good as the Wind Among the Reeds, some of it better, or at least possessed of new qualities. Synge had appeared. There is a new strength in the later Yeats on which he & Synge may have agreed between them.[17]

---

[16] Quoted in Alex Davis, 'Learning to be brutal': Synge, Decadence, and the Modern Movement', *New Hibernia Review/Iris Éireannach Nua*, Vol. 14, No. 3 (Autumn 2010), 33–51, p. 48.

[17] Quoted in Longenbach, *Stone Cottage*, p. 19.

The brutality, 'hardness', and vitality of Synge's work is thus attributed a modernizing power in Pound's critique. Pound himself even incorporated Syngean phrases (which he called 'glorious') into his *Cantos* and his farce *The Consolations of Matrimony* (1916), written under the quasi-Irish pseudonym of 'Oge Terrence O'Cullough', in which two men sit at a table in a remote Irish village and discuss sex.[18] Written in the style of Synge as part of a project to combat the response of the Liverpool Repertory Theatre, which had cancelled its production of *The Playboy of the Western World* in 1913 after Irish nationalist riots, *The Consolations of Matrimony* draws on the plots of *The Shadow of the Glen* and *Playboy* to emphasize the violence, sexuality, and brutality of Synge's plays—qualities which Pound holds up for praise, in part because of their opposition to the nationalist 'mob'. In this way, *Consolations* continues Pound's attack on Irish political culture formulated in his article on 'The Non-existence of Ireland', in which he expressed considerable disdain at the characterization of Synge as a 'decadent' in a Belfast newspaper.[19]

Later artists and writers recognized what we might call Synge's modernism before such a term was coined in criticism, and they also often saw his subversive political potential.[20] Whereas many major modernists across the arts have been studied with regard to the interconnection between Romanticism and modernism, Synge has traditionally been seen in the position that Yeats assigned to him, as one of 'the last Romantics', who 'chose for theme / Traditional sanctity and loveliness'.[21] By drawing out the modernist aspects of his work, and by illustrating their roots in

---

[18] See Longenbach, *Stone Cottage*, pp. 209–10.

[19] Ezra Pound, 'Affirmations: The Non-existence of Ireland', *The New Age*, Vol. 16, No. 17 (25 February 1915), 451–3. For more on Pound's *Consolations of Matrimony* in relation to Synge's works, see James Moran, 'Pound, Yeats, and the Regional Repertory Theatres', in Neal Alexander and James Moran, eds., *Regional Modernisms* (Edinburgh: Edinburgh University Press, 2013), 83–103. *The Consolations of Matrimony*, along with another play Noh play which Pound set in Ireland and modelled on Synge, is published in Ezra Pound, *Plays Modelled on the Noh*, ed. Donald C. Gallup (Toledo: The Friends of the University of Toledo Libraries, 1987).

[20] For a recent account of political uses of Synge, see Susan Cannon Harris, *Irish Drama and the Other Revolutions*.

[21] From W. B. Yeats, 'Coole Park and Ballylee, 1931', *VP*, 490–2, p. 491. For a wide-ranging study of the interplay between Romanticism and modernism, see Alexandra Harris, *Romantic Moderns: English Writers, Artists and the Imagination from Virginia Woolf to John Piper* (London: Thames & Hudson, 2010). For a synoptic overview of Yeats's Romanticism, see George Bornstein, 'Yeats and Romanticism', in Marjorie Howes and John Kelly, eds., *The Cambridge Companion to W. B. Yeats* (Cambridge: Cambridge University Press, 2006), 19–35, and the more recent article by Claire Connolly, 'Counting on the Past: Yeats and Romanticism', *European Romantic Review*, Vol. 28, No. 4 (July 2017), 473–87, which features a discussion of 'Coole Park and Ballylee, 1931'.

contemporary social, political, and aesthetic discourses, the interplay between Revivalism and modernism, or Romanticism and modernism, is illuminated. What is more, such an illumination shows the potential for the modernisms of other key twentieth-century figures to be reappraised.

Uncovering the roots of Synge's drama in the confluence of his leftist politics, his emphasis on spirituality and nature, and the development of a sardonic and 'brutal' irony allows us to posit him as an early leftist modernist. Synge was a writer who explored many of the concerns of other modernists (modes of production, spirituality, primitivism, eugenics, revitalization, irony, and modernization, to name a few) but routed them in line with his own progressive politics. His politics must be contextualized within his aesthetics in order for us to understand them as a form of socialism, and thus his drama develops out of a confluence of aesthetic and political concerns. Likewise, Synge's prioritization of the spiritual element both in literature and in a 'healthy' life can be read alongside, and used to complicate our understanding of, other uses of religion and spirituality that are currently being reassessed in modernist studies.[22] Taken as a whole, the study of Synge's works undertaken in this book emphasizes how fundamental the development of an early set of aesthetic and philosophical values was to his work, and how integral political and social change was to his progression as a dramatist, and thus lays the groundwork for a more wide-ranging reassessment of the relationship between Revivalism and modernism, the relationship between modernization and literary modernism, and a more nuanced exploration of the trajectory towards modernism in the Irish context.

Synge rooted his art in the importance of a 'healthy' engagement with nature and with spirituality, which were combined through his interest in pantheism, and were linked through this to an amalgamation of socialist politics which led him to oppose industrialist capitalism and the homogenizing effects of modernization. Furthermore, through his reading in various evolutionary theories, he was able to oppose certain forms of modernization and restrictive politics of national identity as working against the natural progression of life from a homogeneous to a heterogeneous state. Individuality, individual freedom, and the importance of 'organic' thought became fundamental tools of protest against what he perceived as a limiting

---

[22] For reassessments of the role of religion and spirituality in modernism, see Suzanne Hobson, *Angels of Modernism: Religion, Culture, Aesthetics, 1910–1960* (Basingstoke: Palgrave, 2011); Lewis, *Religious Experience and the Modernist Novel*; and Tonning, *Modernism and Christianity*.

view of Irishness and a limiting literary presentation of Irishness. The threat of both national and literary decadence and degeneration formed the impetus for his increasingly combative drama, which acts as a discursive retribution against the Romantic strains of cultural Revivalism. Synge was a dynamic and sophisticated artist whose theory was constantly being adapted and seeking new forms of expression. His trajectory towards modernism, and his characteristic irony and undercutting of Romanticism, are symptomatic of the tension between the political pressures of his Ireland (and of literary Revivalism) and his own aesthetic and philosophical values. Over his career, as his own political and social consciousness developed in nuance, this fundamental conflict became more pressing, and led him to the production of a literature which was as much a form of artistic as political protest.

Bibliography

Manuscript sources

John Rylands Library, University of Manchester
Manchester Guardian archive

New York Public Library
Berg Collection

Trinity College, Dublin
Papers of John Millington Synge
Synge-Stephens Collection

Newspapers, Magazines, and Periodicals

The Academy and Literature
The Arrow
The Belfast Evening Standard
Birmingham Daily Gazette
Dana
Dublin Daily Express
Dublin Evening Mail
Freeman's Journal
The Gael
The Green Sheaf
Irish Homestead
Irish Independent
Irish Statesman
The Irish Times
The Leader
Le Décadent
L'Européen
The Manchester Guardian
The New Age
New York Morning Telegraph
Nineteenth Century
The Phonetic Journal

Revue des Deux Mondes
The Savoy
Sinn Féin
The Speaker
The United Irishman

Electronic Sources

The Abbey Theatre Online Archive: https://www.abbeytheatre.ie/about/archive/.
Archives de l'Opéra Comique: https://dezede.org.

Primary Sources

AE [George William Russell], *The Building Up of a Rural Civilization* (Dublin: Sealy, Bryers & Walker, 1910).

AE [George William Russell], *Imaginations and Reveries*, 2nd edn. (Dublin and London: Maunsel & Roberts, 1921).

AE [George William Russell], *Letters from AE.*, ed. and selected by Alan Denson (London: Abelard-Schuman, 1961).

AE [George William Russell], *Selections from the contributions to the Irish Homestead*, 2 vols., ed. Henry Summerfield (Gerrards Cross: Colin Smythe, 1978).

Arnold, Matthew, *On the Study of Celtic Literature and Other Essays*, with an introduction by Ernest Rhys (London: J. M. Dent & Sons, 1976).

Author unknown, *Mr Balfour's Tours in Connemara and Donegal* (Dublin: Dublin Daily Express, 1890).

Barnes, Djuna, *The Book of Repulsive Women: Eight Rhythms and Five Drawings* (Los Angeles: Sun & Moon Press, 1989).

Barnes, Djuna, *Poe's Mother: Selected Drawings of Djuna Barnes*, ed. Douglas Messerli (Los Angeles: Sun & Moon Press, 1996).

Besant, Annie, *The Ancient Wisdom: An Outline of Theosophical Teachings* (London: Theosophical Publishing House, 1897).

Besant, Annie, *Esoteric Christianity* (London: Theosophical Publishing House, 1901).

Besant, Annie, *Reincarnation* (London: Theosophical Publishing House, 1910).

Birmingham, George A., *Hyacinth*, 2nd impression (London: Edward Arnold, 1906).

Birmingham, George A., *The Seething Pot*, 7th impression (New York: George H. Doran, 1913).

Blavatsky, Helena, *Isis Unveiled: A Master-Key to the Mysteries of Ancient and Modern Science and Theology, Vol. I: Science* (London: Bernard Quaritch, 1877).

Blavatsky, Helena, *The Secret Doctrine: The Synthesis of Science, Religion, and Philosophy* (London: Theosophical Publishing Society, 1888–97).

Blavatsky, Helena, *The Voice of Silence, Being Chosen Fragments from the 'Book of Golden Precepts', for the daily use of Lanoos Disciples* (London: Theosophical Publishing Company, 1889).

Boehme, Jacob, *The Confessions of Jacob Boehme*, edited and compiled by W. Scott Palmer, with an introduction by Evelyn Underhill (London: Methuen, 1920).

Bois, Jules, *Le Satanisme et la magie* (Paris: E. Flammarion, 1895).

Brissac, Henri, and Alfred Naquet, *Pour et contre le collectivisme*, with a preface by A. Millerand (Paris: Petite République, 1895).

Brunetière, Ferdinand, 'Le symbolisme contemporain', Revue des Deux Mondes, 1 April 1891, 681–92.

Buckley, Robert John, *Ireland as it is and as it would be under Home Rule: Sixty-two letters written by the Special Commissioner of the Birmingham Daily Gazette, Between March and August, 1893* (Birmingham: Birmingham Daily Gazette Company, 1893).

Burke, Oliver J., *The South Isles of Aran, County Galway* (London: Kegan Paul, Trench & Co., 1887).

Caird, Edward, *Individualism and Socialism* (Glasgow: James Maclehose, 1897).

Carlyle, Thomas, *Past and Present* (London: Chapman & Hall, 1870).

Charbonnel, Victor, *Les mystiques dans la littérature présente* (Paris: Edition du Mercure de France, 1897).

Collins, Mabel, *Light on the Path* (London: George Redway, 1888).

Comte, Auguste, *The Positive Philosophy of Auguste Comte*, trans. Harriet Martineau, Vol. I (London: John Chapman, 1853).

Connolly, James, *Collected Works*, Vol. I (Dublin: New Books, 1987).

Considerant, Victor, *Principes du Socialisme: Manifeste de la Démocratie au XIX Siècle*, reprinted from the 1847 edition (Osnabrück: Otto Zeller, 1978).

Coyne, William P., ed., *Ireland: Industrial and Agricultural* (Dublin: Browne & Nolan, 1902).

Crowe, Catherine, *The Night Side of Nature; or, Ghosts and Ghost Seers*, Vol. I (London: T.C. Newby, 1848).

Cunningham, D. J., 'The Skeleton of the Irish Giant, Cornelius Magrath', *The Transactions of the Royal Irish Academy*, Vol. 29 (1887–92), 553–612.

Cunningham, D. J., and A. C. Haddon, 'The Anthropometric Laboratory of Ireland', *Journal of the Anthropological Institute*, Vol. 21, 1891, 35–9.

Darwin, Charles, *The Origin of Species*, ed. Gillian Beer (Oxford: Oxford University Press, 1996).

Darwin, Charles, *The Descent of Man, and Selection in Relation to Sex*, with an introduction by James Moore and Adrian Desmond (London: Penguin, 2004).

Deevy, Teresa, *The King of Spain's Daughter*, in Angela Bourke et al., *The Field Day Anthology of Irish Writing, Volume V: Irish Women's Writing and Traditions* (Cork: Cork University Press, 2002), 1001–7.

Deville, Gabriel, 'L'État et le socialisme', in *Principes socialistes par Gabriel Deville*, 2nd edn. (Paris: V. Giard et E. Brière, 1898), 151–212.

Drummond, Henry, *The Ascent of Man* (London: Hodder & Stoughton, 1894).

Duffy, Charles Gavan, George Sigerson, and Douglas Hyde, *The Revival of Irish Literature* (London: T.F. Unwin, 1894).

Editor unknown, *The Shanachie: An Illustrated Irish Miscellany*, Vol. II (Dublin: Maunsel & Co., 1907).

Eglinton, John, *Some Essays and Passages*, selected by W. B. Yeats (Dundrum: Dun Emer Press, 1905).

Eglinton, John, W. B. Yeats, AE, and W. Larminie, *Literary Ideals in Ireland* (London: T. Fisher Unwin, 1899).

Elworthy, Frederick Thomas, *The Evil Eye: The Classic Account of an Ancient Superstition* (New York: Dover Publications, 2004).

Estlake, Allan, *The Oneida Community: A record of an attempt to carry out the principles of Christian unselfishness and scientific race-improvement* (London: George Redway, 1900).

Flower, Robin, *The Western Island, or The Great Blasket*, with illustrations by Ida M. Flower (Oxford: Oxford University Press, 1978).

France, Anatole, *Histoire Comique* (Paris: Calmann-Lévy, 1903).

Frazer, James, *The Golden Bough: A Study in Magic and Religion* (Hertfordshire: Wordsworth Editions, 1993).

Gregory, Lady Augusta, *Poets and Dreamers: Studies and Translations from the Irish* (Dublin: Hodges, Figgis & Co., 1903).

Gregory, Lady Augusta, *Seven Short Plays* (New York: Putnam, 1909).

Gregory, Lady Augusta, *Collected Plays, Volume I: The Comedies*, ed. Ann Saddlemyer (Gerrards Cross: Colin Smythe, 1970).

Gregory, Lady Augusta, *Collected Plays, Volume II: The Tragedies and Tragi-Comedies*, ed. Ann Saddlemyer (Gerrards Cross: Colin Smythe, 1970).

Gregory, Lady Augusta, *Our Irish Theatre* (Colin Smythe: Gerrards Cross, 1972).

Gregory, Lady Augusta, *Collected Plays: Volume III: Wonder and Supernatural Plays*, ed. Ann Saddlemyer (Gerrards Cross: Colin Smythe, 1979).

Griffith, Arthur, *The Resurrection of Hungary: A Parallel for Ireland*, 3rd edn. (Dublin: Whelan & Son, 1918).

Gurney, Edmund, Frederic W. H. Myers, and Frank Podmore, *Phantasms of the Living*, Vol. I, Society for Psychical Research (London: Trübner & Co., 1886).

Gwynn, Stephen, *The Fair Hills of Ireland*, with illustrations by Hugh Thomson (Dublin and London: Maunsel, 1914).

Haddon, A. C., and C. R. Browne, 'The Ethnography of the Aran Islands, County Galway', *Proceedings of the Royal Irish Academy*, Vol. 2 (1891–3), 768–830.

Haeckel, Ernst, *The History of Creation: of, The Development of the Earth and Its Inhabitants by the Action of Natural Causes*, trans. E. Ray Lankester, 2 vols. (London: Henry S. King, 1876).

Hartland, Edwin Sidney, *The Science of Fairy Tales: An Enquiry into Fairy Mythology* (London: Walter Scott, 1891).

Hegel, Georg Wilhelm Friedrich, *Lectures on the History of Philosophy*, trans. Elizabeth S. Haldane and Frances H. Simson, 3 vols. (London: Kegan Paul, Trench, Trübner & Co., 1892–6).

Hobson, John A., *Problems of Poverty: An Inquiry into the Industrial Condition of the Poor* (London: Methuen & Co., 1899).

Hogan, Robert, and James Kilroy, eds., *Lost Plays of the Irish Renaissance* (California: Proscenium Press, 1970).

Hogan, Robert, and Michael J. O'Neill, eds., *Joseph Holloway's Abbey theatre: A Selection from his Unpublished Journal: Impressions of a Dublin Playgoer*, with a preface by Harry T. Moore (Carbondale: Southern Illinois University Press, 1967).

Horkheimer, Max, and Theodor Adorno, *Dialectic of Enlightenment*, trans. John Cumming (New York: Herder & Herder, 1972).

Hull, Eleanor, *The Poem-Book of the Gael* (London: Chatto & Windus, 1912).

Huxley, T. H., *Evidence as to Man's Place in Nature* (New York: Appleton, 1863).

Huxley, T. H., and Julian Huxley, *Evolution and Ethics, 1893–1943* (London: The Pilot Press, 1947).

Huysmans, Joris-Karl, *À Rebours* (Paris: Fasquelle, 1961).

Hyde, Douglas, *Abhráin Grádh Chúige Connacht; or, Love Songs of Connacht, being the fourth chapter of the 'Songs of Connacht'* (Dublin: Gill, 1893).

Hyde, Douglas, *A Literary History of Ireland from the Earliest Times to the Present Day* (London: Ernest Benn, 1967).

Hyde, Douglas, *Selected Plays of Douglas Hyde, 'An Craobhin Aoibhinn'*, trans. Lady Gregory, chosen and with an introduction by Gareth W. Dunleavy and Janet Egleson Dunleavy (Gerrards Cross: Colin Smythe, 1991).

de Jubainville, Marie Henri d'Arbois, *Le cycle mythologique irlandais et la mythologie celtique* (Paris: E. Thorin, 1884).

Keating, Geoffrey, *The History of Ireland, Vol. I, containing the Introduction and First Book of the History*, edited with translation and notes by David Comyn (London: David Nutt, 1902).

à Kempis, Thomas, *The Imitation of Christ*, trans. Rev. Richard Challoner (Rockford, IL: Tan Books, 1989).

Kenny, P. D., *Economics for Irishmen* (Dublin: Maunsel, 1906).

Kidd, Benjamin, *Social Evolution* (New York and London: Macmillan, 1894).

Lang, Andrew, trans., *Aucassin and Nicolette* (London: D. Nutt, 1897).

Lawless, Emily, *Traits and Confidences* (London: Methuen, 1898).

Lawless, Emily, *Grania: The Story of an Island*, ed. with an introduction by Michael O'Flynn (Brighton: Victorian Secrets, 2013).

Le Braz, Anatole, *Essai sur l'histoire du Théâtre Celtique* (Paris: Calmann-Lévy, 1904).

Leland, Charles Godfrey, *Gypsy Sorcery and Fortune Telling* (London: Fisher Unwin, 1891).

Lillie, Arthur, *Madame Blavatsky and Her 'Theosophy'* (London: Swan Sonnenschein & Co., 1895).

MacKenna, Stephen, *Journals and Letters of Stephen MacKenna*, ed. E.R. Dodds, with a preface by Padraic Colum (London: Constable & Co., 1936).

Maeterlinck, Maurice, *Introduction à une psychologie des songes, 1886–1896*, compiled with notes by Stefan Gross (Brussels: Labor, 1985).

Maeterlinck, Maurice, *Pelleas and Melisanda, and The Sightless*, trans. L. Alma Tadema (London: Walter Scott, 1895).

Maeterlinck, Maurice, *The Treasure of the Humble*, trans. Alfred Sutro (London: George Allen, 1903).

Marx, Karl, *Capital: An Abridged Edition*, edited with an introduction by David McLellan (Oxford: Oxford University Press, 1995).

Marx, Karl, and Friedrich Engels, *The Communist Manifesto*, with an introduction and notes by Gareth Stedman Jones (London: Penguin, 2002).

Meilhac, Henri, and Philippe Gille, *Manon: An Opera in Five Acts and Six Tableaux*, music by Jules Massenet (New York: Fred Rullman, no date).

Meyer, Kuno, ed. and trans., *The Voyage of Bran Son of Febal to the Land of the Living: an Old Irish Saga*, with Alfred Nutt, *Essay upon the Irish Vision of the Happy Otherworld and the Celtic Doctrine of Re-birth: Section I, The Happy Otherworld, Vol. I* (London: David Nutt, 1895).

Meyerfeld, Max, 'The Letters of John Millington Synge', *The Yale Review* XIII (July 1924).

Micks, W. L., *An Account of the Constitution, Administration and Dissolution of the Congested Districts Board for Ireland from 1891 to 1923* (Dublin: Eason & Son, 1925).

Mikhail, E. H., ed., *J. M. Synge: Interviews and Recollections* (London and Basingstoke: Macmillan, 1977).

Moore, George, and Edward Martyn, *Selected Plays of George Moore and Edward Martyn*, chosen, with an introduction by David B. Eakin and Michael Case (Gerrards Cross: Colin Smythe, 1995).

Moran, D. P., *The Philosophy of Irish Ireland*, ed. Patrick Maume (Dublin: University College Dublin Press, 2006).

Morris, William, *The Aims of Art* (London: Office of 'The Commonweal', 1887).

Morris, William, *The Political Writings of William Morris*, edited with an introduction by A. L. Morton (London: Lawrence & Wishart, 1979).

Morris, William, *News from Nowhere, and other writings*, ed. Clive Wilmer (Harmondsworth: Penguin, 1993).

Morris, William, *William Morris on Architecture*, ed. Chris Miele (Sheffield: Sheffield Academic Press, 1996).

Morris, William, and E. Belfort Bax, *Socialism: Its Growth and Outcome* (London: Swan Sonnenschein, 1893).

Müller, F. Max, *The Upanishads*, 2 vols. (Oxford: Clarendon Press, 1879–84).

Nic Shiubhlaigh, Maire, and Edward Kenny, *The Splendid Years*, foreword by Padraic Colum (Dublin: James Duffy & Co., 1955).

Nietzsche, Friedrich, *Thus Spoke Zarathustra: A Book for All and None*, ed. Adrian Del Caro and Robert B. Pippin, trans. Adrian Del Caro (Cambridge: Cambridge University Press, 2006, reprinted 2012).

O'Brien, Flann (Myles na Gopaleen), *The Best of Myles: A Selection from 'Cruiskeen Lawn'*, ed. with a preface by Kevin O'Nolan (London: Picador, 1977).

Oliphant, Laurence, *Scientific Religion: or, Higher Possibilities of Life and Practice through the Operation of Natural Forces*, 2nd edn. (Edinburgh and London: William Blackwood & Sons, 1888).

Pater, Walter, *Studies in the History of the Renaissance*, ed. Matthew Beaumont (Oxford: Oxford University Press, 2010).

Paulhan, Frédéric, *Le nouveau mysticisme* (Paris: Felix Alcan, 1891).

Plunkett, Horace, *Ireland in the New Century* (London: John Murray, 1904).

Pound, Ezra, *The Spirit of Romance: An Attempt to Define Somewhat the Charm of the Pre-Renaissance Literature of Latin Europe* (London: J. M. Dent, 1910).

Pound, Ezra, *Jefferson and/or Mussolini: Fascism as I Have Seen It* (London: Stanley Nott, 1935).

Pound, Ezra, *Selected Cantos* (London: Faber, 1976).

Pound, Ezra, *Plays Modelled on the Noh*, ed. Donald C. Gallup (Toledo: The Friends of the University of Toledo Libraries, 1987).

Rabelais, François, *The Histories of Gargantua and Pantagruel*, trans. with an introduction by J. M. Cohen (Harmondsworth: Penguin, 1986).

Renan, Ernest, *Essais de Morale et de Critique* (Paris: Michel Lévy Frères, 1860).

Renan, Ernest, *Poetry of the Celtic Races, and other essays*, trans. William G. Hutchinson (London: Walter Scott Publishing Co., 1896).

Ruskin, John, *The Stones of Venice*, 3 vols. (London: Smith, Elder & Co., 1851–3).

Ryan, William Patrick, *The Irish Literary Revival: Its History, Pioneers and Possibilities* (London: W.P. Ryan, 1894).

Schuré, Édouard, *Les Grands Initiés: Equisse de l'histoire secrète des religions* (Paris: Perrin, 1922).

Shaw, George Bernard, *The Quintessence of Ibsenism* (London: Walter Scott, 1891).

Shaw, George Bernard, *John Bull's Other Island* (Harmondsworth: Penguin, 1984).

Spencer, Herbert, *First Principles*, 6th edn. (London: Watts & Co., 1937).

de Spinoza, Benedict, *On the Improvement of the Understanding, The Ethics, and Correspondence*, trans. R. H. M. Elwes (New York: Dover, 1955).

Stokes, Whitley, and John Strachan, eds., *Thesaurus Paleohibernicus: A Collection of Old-Irish Glosses, Scholia, Prose and Verse*, Vol. II (Cambridge: Cambridge University Press, 1903).

Swedenborg, Emanuel, *Heaven and Hell*, trans. George F. Dole (West Chester, PA: Swedenborg Foundation, 2002).

Symons, Arthur, *Cities and Sea-Coasts and Islands* (New York: Brentano's, 1919).

Synge, John Millington, *The Works of John M. Synge*, 4 vols. (Dublin: Maunsel, 1910).

Synge, John Millington, *Collected Works, Volume II: Prose*, ed. Alan Price (London: Oxford University Press, 1966).

Synge, John Millington, *Collected Works, Volume IV: Plays, Book II*, ed. Ann Saddlemyer (London: Oxford University Press, 1968).

Synge, John Millington, *Letters to Molly: John Millington Synge to Maire O'Neill*, ed. Ann Saddlemyer (Cambridge, MA: Harvard University Press, 1971).

Synge, John Millington, *My Wallet of Photographs: The Collected Photographs of J. M. Synge*, arranged and introduced by Lilo Stephens (Dublin: The Dolmen Press, 1971).

Synge, John Millington, *Collected Works, Volume I: Poems*, ed. Robin Skelton (Gerrards Cross: Colin Smythe, 1982).

Synge, John Millington, *Collected Works, Volume III: Plays, Book I*, ed. Ann Saddlemyer (Gerrards Cross: Colin Smythe, 1982).

Synge, John Millington, *The Collected Letters of John Millington Synge: Vol. I, 1871–1907*, ed. Ann Saddlemyer (Oxford: Clarendon Press, 1983).

Synge, John Millington, *The Collected Letters of John Millington Synge: Volume II, 1907–1909*, ed. Ann Saddlemyer (Oxford: Clarendon Press, 1984).

Synge, John Millington, *The Aran Islands*, edited with an introduction by Tim Robinson (London: Penguin, 1992).

Synge, John Millington, *Travelling Ireland: Essays 1898–1908*, ed. Nicholas Grene (Dublin: Lilliput Press, 2009).

Synge, John Millington, 'More Letters by John Millington Synge', Ann Saddlemyer, *Irish University Review*, Vol. 45, No. 1 (Spring/Summer 2015), 25–30.

Synge, Samuel, *Letters to my daughter: memories of John Millington Synge* (Dublin and Cork: The Talbot Press, 1931).

Taylor, Charles, *Ultimate Civilization, and other essays* (London: Bell & Daldy, 1860).

Trench, Richard Chenevix, *English Past and Present* (New York: Redfield, 1855).

Tuke, James Hack, *The Condition of Donegal: Letters reprinted from The Times of May 20th, 28th, and June 29th, 1889* (London and Dublin: W. Ridgway and Hodges, Figgis & Co., 1889).

Tuke, James Hack, *James Hack Tuke: A Memoir*, compiled by Sir Edward Fry (London: Macmillan, 1899).

Tylor, Edward, *Primitive Culture: Researches in the Development of Mythology, Philosophy, Religion, Language, Art, and Custom*, Vol. I (London: John Murray, 1920)

Wallace, Alfred Russell, *Spiritualism* (Philadelphia: J.B. Lippincott, 1892).

Ward, James, *Naturalism and Agnosticism: The Gifford Lectures Delivered Before the University of Aberdeen in the Years 1896–1898*, 2nd edn., 2 vols. (London: Adam & Charles Black, 1903).

Weber, Max, 'Science as a Vocation', *From Max Weber: Essays in Sociology*, ed. H. H. Gerth and C. Wright Mills (New York and Abingdon: Routledge, 2009), 129–58.

Weismann, August, *The Germ-Plasm: A Theory of Heredity*, trans. W. Newton Parker and Harriet Rönnfeldt (New York: Charles Scribner's Sons, 1893).

Wordsworth, William, and Samuel Taylor Coleridge, *Lyrical Ballads, with a few other poems* (London: Penguin, 2006).

Yeats, Jack Butler, *Life in the West of Ireland* (Dublin: Maunsel, 1912).

Yeats, Jack Butler, *The Selected Writings of Jack B. Yeats*, ed. Robin Skelton (London: André Deutsch, 1991).

Yeats, William Butler, *Ideas of Good and Evil* (London: A.H. Bullen, 1903).

Yeats, William Butler, *Where There is Nothing: Being Volume One of Plays for an Irish Theatre* (London and New York: Macmillan, 1903).

Yeats, William Butler, ed., *Samhain: An occasional review* (Dublin: Maunsel & Co., 1905).

Yeats, William Butler, *Autobiographies: Memories and Reflections* (London: Macmillan, 1955).

Yeats, William Butler, *The Letters of W. B. Yeats*, ed. Allan Wade (New York: Macmillan, 1955).

Yeats, William Butler, *Mythologies* (London: Macmillan, 1959).

Yeats, William Butler, *Essays and Introductions* (New York: Macmillan, 1961).

Yeats, William Butler, *Explorations* (London: Macmillan, 1961).

Yeats, William Butler, *The Variorum Edition of the Plays of W. B. Yeats*, ed. Russell K. Alspach (London: Macmillan, 1966).

Yeats, William Butler, *Uncollected Prose, Volume I: First Reviews and Articles, 1886–1896*, collected and edited by John P. Frayne (London: Macmillan, 1970).

Yeats, William Butler, *Memoirs*, ed. Denis Donoghue (London: Macmillan, 1972).

Yeats, William Butler, *Uncollected Prose, Volume II: Later Reviews, Articles & Other Miscellaneous Prose, 1897–1939*, ed. John P. Frayne and Colton Johnson (London: Macmillan, 1979).

Yeats, William Butler, *The Variorum Edition of the Poems of W. B. Yeats*, eds. Peter Allt and Russell K. Alspach, (London: Macmillan, 1989).

Yeats, William Butler, *The Collected Letters of W. B. Yeats: Volume III, 1901–1904*, ed. John Kelly and Ronald Schuchard (Oxford: Clarendon Press, 1994).

Yeats, William Butler, and Edwin John Ellis, eds., *The Works of William Blake: Poetic, Symbolic, and Critical, edited with lithographs of the illustrated 'Prophetic Books' and a Memoir and Interpretation*, Vol. I (London: Bernard Quaritch, 1893).

Secondary Sources

Aalen, Frederick H. A., 'Constructive Unionism and the Shaping of Rural Ireland, c. 1880–1921', *Rural History*, Vol. 4, No. 2 (October 1993), 137–64.

Alexander, Neal, and James Moran, eds., *Regional Modernisms* (Edinburgh: Edinburgh University Press, 2013).

Armstrong, Tim, *Modernism: A Cultural History* (Cambridge: Polity, 2005).

Arnold, Bruce, *Jack Yeats* (New Haven and London: Yale University Press, 1998).

Arrington, Lauren, *W. B. Yeats, the Abbey Theatre, Censorship, and the Irish State: Adding the Half-Pence to the Pence* (Oxford and New York: Oxford University Press, 2010).

Arrington, Lauren, *Revolutionary Lives: Constance and Casimir Markievicz* (Princeton and Oxford: Princeton University Press, 2016).

Ashley, Scott, 'Primitivism, Celticism and Morbidity in the Atlantic fin de siècle', in Patrick McGuinness, ed., *Symbolism, Decadence and the Fin de Siècle: French and European Perspectives* (Exeter: Exeter University Press, 2000), 175–93.

Ashley, Scott, 'The poetics of race in 1890s Ireland: an ethnography of the Aran Islands', *Patterns of Prejudice*, Vol. 35, No. 2 (2001), 5–18.

Atkin, Warren IV, '"I Just Riz the Loy": The Oedipal Dimension of "The Playboy of the Western World"', *South Atlantic Bulletin*, Vol. 45, No. 4 (November 1980).

Author unknown, *The Synge Manuscripts in the Library of Trinity College Dublin: A Catalogue Prepared on the Occasion of the Synge Centenary Exhibition, 1971* (Dublin: The Dolmen Press, 1971).

Beaumont, Matthew, 'Socialism and Occultism at the Fin de Siècle: Elective Affinities', *Victorian Review*, Vol. 36, No. 1 (Spring 2010), 217–32.

Beer, Gillian, *Open Fields: Science in Cultural Encounter* (Oxford: Clarendon Press, 1996).

Beiser, Frederick C., ed., *The Cambridge Companion to Hegel and Nineteenth-Century Philosophy* (Cambridge: Cambridge University Press, 2008).

Bennett, Jane, *Unthinking Faith and Enlightenment: Nature and the State in a Post-Hegelian Era* (New York and London: New York University Press, 1987).

Bennett, Jane, *The Enchantment of Modern Life: Attachments, Crossings, and Ethics* (Princeton and Oxford: Princeton University Press, 2001).

Benson, Eugene, *J. M. Synge* (London and Basingstoke: Macmillan, 1982).

Berger, Peter, Brigitte Berger, and Hansfried Kellner, *The Homeless Mind: Modernization and Consciousness* (Harmondsworth: Penguin, 1973).

Berlin, Normand, 'Traffic of Our Stage: *DruidSynge*', *The Massachusetts Review*, Vol. 48, No. 1 (Spring 2007), pp. 90–102.

Bhabha, Homi K., *The Location of Culture* (New York: Routledge, 1994).

Bourgeois, Maurice, *John Millington Synge and the Irish Theatre* (London: Constable & Co., 1913).

Bradbury, Malcolm, and James MacFarlane, eds., *Modernism: A Guide to European Literature, 1890–1930* (London: Penguin, 1976).

Bramble, John, *Modernism and the Occult* (Basingstoke: Palgrave Macmillan, 2015).

Brannigan, John, *Race in Modern Irish Literature and Culture* (Edinburgh: Edinburgh University Press, 2009).

Brannigan, John, *Archipelagic Modernism: Literature in the Irish and British Isles, 1890–1970* (Edinburgh: Edinburgh University Press, 2015).

Breathnach, Ciara, *The Congested Districts Board of Ireland, 1891–1923: Poverty and Development in the West of Ireland* (Dublin, 2005).

Breathnach, Ciara, ed., *Framing the West: Images of Rural Ireland, 1891–1920* (Dublin: Irish Academic Press, 2007).

Brooker, Peter, and Andrew Thacker, eds., *The Oxford Critical and Cultural History of Modernist Magazines, Volume I: Britain and Ireland 1880–1955* (Oxford: Oxford University Press, 2009).

Brown, Terence, 'Ireland, Modernism and the 1930s', in Patricia Coughlan and Alex Davis, eds., *Modernism and Ireland: The Poetry of the 1930s* (Cork: Cork University Press, 1995), 24–42.

Bryson, Mary E., 'Metaphors for Freedom: Theosophy and the Irish Literary Revival', *The Canadian Journal of Irish Studies*, Vol. 3, No. 1 (June 1977), 32–40.

Burke, Mary, 'Evolutionary Theory: And the Search for Lost Innocence in the Writings of J. M. Synge', *The Canadian Journal of Irish Studies*, Vol. 30, No. 1, Re-Thinking the 19th Century/Repenser le 19ième siècle (Spring, 2004), 48–54.

Burke, Mary, *'Tinkers': Synge and the Cultural History of the Irish Traveller* (Oxford: Oxford University Press, 2009).

Bushrui, Suheil Badi, ed., *Sunshine and the Moon's Delight: A Centenary Tribute to John Millington Synge, 1871–1909* (Gerrards Cross and Beirut: Colin Smythe and American University of Beirut, 1972).

Carden, Siún, 'Cable Crossings: The Aran Jumper as Myth and Merchandise', *Costume: Journal of the Costume Society*, Vol. 48, No. 2 (2014), 260–75.

Carpenter, Andrew, ed., *Place, Personality and the Irish Writer* (New York: Barnes & Noble, 1977).

Carville, Justin, 'Visible Others: Photography and Romantic Ethnography in Ireland', in Maria McGarrity and Claire A. Culleton, eds., *Irish Modernism and the Global Primitive* (New York: Palgrave Macmillan, 2009), 93–115.

Casey, Daniel J., and Robert E. Rhodes, eds., *Views of the Irish Peasantry 1800–1916* (Hamden, CT: Archon, 1977).

Castle, Gregory, *Modernism and the Celtic Revival* (Cambridge: Cambridge University Press, 2001).

Castle, Gregory, and Patrick Bixby, eds., *A History of Irish Modernism* (Cambridge: Cambridge University Press, 2019).

Charnow, Sally Debra, *Theatre, Politics, and Markets in Fin-de-Siècle Paris* (Basingstoke: Palgrave Macmillan, 2005).

Chaudhuri, Una, 'The Dramaturgy of the Other: Diegetic Patterns in Synge's *The Playboy of the Western World*', *Modern Drama*, Vol. 32, No. 3 (Fall 1989), 374–86.

Childs, Donald J., *Modernism and Eugenics: Woolf, Eliot, Yeats, and the Culture of Degeneration* (Cambridge: Cambridge University Press, 2001).

Churchill, Suzanne W., and Adam McKible, eds., *Little Magazines & Modernism: New Approaches* (Hampshire: Ashgate, 2007).

Cleary, Joe, *Outrageous Fortune: Capital and Culture in Modern Ireland* (Dublin: Field Day Publications, 2007).

Cleary, Joe, ed., *The Cambridge Companion to Irish Modernism* (Cambridge: Cambridge University Press, 2014).

Cleary, Joe, and Claire Connolly, eds., *The Cambridge Companion to Modern Irish Culture* (Cambridge: Cambridge University Press, 2005).

de Cléir, Síle, 'Creativity in the Margins: Creativity and Locality in Ireland's Fashion Journey', *Fashion Theory: The Journal of Dress, Body & Culture*, Vol. 15, No. 2 (2011), 204–24.

Cliff, Brian, and Nicholas Grene, eds., *Synge and Edwardian Ireland* (Oxford: Oxford University Press, 2012).

Coldwell, Joan, 'Pamela Colman Smith and the Yeats Family', *The Canadian Journal of Irish Studies*, Vol. 3, No. 2 (November 1977), 27–34.

Cole, Sarah, *At the Violet Hour: Modernism and Violence in England and Ireland* (Oxford: Oxford University Press, 2012).

Collins, Christopher, '"The Cries of Pagan Desperation": Synge, *Riders to the Sea* and the Discontents of Historical Time', *Irish Theatre International*, Vol. 3, No. 1 (2014), 7–24.

Collins, Christopher, *Theatre and Residual Culture: J. M. Synge and Pre-Christian Ireland* (London: Palgrave Macmillan, 2016).

Connolly, Claire, 'Counting on the Past: Yeats and Romanticism', *European Romantic Review*, Vol. 28, No. 4 (July 2017), 473–87.

Contini, Roberto, Sergio Marinelli, and Angelo Mazza, eds., *Paolo Piazza: pittore cappuccino nell'età della Controriforma tra conventi e corti d'Europa* (Verona: Banco Popolare di Verona e Novara, 2002).

Corkery, Daniel, *Synge and Anglo-Irish Literature: A Study* (Dublin and Cork: Cork University Press, 1931).

Coughlan, Patricia, and Alex Davis, eds., *Modernism and Ireland: The Poetry of the 1930s* (Cork: Cork University Press, 1995).

Cox, Catherine, *Negotiating Insanity in the Southeast of Ireland, 1820–1900* (Manchester: Manchester University Press, 2012).

Coxhead, Elizabeth, *Lady Gregory: A Literary Portrait* (London: Macmillan, 1961).

Coxhead, Elizabeth, *J. M. Synge and Lady Gregory* (Harlow: Longmans, Green & Co., 1969).

Crawford, Nicholas, 'Synge's *Playboy* and the Eugenics of Language', *Modern Drama*, Vol. 51, No. 4 (Winter 2008), 482–500.

Cullingford, Elizabeth, *Yeats, Ireland, and Fascism* (London and Basingstoke: Macmillan, 1981).

Cusack, George, '"In the gripe of the ditch": nationalism, famine and *The Playboy of the Western World*', in George Cusack and Sarah Goss, eds., *Hungry Words: Images of Famine in the Irish Canon* (Dublin and Portland, OR: Irish Academic Press, 2006), 133–58.

Dalsimer, Adele M., '"The Irish Peasant Had All His Heart": J. M. Synge in *The Country Shop*', in Adele M. Dalsimer, ed., *Visualising Ireland: National Identity and the Pictorial Tradition* (Winchester, MA: Faber & Faber, 1993), 201–30.

Daly, Nicholas, *Modernism, Romance and the Fin de Siècle* (Cambridge: Cambridge University Press, 1999).

Daly, Nicholas, *Literature, Technology, and Modernity, 1860–2000* (Cambridge: Cambridge University Press, 2004).

Davis, Alex, 'Learning to be Brutal: Synge, Decadence, and the Modern Movement', *New Hibernia Review*, Vol. 14, No. 3 (Autumn 2010), 33–51.

Davis, Alex, 'J. M. Synge's *Vita Vecchia* and *Aucassin et Nicolette*', in *Notes & Queries*, Vol. 58, No. 1 (March 2011), 125–7.

Dean, Joan Fitzpatrick, and José Lanters, eds., *Beyond Realism: Experimental and Unconventional Drama since the Revival* (Leiden: Brill, 2014).

Deane, Seamus, *Celtic Revivals: Essays in Modern Irish Literature, 1880–1980* (London: Faber & Faber, 1985).

Deane, Seamus, ed., *The Field Day Anthology of Irish Writing*, Vol. II (Derry: Field Day Publications, 1991).

Deane, Seamus, *Strange Country: Modernity and Nationhood in Irish Writing since 1790* (Oxford: Clarendon Press, 1997).

Devlin, Joseph, 'J. M. Synge's *The Playboy of the Western World* and the Culture of Western Ireland under Late Colonial Rule', *Modern Drama*, Vol. 41, No. 3 (Fall 1998), 371–835.

Dillenberger, John, *Protestant Thought and Natural Science: A Historical Interpretation* (Nashville and New York: Abingdon Press, 1960).

Doane, Mary Ann, *The Emergence of Cinematic Time: Modernity, Contingency, the Archive* (Cambridge, MA: Harvard University Press, 2002).

Dowling, Linda C., *The Vulgarization of Art: The Victorians and Aesthetic Democracy* (London and Charlottesville, VA: University Press of Virginia, 1996).

Eagleton, Terry, *Heathcliff and the Great Hunger: Studies in Irish Culture* (London: Verso, 1995).

Eagleton, Terry, 'The Flight to the Real', in *Cultural Politics at the Fin de Siècle*, ed. Sally Ledger and Scott McCracken (Cambridge: Cambridge University Press, 1995), 11–21.

Eagleton, Terry, *Crazy John and the Bishop and Other Essays on Irish Culture* (Cork: Cork University Press, 1998).

Fallis, Richard, *The Irish Renaissance: an Introduction to Anglo-Irish Literature* (Dublin: Gill and Macmillan, 1978).

Fallis, Richard, 'Art as Collaboration: Literary Influences on J. M. Synge', in Edward A. Hopper, Jr., ed., *A J. M. Synge Literary Companion* (New York and London: Greenwood Press, 1988), 145–60.

Ferrall, Charles, *Modernist Writing and Reactionary Politics* (Cambridge: Cambridge University Press, 2001).

FitzSimon, Betsey Taylor, and James H. Murphy, eds., *The Irish Revival Reappraised* (Dublin: Four Courts Press, 2004).

Flannery, James W., *W. B. Yeats and the Idea of a Theatre: The Early Abbey Theatre in Theory and Practice* (New Haven and London: Yale University Press, 1976).

Fleming, Deborah, *'A man who does not exist': The Irish Peasant in the Work of W. B. Yeats and J. M. Synge* (Ann Arbor: University of Michigan Press, 1995).

Foster, John Wilson, *Fictions of the Irish Literary Revival: A Changeling Art* (Syracuse, NY: Syracuse University Press, 1987).

Foster, John Wilson, and Helena C. G. Chesney, eds., *Nature in Ireland: A Scientific and Cultural History* (Dublin: Lilliput Press, 1997).

Foster, Roy, *W. B. Yeats: A Life, I: The Apprentice Mage, 1865–1914* (Oxford and New York: Oxford University Press, 1997).

Fraser, Robert, ed., *Sir James Frazer and the Literary Imagination: Essays in Affinity and Influence* (London and Basingstoke: Macmillan, 1990).

Frawley, Oona, *Irish Pastoral: Nostalgia and Twentieth-Century Irish Literature* (Dublin and Portland, OR: Irish Academic Press, 2005).

Frazier, Adrian, *Behind the Scenes: Yeats, Horniman, and the Struggle for the Abbey Theatre* (California: University of California Press, 1990).

Freeman, T. W., 'The Congested Districts of Western Ireland', *Geographical Review*, Vol. 33, No. 1 (January 1943), 1–14.

Gailey, Andrew, *Ireland and the Death of Kindness: The Experience of Constructive Unionism, 1890–1905* (Cork: Cork University Press, 1987).

Gandhi, Leela, *Postcolonial Theory: A Critical Introduction* (New York: Columbia University Press, 1998).

Gerstenberger, Donna, 'Yeats and Synge: "A Young Man's Ghost"', in D. S. Maxwell and S. B. Bushrui, eds., *W. B. Yeats, 1865–1965: Centenary Essays on the Art of W. B. Yeats* (Ibadan: Ibadan University Press, 1965), 79–87.

Gerstenberger, Donna, *John Millington Synge* (Boston: Twayne, 1990).

Gibbons, Luke, *Transformations in Irish Culture* (Cork: Cork University Press, 1996).

Goodin, Robert, *Green Political Theory* (Oxford: Polity Press, 1992).

Gould, Peter, *Early Green Politics: Back to Nature, Back to the Land, and Socialism in Britain, 1880–1900* (Brighton: Harvester Press, 1988).

Greene, David H., and Edward M. Stephens, *J. M. Synge, 1871–1909* (New York: Macmillan, 1959).

Grene, Nicholas, *Synge: A Critical Study of the Plays* (London: Macmillan, 1975).

Grene, Nicholas, *The Politics of Irish Drama: Plays in Context from Boucicault to Friel* (Cambridge: Cambridge University Press, 1999).

Grene, Nicholas, ed., *Interpreting Synge: Essays from the Synge Summer School, 1991–2000* (Dublin: Lilliput Press, 2000).

Grene, Nicholas, and Chris Morash, eds., *The Oxford Handbook of Modern Irish Theatre* (Oxford: Oxford University Press, 2016).

Grene, Nicholas, 'J. M. Synge: Late Romantic or Protomodernist?', in Gregory Castle and Patrick Bixby, eds., *A History of Irish Modernism* (Cambridge: Cambridge University Press, 2019), 78–90.

Guinnane, Timothy W., and Ronald I. Miller, 'The Limits to Land Reform: The Land Acts in Ireland, 1870–1909', *Economic Development and Cultural Change*, Vol. 45, No. 3 (April 1997), 591–612.

Guinness, Selina, '"Protestant Magic" Reappraised: Evangelicalism, Dissent, and Theosophy', *Irish University Review*, Vol. 33, No. 1, Special Issue: New Perspectives on the Irish Literary Revival (Spring/Summer 2003), 14–27.

Haldane, Elizabeth S., 'Jacob Böhme and his Relation to Hegel', *The Philosophical Review*, Vol. 6, No. 2 (March 1897), 146–61.

Hammond, J. L., *C.P. Scott of the Manchester Guardian* (London: G. Bell & Sons, 1934).

Harmon, Maurice, ed., *The Celtic Master, Being Contributions to the First James Joyce Symposium in Dublin* (Dublin: Dolmen Press, 1969).

Harmon, Maurice, ed., *J. M. Synge Centenary Papers, 1971* (Dublin: Dolmen Press, 1972).

Harmon, Maurice, 'Cobwebs before the Wind: Aspects of the Peasantry in Irish Literature from 1800–1916', in Daniel J. Casey and Robert E. Rhodes, eds., *Views of the Irish Peasantry 1800–1916* (Hamden, CT: Archon, 1977), 129–59.

Harris, Alexandra, *Romantic Moderns: English Writers, Artists and the Imagination from Virginia Woolf to John Piper* (London: Thames & Hudson, 2010).

Harris, Susan Cannon, 'More than a Morbid, Unhealthy Mind: Public Health and the *Playboy* riots', in Stephen Watt, Eileen Morgan, and Shakir Mustafa, eds., *A Century of Irish Drama: Widening the Stage* (Indianapolis: Indiana University Press, 2000), 72–94.

Harris, Susan Cannon, *Gender and Modern Irish Drama* (Bloomington and Indianapolis: Indiana University Press, 2002).

Harris, Susan Cannon, *Irish Drama and the Other Revolutions: Playwrights, Sexual Politics, and the International Left, 1892–1964* (Edinburgh: Edinburgh University Press, 2017).

Hawkins, Mike, *Social Darwinism in European and American Thought, 1860–1945: Nature as Model and Nature as Threat* (Cambridge: Cambridge University Press, 1997).

Hayter, Althea, *Opium and the Romantic Imagination* (London: Faber & Faber, 1968).

Helland, Janice, '"Caprices of Fashion": Handmade Lace in Ireland, 1883–1907', Textile History, Vol. 39, No. 2 (2008), 193–222.

Helland, Janice, '"A Delightful Change of Fashion": Fair Trade, Cottage Craft, and Tweed in Late Nineteenth-Century Ireland', The Canadian Journal of Irish Studies, Vol. 36, No. 2 (Fall 2010), 34–55.

Henn, T. R., Last Essays (Gerrards Cross: Colin Smythe, 1976).

Higgins, Geraldine, Heroic Revivals from Carlyle to Yeats (Basingstoke: Palgrave Macmillan, 2012).

Hirsch, Edward, 'The Imaginary Irish Peasant', in PMLA, Vol. 106, No. 5 (October 1991), 1116–33.

Hobson, Suzanne, Angels of Modernism: Religion, Culture, Aesthetics, 1910–1960 (Basingstoke: Palgrave, 2011).

Hogan, Robert, and James Kilroy, The Irish Literary Theatre, 1899–1901 (Dublin: The Dolmen Press, 1975).

Hogan, Robert, and James Kilroy, Laying the foundations, 1902–1904 (Dublin: The Dolmen Press, 1976).

Hogan, Robert, and James Kilroy, eds., The Abbey Theatre: The Years of Synge, 1905–1909 (Dublin: The Dolmen Press, 1978).

Howarth, Herbert, 'The Realist Basis of Surreality', in Thomas R. Whitaker, ed., Twentieth-Century Interpretations of The Playboy of the Western World: A Collection of Critical Essays (Englewood Cliffs, NJ: Prentice-Hall, 1969), 106–11.

Howes, Marjorie, and John Kelly, eds., The Cambridge Companion to W. B. Yeats (Cambridge: Cambridge University Press, 2006).

Howkins, Alun, Reshaping rural England: a social history, 1850–1925 (London: Routledge, 1991).

Hutchinson, John, The Dynamics of Cultural Nationalism: The Gaelic Revival and the Creation of the Irish Nation State (London: Allen & Unwin, 1987).

Johnson, Toni O'Brien, Synge: The Medieval and the Grotesque (Gerrards Cross: Colin Smythe, 1982).

Jones, Greta, 'Eugenics in Ireland: The Belfast Eugenics Society, 1911–15', Irish Historical Studies, Vol. 28, No. 109 (May 1992), 81–95.

Jones, Greta, 'Contested Territories: Alfred Cort Haddon, Progressive Evolutionism and Ireland', History of European Ideas, Vol. 24, No. 3 (1998), 195–211.

Jones, Susan, Literature, Modernism, and Dance (Oxford: Oxford University Press, 2013).

Kearney, Richard, Transitions: Narratives in Modern Irish Culture (Manchester: Manchester University Press, 1988).

Kelsall, Malcolm, 'Synge in Aran', Irish University Review, Vol. 5, No. 2 (Autumn 1975), 254–70.

Kennedy, S. B., 'An Enduring View of Irish Identity: Paul Henry and the Realism of Fiction', Irish Arts Review Yearbook, Vol. 15 (1999), 98–107.

Kermode, Frank, Modern Essays (London: Fontana, 1971).

Kern, Stephen, The Culture of Time and Space, 1880–1918 (Cambridge, MA: Harvard University Press, 1983).

Kiberd, Declan, *Synge and the Irish Language*, 2nd edn. (Dublin: Gill & Macmillan, 1993).

Kiberd, Declan, *Inventing Ireland: The Literature of a Modern Nation* (London: Vintage, 1996).

Kiberd, Declan, *Irish Classics* (London: Granta, 2000).

Kilroy, James, *The 'Playboy' Riots* (Dublin: Dolmen, 1971).

King, Carla, '"Our Destitute Countrymen on the Western Coast": Relief and Development Strategies in the Congested Districts in the 1880s and 90s', in King and McNamara, eds., *The West of Ireland: New Perspectives on the Nineteenth Century* (Dublin: History Press Ireland, 2011), 161–84.

King, Carla, and Conor McNamara, eds., *The West of Ireland: New Perspectives on the Nineteenth Century* (Dublin: The History Press, 2011).

King, Mary C., *The Drama of J. M. Synge* (New York: Syracuse University Press, 1985).

King, Mary C., 'Conjuring past or Future? Versions of Synge's 'Play of '98'', *The Irish Review*, No. 26 (Autumn 2000), 71–9.

Knapp, James F., 'Primitivism and Empire: John Synge and Paul Gauguin', *Comparative Literature*, Vol. 41, No. 1 (Winter 1989).

Kopper, Edward A., Jr., ed., *A J. M. Synge Literary Companion* (New York and London: Greenwood Press, 1988).

Krause, David, '"The Rageous Ossean": Patron-Hero of Synge and O'Casey', *Modern Drama*, Vol. 4, No. 3 (Fall 1961), 268–91.

Kuch, Peter, *Yeats and A.E.: 'The antagonism that unites Dear Friends'* (Gerrards Cross: Colin Smythe, 1986).

Lane, Fintan, *The Origins of Modern Irish Socialism, 1881–1896* (Cork: Cork University Press, 1997).

Lane, Leeann, '"There are compensations in the congested districts for their poverty": AE and the idealized peasant of the agricultural co-operative movement', in Betsey Taylor FitzSimon and James H. Murphy, eds., *The Irish Revival Reappraised* (Dublin: Four Courts Press, 2004), 33–48.

Largier, Niklaus, 'Mysticism, Modernity, and the Invention of Aesthetic Experience', *Representations*, Vol. 105, No. 1 (Winter 2009), 37–60.

Leder, Judith Remy, 'Synge's *Riders to the Sea*: Island as Cultural Battleground', *Twentieth-Century Literature*, Vol. 36, No. 2 (Summer 1990), 207–24.

Lee, Joseph, *The Modernisation of Irish Society, 1848–1918* (Dublin: Gill & Macmillan, 1973).

Leeney, Cathy, *Irish Women Playwrights, 1900–1939: Gender & Violence On Stage* (New York: Peter Lang, 2010).

Leerssen, Joep, *Mere Irish and Fíor-Ghael: Studies in the Idea of Irish Nationality, its Development and Literary Expression prior to the Nineteenth Century* (Cork: Cork University Press, 1996).

Leerssen, Joep, *Remembrance and Imagination: Patterns in the Historical and Literary Representation of Ireland in the Nineteenth Century* (Cork: Cork University Press, 1996).

Lennon, Joseph, *Irish Orientalism: A Literary and Intellectual History* (New York: Syracuse University Press, 2004).

Levine, George, *Darwin Loves You: Natural Selection and the Re-Enchantment of the World* (Princeton and Oxford: Princeton University Press, 2006).

Levitas, Ben, '"The Loy in Irish Politics": The Abbey Theatre in the Wake of the Playboy, 1907–1910', *The Irish Review*, No. 29, Irish Theatre (Autumn 2002), 38–50.

Levitas, Ben, *The Theatre of Nation: Irish Drama and Cultural Nationalism, 1890–1916* (Oxford: Clarendon Press, 2002).

Levitas, Ben, 'A Temper of Misgiving: W. B. Yeats and the Ireland of Synge's Time', in Senia Pašeta, ed., *Uncertain Futures: Essays about the Irish Past for Roy Foster* (Oxford: Oxford University Press, 2016), 110–22.

Lewis, Pericles, *The Cambridge Introduction to Modernism* (Cambridge: Cambridge University Press, 2007).

Lewis, Pericles, *Religious Experience and the Modernist Novel* (Cambridge: Cambridge University Press, 2010).

Linehan, Thomas, *Modernism and British Socialism* (Basingstoke and New York: Palgrave Macmillan, 2012).

Livesey, Ruth, 'Socialism in Bloomsbury: Virginia Woolf and the Political Aesthetics of the 1880s', *The Yearbook of English Studies*, Vol. 37, No. 1 (2007), 126–44.

Livingstone, David, 'Darwin in Belfast: The Evolution Debate', in John Wilson Foster and Helena C. G. Chesney, eds., *Nature in Ireland: A Scientific and Cultural History* (Dublin: Lilliput, 1997), 387–408.

Lloyd, David, *Irish Times: Temporalities of Modernity* (Dublin: Keough-Naughton Institute for Irish Studies, University of Notre Dame/Field Day, 2008).

Lochlainn, Colm O., 'Lúireach Phádraic: St. Patrick's Breastplate', in *Studies: An Irish Quarterly Review*, Vol. 50, No. 197 (Spring 1961), 1–4.

Lonergan, Patrick, ed., *Synge and His Influences: Centenary Essays from the Synge Summer School* (Dublin: Carysfort Press, 2011).

Longenbach, James, *Stone Cottage: Pound, Yeats and Modernism* (New York and Oxford: Oxford University Press, 1988).

Luckhurst, Roger, *The Invention of Telepathy, 1870–1901* (Oxford: Oxford University Press, 2002).

McAteer, Michael, *Yeats and European Drama* (Cambridge: Cambridge University Press, 2010).

MacCarthy, Fiona, *William Morris: A Life for Our Time* (London: Faber & Faber, 1994).

McCormack, W. J., *Fool of the Family: A Life of J. M. Synge* (London: Weidenfeld & Nicolson, 2000).

McCormack, W. J., *Blood Kindred: W. B. Yeats: The Life, The Death, The Politics* (London: Pimlico, 2005).

McDonald, Ronan, 'A gallous story or a dirty deed?: J. M. Synge and the Art of Guilt', *Irish Studies Review*, Vol. 5, No. 17 (Winter 1996), 25–30.

McDonald, Ronan, *Tragedy and Irish Literature: Synge, O'Casey, Beckett* (Basingstoke: Macmillan, 2002).

McDonald, Ronan, '"With Weariness More than of Earth": Degeneration and the Listless Male in the Mythic Poems of W. B. Yeats', *The Yeats Journal of Korea*, Vol. 41 (2013), 67–82.

McGarrity, Maria, and Claire A. Culleton, eds., *Irish Modernism and the Global Primitive* (New York: Palgrave Macmillan, 2009).

McGuinness, Patrick, *Maurice Maeterlinck and the Making of Modern Theatre* (Oxford: Oxford University Press, 2000).

McGuinness, Patrick, ed., *Symbolism, Decadence and the Fin de Siècle: French and European Perspectives* (Exeter: Exeter University Press, 2000).

Materer, Timothy, *Modernist Alchemy: Poetry and the Occult* (New York: Cornell University Press, 1995).

Mathews, P. J., *Revival: The Abbey Theatre, Sinn Féin, the Gaelic League and the Co-operative Movement* (Cork: Cork University Press, 2003).

Mathews, P. J., ed., *The Cambridge Companion to J. M. Synge* (Cambridge: Cambridge University Press, 2009).

Mattar, Sinéad Garrigan, *Primitivism, Science, and the Irish Revival* (Oxford: Clarendon Press, 2004).

Mattar, Sinéad Garrigan, 'Yeats, Fairies, and the New Animism', *New Literary History*, Vol. 43, No. 1 (Winter 2012), 137–57.

Maume, Patrick, *The Long Gestation: Irish Nationalist Life, 1891–1918* (New York: St. Martin's Press, 1999).

Mercier, Vivian, *The Irish Comic Tradition* (Oxford: Clarendon Press, 1962).

Mercier, Vivian, *Modern Irish Literature: Sources and Founders*, ed. Eilís Dillon (Oxford: Clarendon Press, 1994).

Mitchell, Robery, *Experimental Life: Vitalism in Romantic Science and Literature* (Baltimore: John Hopkins University Press, 2013).

Montague, C. E., *Dramatic Values* (London: Methuen, 1911).

Monteith, Ken, *Yeats and Theosophy* (London and New York: Routledge, 2008).

Moore, James R., *The Post-Darwinian Controversies: A Study of the Protestant struggle to come to terms with Darwin in Great Britain and America, 1870–1900* (Cambridge: Cambridge University Press, 1979).

Morash, Christopher, *A History of the Irish Theatre, 1601–2000* (Cambridge: Cambridge University Press, 2002).

Morash, Christopher, and Shaun Richards, *Mapping Irish Theatre: Theories of Space and Place* (Cambridge: Cambridge University Press, 2013).

Morrison, Mark S., *The Public Face of Modernism: Little Magazines, Audiences, and Reception, 1905–1920* (Wisconsin: University of Wisconsin Press, 2000).

Moses, Omri, *Out of Character: Modernism, Vitalism, Psychic Life* (Stanford: Stanford University Press, 2014).

Mulhern, Francis, *The Present Lasts a Long Time: Essays in Cultural Politics* (Cork: Cork University Press, 1998).

Muratori, Cecelia, *The First German Philosopher: The Mysticism of Jakob Böhme as Interpreted by Hegel, International Archives of the History of Ideas Archives*, Vol. 217 (2016).

Murphy, Brenda, '"The Treachery of Law": Reading the Political Synge', *Colby Quarterly*, Vol. 28, No. 1 (March 1992), 45–51.

Murphy, Paul, *Hegemony and Fantasy in Irish Drama, 1899–1949* (Basingstoke: Palgrave Macmillan, 2008).

Neff, D. S., 'Synge, Spinoza, and *The Well of the Saints*', *ANQ*, Vol. 2, No. 4 (1989), 138–45.

North, Michael, *The Political Aesthetic of Yeats, Eliot, and Pound* (Cambridge: Cambridge University Press, 1991).

O'Brien, John, ed., *The Cambridge Companion to Rabelais* (Cambridge: Cambridge University Press, 2010).

O'Connell, Helen, *Ireland and the Fiction of Improvement* (Oxford: Oxford University Press, 2006).

O'Donnell, Frank Hugh, *The Stage Irishman of the Pseudo-Celtic Drama* (London: John Long, 1904).

Oerlemans, Onno, *Romanticism and the Materiality of Nature* (Toronto: University of Toronto Press, 2002).

O'Leary, Philip, *The Prose Literature of the Gaelic Revival, 1881–1921: Ideology and Innovation* (Pennsylvania: Pennsylvania State University Press, 1994).

Oppenheim, Janet, *The Other World: Spiritualism and Psychical Research in England, 1850–1914* (Cambridge: Cambridge University Press, 1985).

Osborne, Peter, *The Politics of Time: Modernity and the Avant-Garde* (London: Verso, 1995).

Owen, Alex, *The Place of Enchantment: British Occultism and the Culture of the Modern* (Chicago and London: University of Chicago Press, 2004).

Parsons, Cóilín, *The Ordnance Survey and Modern Irish Literature* (Oxford: Oxford University Press, 2016).

Pašeta, Senia, ed., *Uncertain Futures: Essays about the Irish Past for Roy Foster* (Oxford: Oxford University Press, 2016).

Patten, Eve, 'Ireland's "Two Cultures" Debate: Victorian Science and the Literary Revival', *Irish University Review*, Vol. 33, No. 1 (Spring/Summer 2003), 1–13.

Pick, Daniel, *Faces of Degeneration: A European Disorder, c.1848–c.1918* (Cambridge: Cambridge University Press, 1989).

Pilkington, Lionel, *Theatre and the State in Twentieth-Century Ireland: Cultivating the People* (London and New York: Routledge, 2001).

Pilkington, Lionel, '"The Most Unpopular Man in Ireland": P. D. Kenny, J. M. Synge and Irish Cultural History', *The Irish Review*, No. 29 (Autumn 2002), 51–7.

Price, Alan, *Synge and Anglo-Irish Drama* (London: Methuen, 1961).

Price, Alan, 'Synge's Prose Writings: A First View of the Whole', *Modern Drama*, Vol. 11, No. 3 (December 1968), 221–6.

Randall, Bryony, *Modernism, Daily Time and Everyday Life* (Cambridge: Cambridge University Press, 2007).

Redman, Tim, *Ezra Pound and Italian Fascism* (Cambridge: Cambridge University Press, 1991).

Reynolds, Paige, 'Reading Publics, Theater Audiences, and the Little Magazines of the Abbey Theatre', *New Hibernia Review/Iris Éireannach Nua*, Vol. 7, No. 4 (Winter 2003), 63–84.

Reynolds, Paige, *Modernism, Drama, and the Audience for Irish Spectacle* (Cambridge: Cambridge University Press, 2007).

Ritschel, Nelson O'Ceallaigh, *Productions of the Irish Theatre Movement, 1899–1916: A Checklist* (Westport, CT, and London: Greenwood Press, 2001).

Ritschel, Nelson O'Ceallaigh, *Synge and Irish Nationalism: The Precursor to Revolution* (Westport, CT, and London: Greenwood Press, 2002).

Ritschel, Nelson O'Ceallaigh, *Shaw, Synge, Connolly, and Socialist Provocation* (Gainesville, FL: University of Florida Press, 2011).

Roberts, Richard H., ' "Nature", Post/Modernity and the Migration of the Sublime', *Ecotheology: Journal of Religion, Nature & the Environment*, Vol. 9, No. 3 (December 2004), 315–37.

Robinson, Lennox, *Ireland's Abbey Theatre: A History, 1899–1951* (London: Sidgwick & Jackson, 1951).

Roche, Anthony, 'The Two Worlds of Synge's *The Well of the Saints*', in Ronald Schleifer, ed., *The Genres of the Irish Literary Revival* (Dublin: Wolfhound Press, 1980), 27–38.

Roche, Anthony, *Synge and the Making of Modern Irish Drama* (Dublin: Carysfort Press, 2013).

Roche, Anthony, *The Irish Dramatic Revival, 1899–1939* (London: Bloomsbury, 2015).

Rubenstein, Michael, *Public Works: Infrastructure, Irish Modernism, and the Postcolonial* (Notre Dame, IN; University of Notre Dame Press, 2010).

Saddlemyer, Ann, 'Synge to MacKenna: The Mature Years', *The Massachusetts Review*, Vol. 5, No. 2 (Winter 1964), 279–96.

Saddlemyer, Ann, "A Share in the Dignity of the World": J. M. Synge's Aesthetic Theory', in Robin Skelton and Ann Saddlemyer, eds., *The World of W. B. Yeats: Essays in Perspective* (Dublin: The Dolmen Press, 1965).

Saddlemyer, Ann, *In Defence of Lady Gregory, Playwright* (Dublin: Dolmen Press, 1966).

Saddlemyer, Ann, *J. M. Synge and Modern Comedy* (Dublin: Dolmen Press, 1968).

Saddlemyer, Ann, 'Art, Nature, and "The Prepared Personality": A Reading of *The Aran Islands* and Related Writings', in S. B. Bushrui, ed., *Sunshine and the Moon's Delight: A Centenary Tribute to John Millington Synge, 1871–1909* (Gerrards Cross and Beirut: Colin Smythe and American University of Beirut, 1972), 107–20.

Saddlemyer, Ann, 'Synge and Doors of Perception', in Andrew Carpenter, ed., *Place, Personality and the Irish Writer* (New York: Barnes & Noble, 1977), 91–120.

Schleifer, Ronald, *Modernism and Time: The Logic of Abundance in Literature, Science, and Culture: 1880–1930* (Cambridge: Cambridge University Press, 2000).

Schleifer, Ronald, ed., *The Genres of the Irish Literary Revival* (Dublin: Wolfhound Press, 1980).

Schmidt, Eric Leigh, 'The Making of Modern "Mysticism"', *Journal of the American Academy of Religion*, Vol. 71, No. 2 (June 2003), 273–302.

Sessions, George, ed., *Deep Ecology for the Twenty-First Century* (Boston: Shambhala, 1995).

Setterquist, Jan, *Ibsen and the Beginnings of Anglo-Irish Drama, Volume I: John Millington Synge* (New York: Oriole, 1973).

Shackford, Martha Hale, 'A Definition of the Pastoral Idyll', *PMLA*, Vol. 19, No. 4 (1904), 583–92.

Sheils, Barry, W. B. *Yeats and World Literature: The Subject of Poetry* (Abingdon and New York: Routledge, 2016).

Sheldrake, Rupert, *The Rebirth of Nature: The Greening of Science and God* (London: Century, 1990).

Sherman, Stuart P., *On Contemporary Literature* (New York: Henry Holt, 1917).

Singer, Katherine, 'Stoned Shelley: Revolutionary Tactics and Women Under the Influence', *Studies in Romanticism*, Vol. 48, No. 4 (Winter 2009), 687–707.

Skelton, Robin, *J. M. Synge and His World* (London: Thames & Hudson, 1971).

Skelton, Robin, *The Writings of J. M. Synge* (London: Thames & Hudson, 1971).

Skelton, Robin, 'The Politics of J. M. Synge', *The Massachusetts Review*, Vol. 18, No. 1 (Spring 1977), 7–22.

Skelton, Robin, *Celtic Contraries* (Syracuse, NY: Syracuse University Press, 1990).

Smith, Stan, *The Origins of Modernism: Eliot, Pound, Yeats and the Rhetorics of Renewal* (Hemel Hempstead: Harvester Wheatsheaf, 1994).

Smyth, Gerry, *Space and the Irish Cultural Imagination* (Basingstoke: Palgrave Macmillan, 2001).

Soper, Kate, *What is Nature?: Culture, Politics, and the Non-Human* (Oxford: Blackwell, 1995).

Stephens, Edward, *My Uncle John: Edward Stephens's Life of J. M. Synge*, ed. Andrew Carpenter (London: Oxford University Press, 1974).

Strong, L. A. G., *John Millington Synge* (London: George Allen & Unwin, 1941).

Styers, Randall, *Making Magic: Religion, Magic, and Science in the Modern World* (New York: Oxford University Press, 2004).

Sultan, Stanley, 'A Joycean Look at The Playboy of the Western World', in Maurice Harmon, ed., *The Celtic Master, Being Contributions to the First James Joyce Symposium in Dublin* (Dublin: Dolmen Press, 1969), 45–55.

Surette, Leon, and Demetres Tryphonopoulos, eds., *Literary Modernism and the Occult Tradition* (Maine: The National Poetry Foundation, 1996).

Sword, Helen, *Ghostwriting Modernism* (Ithaca and London: Cornell University Press, 2002).

Taylor, Charles, *Sources of the Self: The Making of Modern Identity* (Cambridge: Cambridge University Press, 1989).

Taylor, Charles, *A Secular Age* (Cambridge, MA, and London: Harvard University Press, 2007).

Thacker, Andrew, *Moving Through Modernity: Space and Geography in Modernism* (Manchester and New York: Manchester University Press, 2003).

Thornton, Weldon, *J. M. Synge and the Western Mind* (Gerrards Cross: Colin Smythe, 1979).

Thurschwell, Pamela, *Literature, Technology and Magical Thinking, 1880–1920* (Cambridge: Cambridge University Press, 2001).

Tonning, Erik, *Modernism and Christianity* (Basingstoke: Palgrave Macmillan, 2014).

Toomey, Deirdre, '"Killing the da": J. M. Synge and *The Golden Bough*', in Robert Fraser, ed., *Sir James Frazer and the Literary Imagination: Essays in Affinity and Influence* (London and Basingstoke: Macmillan, 1990), 154–71.

Toomey, Deirdre, ed., *Yeats and Women* (Basingstoke: Macmillan, 1997).

Trotter, Mary, *Ireland's National Theaters: Political Performance and the Origins of the Irish Dramatic Movement* (New York: Syracuse University Press, 2001).

Turda, Marius, *Modernism and Eugenics* (New York: Palgrave Macmillan, 2012).

Vandevelde, Karen, '"What's All the Stir about?": Gerald MacNamara, Synge, and the Early Abbey Theatre', *New Hibernia Review/Iris Éireannach Nua*, Vol. 10, No. 3 (Autumn 2006), 108–21.

Velissariou, Aspasia, 'The Dialectics of Space in Synge's *The Shadow of the Glen*', *Modern Drama*, Vol. 36, No. 3 (Fall 1993), 409–19.

Vickery, John B., *The Literary Impact of the Golden Bough* (Princeton, NJ: Princeton University Press, 1973).

Volpicelli, Robert A., 'Bare Ontology: Synge, Beckett, and the Phenomenology of Imperialism', *New Hibernia Review*, Vol. 17, No. 4 (Winter 2013), 110–29.

Watson, G. J., *Irish Identity and the Literary Revival: Synge, Yeats, Joyce and O'Casey*, 2nd edn. (Washington, DC: The Catholic University Press of America, 1994).

Watt, Stephen, Eileen Morgan, and Shakir Mustafa, eds., *A Century of Irish Drama: Widening the Stage* (Indianapolis: Indiana University Press, 2000).

Weir, David, *Decadence and the Making of Modernism* (Amherst, MA: University of Massachusetts Press, 1995).

Weiskel, Thomas, *The Romantic Sublime: Studies in the Structure and Psychology of Transcendence* (Baltimore and London: The John Hopkins University Press, 1976).

Welch, Robert, *Changing States: Transformations in Modern Irish Writing* (London and New York: Routledge, 1993).

Welch, Robert, *The Abbey Theatre, 1899–1999: Form and Pressure* (Oxford: Oxford University Press, 1999).

Whitaker, Thomas R., ed., *Twentieth Century Interpretations of The Playboy of the Western World: A Collection of Critical Essays* (Englewood Cliffs, NJ: Prentice-Hall, 1969).

White, Harry, *Music and the Irish Literary Imagination* (Oxford: Oxford University Press, 2008).

Whyte, Nicholas, *Science, Colonialism and Ireland* (Cork: Cork University Press, 1999).

Willwerscheid, Jason, 'Migratory movements: evolutionary theory in the works of J. M. Synge', *Irish Studies Review*, Vol. 22, No. 2 (2014), 129–46.

Wilson, Leigh, *Modernism and Magic: Experiments with Spiritualism, Theosophy and the Occult* (Edinburgh: Edinburgh University Press, 2013).

Wilson, Steve, '"His Native Homespuns... Become Him": Synge's *The Playboy of the Western World* and Performative Identity', *Midwest Quarterly*, Vol. 48, No. 2 (Winter 2007), 233–46.

Worth, Katharine, *The Irish Drama of Europe from Yeats to Beckett* (London: The Athlone Press, 1986).

Yahata, Masahiko, 'George A. Birmingham, "Hyacinth" (1906): What Turns a Patriot into an Exile', *The Harp*, Vol. 10 (1995).

Yeo, Stephen, 'A New Life: The Religion of Socialism in Britain, 1883–1896', *History Workshop Journal*, 4 (1977), 5–55.

Zox-Weaver, Annalisa, *Women Modernists and Fascism* (Cambridge: Cambridge University Press, 2011).

King, Anthony, 'Overload: Problems of Governing in the 1970's',
Political Studies, XXIII (1975).

Wheare, K. C., *Maladministration and its Remedies* (1973).

Younger, Kenneth, *Changing Perspectives in British Foreign
Policy* (1964).

Index

Note: Figures are indicated by an italic "*f*", respectively, following the page number.

For the benefit of digital users, indexed terms that span two pages (e.g., 52–53) may, on occasion, appear on only one of those pages.